CONTEMPORARY AMERICAN LITERATURE AND RELIGION

By HALFORD E. LUCCOCK

Professor in Yale University Divinity School

WILLETT, CLARK & COMPANY

CHICAGO   NEW YORK

1934

150S-4D34

PS
221
L8

To
ROBERT
AND
MARY ETTA

CONTENTS

CONTEMPORARY
AMERICAN LITERATURE
AND RELIGION

CHAPTER ONE

MORNING AFTER AN EARTHQUAKE

ONE of the most moving passages in Lord Grey's autobiography, *Twenty-Five Years,* is that in which he describes the night of August 3, on which Great Britain declared war on Germany. After the historic debate in the House of Commons had been concluded and the vote taken, he went to the Foreign Office in Whitehall street and spent the early morning hours there. As dawn broke over the city he looked out of the window and watched the street lights being extinguished one after another up the street. He turned to a friend with him and said, " The lamps are going out all over Europe; we shall not see them lit again in our lifetime." [1]

Lord Grey little realized how wide was to be the application of his prophecy. It is not only Europe but all the world which has seen lights of many sorts blink out. Twenty years later the darkness is still deepening. That blinking out of lights is the primary fact of the post-war years. It has affected every trend in the world of religion and literature. It is the vast back-drop in front of which the whole drama has been played. The quenching or dimming of many of the lights has, of course, been a real moral and spiritual gain; for many hopes and faiths extinguished by the war were but the blaring lights of some Great White Way, confusing the eye

I

and shutting out the stars. Some blinking lights, however, were those of high faith and spiritual resource. But whether gain or loss, the sputtering and going out of what had been sustaining beliefs and faiths for millions is a major feature of the last fifteen years in America as in Europe. The phrase of Newman's hymn, " Amid th' encircling gloom," has a close relation to the life, literature and religion of our time.

We have undertaken to look at some of the creative literature of America since the war and its relation to religion, not as an exercise in literary criticism, but looking at literature as the expression of life, the symptoms of the moods of the time, its health and its sickness, its despairs and its hopes; the wrist of the common body of life, as it were, where we can count its heartbeats. All of these things are primary concerns of religion. The period is that which has of late proved strangely fascinating to America, the record of yesterday and the day before yesterday, that " intermediate state " which has not yet got into history and which has just ceased being present experience. Such works as Mark Sullivan's *Our Times,* Frederick L. Allen's *Only Yesterday,* and more recently Gaius Glenn Atkins' *Religion in Our Times,* Gilbert Seldes' *The Years of the Locust,* and Winfred Ernest Garrison's *The March of Faith* have both indicated and stimulated the interest in that period.

Organized religion can neglect the literature of its time only at its peril. To say that seems an utter commonplace, yet it is a tragedy which has often happened, and which has been by no means absent in the last fifteen years. The creative writing of any time is one of the most authentic sources of knowledge of the tempers and distempers of that time, in

which religion must live and move and do whatever work of
redemption it is to achieve. To neglect it is like a physician
neglecting to take a patient's pulse or temperature; for literature is both. A striking expression of the unique value of
fiction as source material for the understanding of an historical period is to be found in St. John Ervine's novel, *Changing
Winds*. A social worker has been disparaging novels as use-
less to her in her work. Mr. Ervine thus describes the comments of another character:

"No wonder, he thought to himself, all reformers and serious
people make such a mess of the social system when they despise and
ignore the principal means of knowing the human spirit (*i.e.* literature).

"'That's a pity,' he said aloud, 'I should have thought that you'd
find novels useful to you in your work. I mean, there's surely more
chance of understanding the people of the eighteenth century if you
read Fielding's *Tom Jones* than there is if you read Lecky's *England
in the Eighteenth Century.*'

"'Is there?' said Rachel. 'Of course there is,' Gilbert hurled at
her from the other side of the table. 'Fielding was an artist, inspired
by God, but Lecky was simply a fact-pedlar, inspired by the Board
of Education. Why, even that dull ass, Richardson, makes you understand more about his period than Lecky does.'"

Often we hear ministers and others cry out at the low
tone of literature, seemingly oblivious that their criticism
is not so much of literature, which is a symptom, as of the
life of a generation, which is a cause. We repeatedly hear
the question, for instance, Where have the heroes of literature gone? A pertinent question, which we shall try to
face. But many forget, in asking it, that the real answer
is not that authors are degenerate and perverse, but that
they are voices of their time; and ours has not been a moral

climate in which heroes are nourished as naturally and luxuriantly as daisies in June. Whatever we have done for democracy, we have not made a world safe for heroes. As T. S. Eliot said, in the early 1920's, " The age objects to the heroic." Whatsoever a generation soweth that shall it also reap; and a generation that soweth to the flesh shall of the flesh also reap the neurotic alcoholics who stagger through the novels of Ernest Hemingway and Theodore Dreiser.

The literature of a period is significant, also, because it is often the most sensitive barometer, indicating what shall be some dominating trends of the immediate future. The encyclopedists, Voltaire and Rousseau, were authentic indications of the atmospheric pressure which preceded the storm of the French Revolution. In Great Britain the novels of the 1840's and 1850's pointed toward many of the molding forces of the latter half of the nineteenth century. *Oliver Twist* was published in 1838, *David Copperfield* in 1850, Charles Kingsley's *Alton Locke* in 1850 and *Yeast* in 1852. They were all foregleams of that chapter in social and political legislation which was opened up with the passage of the Reform Bill of 1867. In like manner it is very interesting today, in the light of Russian history since 1917, to reread Tolstoi, Dostoievsky and Chekhov, and see the sure manner in which fiction was a prophecy of political history, and also a force in making it.

I

The present moment furnishes an advantageous time for an attempt to estimate some of the spiritual and moral significance of American literature in the past fifteen years, for we are very definitely at the end of a literary period. The word " era " is, no doubt, too pretentious and glittering a title with which to baptize a modest little period of half a generation. We have become coldly skeptical of watchmen on the housetops proclaiming new eras and new ages every two weeks, particularly since the debacle of the New Economic Era, gaudily inaugurated by such a solemn March of the Priests (of Wall street) when the Golden Age of the Bull Market was ushered in in 1922, just twelve years ago. But we have reached a point at which the predominant post-war moods and fashions in literature have definitely exhausted themselves. In the sacred language of the market, they have passed the saturation point. Sad-eyed revelry, stark disillusion, the titillation of bold, bad cynicism, have played their hour and yielded the spotlight to drama in a different key. The very words of the early 1920's — " flapper," " the revolt of youth " and a score of others — have a quaintly archaic flavor, like something out of early Anglo-Saxon or, at least, Chaucer. Scott Fitzgerald, the godfather of the " highball school " of fiction, begun with *This Side of Paradise* and encored in *Tales of the Jazz Age* and *The Beautiful and Damned,* declared in the autumn of 1932 that " the 1920's are as dead as Dickens' doornail." E. Merrill Root says that H. L. Mencken today " has to speak through a ouija board." But yesterday the word of Mencken might have stood against the world, now he lies low with few so poor to do him reverence.

The earliest flapper heroines, like Floyd Dell's Janet March, who crawled out from under the ruins left by the war in 1923, seem much more distant in time than Jane Eyre or even Jane Austen. Much of the adolescent revolt of the 1920's is more distant and dead today than the Victorian era. This has been a vast relief to multitudes of young people who have heard the news that they can now drop the rôle of disillusioned Byrons, with "impotently folded hands and articulately opened mouth," a pose of which many had become infinitely weary. As Stuart Chase has cogently put it in his essay entitled, significantly, *The End of an Era:* "There is reason to believe that the period of cynicism and moral frustration caused by the war is drawing to its close. Youth is beginning to believe in something again. The flapper in her more hard-boiled aspects passes. After a decade of roaring materialism we may be on the threshold of more consideration for art, esthetics, literature, things of the spirit." [2]

One obvious factor making definitely for the beginning of a new period of literature is that the younger writers now emerging into prominence and influence were children during the war. They had no personal experience of it; their minds are directed to the future, rather than the past. The stock "rebellions" of the 1920's have become merely part of the history of their elders, like the crusade to make the world safe for democracy. To a large number of young people, as well as older ones, an orthodoxy of rebellion became as empty and static as the established orthodoxy against which it was originally directed.

It is just as obvious, of course, that an even later mood which possessed large numbers, that of the confident optimism of the boom years 1925–1929, and which found expression in a vast amount of reading matter with which the public addled its wits and smothered its soul, has also passed into history. Perhaps, like the glittering image of

Prosperity which it celebrated, it has fallen like Humpty Dumpty, never again to be put together in recognizable shape. For these reasons, some glimpse of that period, both for literature and religion, comes today as from the top of a rather definite watershed, dividing yesterday from today and tomorrow.

II

At first glance, the outstanding fact about the relation of contemporary literature and religion may well seem to be that there isn't any. So the very title of this book may look like the prospectus of a voyage along the seacoast of Bohemia. There is much that drives us to that conclusion. One of the major facts in the whole field of present day fiction is the large number of novels in which, from start to finish, there seems to be no recognition of the fact that there has ever been such a thing as religion in human experience, or that such an institution as the church is still in existence today. For any indicated awareness of the whole religious area of experience, or even its institutional life, the novels might as well be located in upper Greenland, in the more remote of the South Sea Islands, or that ice expanse near the south pole to which Byrd gave the name " Little America." It is, in that sense, emphatically a " little America " which scores and hundreds of novels have portrayed.

This may be partly due to the significant fact that most of the novelists, with such exceptions as Willa Cather, and many of the poets, with such exceptions as Vachel Lindsay, are entirely without connection with the churches or institutions of religion. At any rate, that absence of religion as

even a minor theme from the creative literature of the period
is one of large meaning for any interpretation. For in a
subtle and indirect but effective way that very gap, that
ignoring not only of religion but of those areas of life in
which religion has played a significant part, has acted as a
force itself making for a further disregard of religion. As
Joseph Wood Krutch has pointed out, speaking frankly to
a group of radicals on how to bring about a change of economic attitudes through literary expression: " The current
drama of today makes, for instance, for agnosticism. But
it does not do so because it is concerned with attacks on
God; it does so rather because it never occurs to most of the
characters in most plays to try to pray themselves out of
their difficulties. If the drama of tomorrow is socially radical, it will be socially radical in a similar way; it will, that
is to say, get its effect by what it takes for granted as much
as by what it says."

There we have it — " getting effect by what it takes for
granted." A hundred novels and more have apparently
taken for granted that religion does not exist. One large
exception must be made — God is still necessary for purposes of profanity.

It is obvious that we have nothing like the wide reading
given to such distinctively religious verse as that given to
Keble's *Christian Year* in the mid-nineteenth century, to
such a disguised tract as *Robert Elsmere* a generation later,
or Samuel Butler's *The Way of All Flesh* at the turn of the
century, or even in 1913 to Winston Churchill's *The Inside
of the Cup*. The only book comparable with these in general attention is the sorry exhibit of *Elmer Gantry,* balanced somewhat by a novel off the main line of recent fiction — Willa Cather's *Death Comes to the Archbishop.*

This judgment on the absence of religion from literature stands, however, only as long as we confine our definition of religion within the rigid and traditional limits of articulate belief and theology. When we refuse to accept the strict demarcation of religion into an isolated province on the map of life and think of it as an attitude and spirit which pervades the whole, a total response to life, we find much of the literature of today occupied with the examination and interpretation of those experiences which are and have been of vital concern, historically, to religion. It is merely a commonplace to observe that one of the continuing and most significant marks of fifty years in religious thought and life has been the overflowing of the artificial canal banks with which religion has been enclosed. The history has been a parallel to the Niagara river, flowing through a deeply cut gorge, against the banks of which it bounds and surges in restraint, finally making its way out into the broad expanse of Lake Ontario. Perhaps the figure of speech will hold a bit further. For waters enclosed in the Niagara gorge were not always thus narrowly confined; back of the temporarily compressed river lay the spaciousness of lakes Erie, Huron and Superior. Men have caught a fresh glimpse of the range of religion in the last half century, as they have reread with unbandaged eyes the charter of Christianity as proclaimed by Jesus:

The spirit of the Lord is upon me,
Because he anointed me to preach good tidings to the poor;
He hath sent me to proclaim release to the captives,
And recovering of sight to the blind,
To set at liberty them that are bruised,
To proclaim the acceptable year of the Lord.

The Christian religion has broken its theological jail.
It is loose in the world. Nothing human is foreign to it.
Its broken dams are pictured in the words of Dr. Fosdick:
"To talk of redeeming personality while one is careless of
the social environments which ruin personality; to talk of
building Christlike character while one is complacent about
an economic system that is definitely organized about the
idea of selfish profit; to praise Christian ideals while one is
blind to the inevitable urgency with which they insist on
getting themselves expressed in social programs — all this
is vanity."

Definitions of religion have very often been like the bed
described by Isaiah — "too short for a man to stretch himself in." They have often been over-intellectualized, too exclusively focused on the formulation of opinion to represent
the part played by religion in life. If an exploration of the
relationship of religion and literature is to have any real, as
opposed to a merely formal, significance, the conception of
religion must be widened to include factors much more
vital than formulated beliefs and ceremonial practices. A
generation of the study of religion has laid emphasis on the
deeper and wider aspects of religion. Such a definition as
that of G. M. Stratton, for instance, "Religion is a man's
whole bearing toward what seems to him the Best or the
Greatest," [3] expresses a conception of religion based on a
wide examination of the manifestations of religion in various races and cultures. Similar in range is the definition of
Catlin: "Religion is that sense of something greater than
ourselves with which we may identify ourselves." [4] William
E. Hocking's definition of religion gives a different emphasis: "Religion is a passion for righteousness and the

spread of righteousness felt as a cosmic demand." [5] This last conception of religion is one particularly useful for the interpretation of a large amount of post-war American literature, in poetry, fiction and criticism.

These citations are sufficient to indicate that the judgment that religion has been almost entirely absent from contemporary literature is hasty, superficial and based on an inadequate idea of religion and its expression in human life. If, as Professor H. N. Wieman claims, "the human drive toward more abundant living is the root of religion in human nature," [6] its roots are sunk deep in present day life, and are easily discernible in current expression of the life in literature.

It is this expansion of the conception of the field, function and nature of religion which must color our whole interpretation of the spiritual significance of contemporary literature. The Christian religion is good news about God, completed and made concrete in good news about man, about the significance and the worth of human personality, about a kingdom of God in which personality may come to abundant fruition. Consequently we find a striking contrast between evaluations of the religious element in literature done in the 1880's, for instance, and those made today. Stopford Brooke, R. H. Hutton and many others were largely occupied in tracing the expression of theological assumptions and belief in Tennyson and Browning, in Arnold and Carlyle.

Today our conception of the definitely religious takes in a much wider territory. If religion is "the life of God in the soul of man," all that plays on man, all that blights and maims and frustrates men, all that, in the words of Jesus,

" injures one of these little ones," all the wistfulness and yearnings of the spirit, the life of the soul in a machine world, the cry for justice, the death-rattle of hunger — all this is the field of religious conceptions and attitudes.   When Vachel Lindsay puts into music the life and faith of William Booth, that is religion in literature.   But when a man ordinarily accounted and self-proclaimed non-religious, such as Sherwood Anderson, by a clairvoyant sympathy creeps under the other man's skin and shows the frustration of dreams, the demoralization of life by the ugly and sordid effects of a money-obsessed civilization, that too is religious literature. And the church had better pay attention to it!   For Sherwood Anderson in some of his moods is not far from the kingdom of God, as we have a glimpse of its spirit in Jesus, as pictured in Matthew 9:36: " But when he saw the multitudes he was moved with compassion for them, because they were distressed and scattered, as sheep not having a shepherd."

Take that novel, for instance, which marked a definite turning point in the literary treatment of the war, *Three Soldiers* by John Dos Passos, published in 1921. To call it a religious book, in the accepted sense of that term, would be stretching language out of all rational meaning. Religious faith does not come within its circumference. Yet it pictures a slice of human experience of the utmost concern for religion.   In its realistic picturing of the most irreligious force in the world — war — it is far more of a religious asset than scores of formal discussions of the war and religion, many of which were marked by a spiritual dimness which can only be described as a total eclipse.   It is an ugly, coarse, brutally frank recording of the history of a platoon of everyday Americans through the war. It let in the daylight on the obscene spectacle which war is. It helped mightily to start the deflating of the prestige of war, which is one of the primary tasks of religion in this century. It is interesting in this connection to remember that the first realistic drama on war after the armistice, *What Price Glory* by Maxwell Anderson and Laurence Stallings, another immense contribution to spiritual understanding, was greeted with a storm of protests by ministers and other religious people on account of its profanity. They called it blasphemous, entirely overlooking the far more profound blasphemy of war itself against which the play was dealing terrific blows. That was as perfect an example of straining at a gnat and swallowing a camel as can be conceived.

Take quite another sort of work, a novel of 1931, *Call Home the Heart,* by Olive Tilford Dargan. Here again is a novel into which religion as a distinct theme comes very little. It describes the hill people of western North Carolina and Tennessee, driven by economic distress down into the mill towns. The novel shows real knowledge of a group of people, deep sympathy and understanding, and an anguish over the degradation and exploitation of these helpless children of the hills — a viewpoint and mood which prophetic religion has made its own in its highest hours. It is deeply religious in the sense that it shows a passionate sympathy and a conscience sensitive to injustice, which are at the heart of any authentic Christianity or Judaism. It also presents aspects of life with which any religion not in full retreat from its world must deal.

III

A study of the literature of today ought to show three real relationships to religion. For one thing, it will disclose much of what might be called "implicit religion." The voice of the day in poetry, drama and novel includes much that expresses attitudes and spirit which mark the Christian conception of life. It will not often be labeled formal religion. Some of it may even be listed, because of one feature or another, as an irreligious or immoral influence. One looking only at the surface, or interested only in pasting labels, may easily overlook or wrongly identify it. But those who are looking for the thing itself, for the understanding of life, for the sensitiveness to injustice, for the pity and sympathy born of love and of respect for the capacities of the soul, a devotion to truth which makes men free from the blight of lies, will find this attitude and spirit an inseparable part of religion in human life. They will find much of it, often strangely stirring and beautiful, in unlikely places. It will be found in Dreiser as well as Upton Sinclair, in Eugene O'Neill as well as Carl Sandburg.

Literature is of first concern for religion also in that it shows the symptoms of a time, its need, its voids, its sore spots, its hopes, its despairs. The competent novelist of any period is an indispensable diagnostician for anyone who would seek to heal the hurt of humanity. We can learn far more of the soul of nineteenth century England from Charles Dickens than from John Henry Newman. We can learn more, to taken an extreme example, of the sickness of soul of New York City from Michael Gold's *Jews*

Without Money than from all the reports of the Federation of Churches published in the last thirty years. If more religious leaders had had the wisdom to see life through the eyes of dramatists and novelists, and had not exhausted so much of their spiritual energies in denunciation, they would have felt more deeply and known more accurately the sickness they desired to heal.

In addition to these services, contemporary literature renders an indispensable ministry to religion in the challenge which it presents. It holds out to organized religion the sacrament of disturbance. It saves religion from the soporific of its own anthems. Literature acts as an open window into the sanctuary, through which the screams of life, its wails, its fighting cries, its hollow revelry, come in to mix with the " Peace, perfect peace," of the hymnbook. Its often unconscious pictures of the futility of life empty of faith come as a challenge to faith; its dramas of the bankruptcy of hope may confront and stir those who believe in divine resources in life; its aching portrayals of the oppressed may bring rebirth to those who pray to the God of Amos and of Jesus; its deep etchings of the loneliness of man without God may act as a divine recommissioning to those not wholly dead.

In order to help get the picture in the frame, let us recall swiftly some of the forces which during these fifteen years have been playing upon both literature and religion in America, because they have been playing upon life. Swift and far-reaching changes have marked every realm. In one of Conan Doyle's stories published during the war, Sherlock Holmes says to Dr. Watson, " Good old Watson, you're the one fixed point in a world of change! " There have not been very many Dr. Watsons in that respect. A man recently lost his life in the attempt to prove that Greenland was drifting. It requires no hazardous risk of life to demonstrate that the United States has been drifting. In just a few years, to cite but one of a thousand instances, we have moved from an attitude of lyric ecstacy toward machinery — a mood not far from that of Simeon in the temple, "Now lettest thou thy servant depart in peace, for mine eyes have seen thy salvation" — to the startled contemplation of the twentieth century equivalent of Dante's vision of hell, as presented in the phrase "technological unemployment."

The surest way to misinterpret the whole post-war period is to ascribe all the changing forces to the war. In this period the war has played the part of the scapegoat in the Mosaic ritual. All the sins of a generation have been carefully bound on its head and it has been driven out to the wilderness bearing the sins of us all. This has been very convenient, but it involves the fallacy of over-simplification — a pit into which the clergy fall with the greatest ease in dealing with social or moral problems. Many of the most important developments of the post-war era have come from the working of causes that were in operation long before the war. In many respects, for instance, the war was but the last step in the deflation of Victorian optimisms, a process which had been going on for a generation. There is a much wider significance than appears on the surface in the scene in the early part of the moving picture made from Noel Coward's play *Cavalcade,* showing the funeral of Queen Victoria. For the whole generation, 1900–1930, pictured in that film, was marked by a more or less continuous funeral of the Victorian age. Like the characters in the play, a whole generation stood on a balcony and watched the passing of sanctified orthodoxies, in economics, in politics and diplomacy, many of which were directly responsible for the turmoil, the waste and the agony which the first generation of the twentieth century saw.

IV

Just as in economics the war has been a too easy explanation of the whole collapse which we euphemistically call the " depression," so in literature there has been a tendency to undervalue the impact of other forces.

It has not been what history will call a great age. With truth it may well be called a dreary age, as dreary in its prosperity as it has been dreary in its disillusionment. It is interesting to see it called a dark and dreary age by one to whom is usually awarded the crown of pessimism, Thomas Hardy. It seems black even to one to whom black is a native color. In what he calls an "apology" for his last volume of poems, *Late Lyrics and Earlier* (1922), Hardy says: "Whether owing to the barbarizing of taste in the younger minds by the dark madness of the late war, the unabashed cultivation of selfishness in all classes, the plethoric growth of knowledge simultaneously with the stunting of wisdom, 'a degrading thirst after outrageous stimulation,' or from any other cause, we seem threatened with a new Dark Age . . . men's minds appear to be moving backwards rather than on."

Perhaps the tone is the familiar one in octogenarians commenting on the scene of their last days. His estimate, however, has features recognizable to anyone who has lived the last fifteen years in the United States.

Yet we may wonder whether these years may not later appear as a formative period in which old delusions were shattered, some sanctified stupidities crumbled, new pathways for future traveling opened up, new values and standards set up.

> There is a day in spring,
> When under all the earth the secret germs
> Begin to stir and glow before they bud.
> The wealth and festal pomps of midsummer
> Lie in the heart of that inglorious hour
> Which no man names with blessing, though its work
> Is blessed by all the world.

It is at least a fair hope for all our travail that the seeds of some distant midsummer pomp of the spirit may lie in our " inglorious hour."

In any roll of the forces under the pressure of which postwar literature and religion have developed, there may well come, first, that spiritual dislocation which may be called " shell-shock." It is not the whole story of the post-war era; it *is* an inseparable part of it. Some shells detonate by impact; others by time. Many of the shells of the war are detonating only today and their repercussion will shake the next generation. The emotional and spiritual effects of the war on multitudes, to some extent setting the tempo and mood of a whole generation, had many resemblances to the physical and nervous effects of shell-shock — a battered stupor, a moral apathy and lethargy, disgust, headache and paralysis. It affected not only those exposed to physical shell-shock; it was a highly contagious disease; it seized multitudes who never crossed the Atlantic. Of course, it must be added, it was a highly fashionable pose as well, and it is often impossible to separate the real shock from the pose. But even as a pose it affected deeply the intellectual climate and mood of the period.

Obvious also is the omnipresent effect of the progress and prestige of science, both in theory and in applied technology. Joseph Wood Krutch tosses off in one jaunty sentence what has been a widespread attitude: " Biology and psychology explain away the awe of emotional existence." Just like that! C. E. M. Joad, the prolific British critic, gives expression to a feeling rather widely held: " So far as present indications go, it seems not unlikely that science will deliver the *coup de grace* to organized Christianity within the next hundred years." [7] He softens the blow by admitting that possibly the Church of England, with the House of Commons and the royal family, may be kept going for the entertainment of American tourists.

In the 1930's, of course, that type of dogmatism is meeting a rising chorus of " Is that so? " The developments of physics in the last few years have carried science far beyond the trick of trapping the universe in a neat little epigram. The confident materialism so fashionable twenty years ago, which finds such quaint, outdated fixation in the psychology of Dreiser, has been undergoing a deflation very parallel to that which the Victorian optimisms in economics and politics have had in the last generation. The new physics has given to the assurance of an all-explaining scientific naturalism, elevated to the throne of a philosophy, a far more devastating upset than Darwin and Huxley gave to Victorian religious orthodoxy in the nineteenth century. Yet during

the post-war period in America, the influence of a scientific
cast of thought, which was supposed to have written a flour-
ishing " Finis " to the history of God and religion, was a
major one. The change of atmosphere, as it has spread
widely, is amusingly pictured in two verses by Walter
Prichard Eaton:

> When Grandma and Grandpa had a guest over night;
> They gave him at ten o'clock a kerosene light;
> Then the poor victim, shivering, repaired
> To an icy spare room that never was aired;
> Gooseflesh all over as he washed in a bowl;
> Very brief commune with God about his soul —
> Then he dove hastily into the bed,
> And reached for the solace on the stand by its head;
> There he found always the excellent books
> Of Talmage, Martineau, Beecher, and Brooks!
>
> Grandma, Grandpa, my great-aunts are dead,
> But still stands the table by the guest room bed;
> Steam heat, electric light, flowers and fresh air
> Make the job of going up not so hard to bear;
> Hot bath, shower bath, needle bath and spray
> Give you such comfort that you don't need to pray;
> Sink on the box springs and reach for a book;
> Don't you want that one? Have another look;
> Culture our watchword, and this is what it means —
> Einstein, Eddington, Millikan, and Jeans! [8]

The four scientists whom Mr. Eaton groups in his last
line are by no means among the anti-religious forces of the
generation, but the picture does express a change of intellectual climate.

With insight and sincerity Walter Lippmann puts a central fact of the time: " God is the supreme symbol in which

man expresses his destiny, and if that symbol is confused, his life is confused."

The change which has gradually been coming over the minds of multitudes of people, partly as a result of the progress of science and the prestige given to science by its practical applications, may be described as the change from a God-centered universe to a man-centered world. To a degree never realized by the Greek philosopher who first said it, " Man is the measure of all things." In relation to the place of religious beliefs in the minds of men, it is like a change from a Copernican universe, in which the earth goes around the sun, to a Ptolemaic one, in which everything goes around the earth. Men's minds and lives do not revolve around God. Man himself — his powers, his interests, his problems and human resources for meeting them — is the center. The classic remark of Professor J. B. Pratt, of Williams, speaking of college students of the present day, interprets the situation: " Their grandfathers believed the creed; their fathers a little doubted the creed; they have never read it." The old picture of the Fates spinning the thread of man's destiny has been replaced by one in which man handles all the threads with his own fingers.

It is easily possible, of course, to overestimate the influence of scientific thinking on the popular mind. The so-called secularization of life is doubtless due in far less measure to science directly than is frequently estimated. It is the preoccupations of men, activity rather than thought, which are among the chief causes of a reduced place for religion in the lives of millions. "The world is so full of a number of things " that they absorb the attention, as a child is absorbed by a succession of brightly lighted and well filled store windows. Professor Charles G. Shaw, of New York University, has listed some of these omnipresent and well nigh omnipotent preoccupations in his evaluation of civilization in terms of the " seven deadly values " of " communication, speed, entertainment, health, psychology, sex and youth," to which the present American mind is keyed.[9]

In the confusion morals are, for multitudes, no longer a compulsory code. That fact finds crude but fairly accurate expression in the words of one of Scott Fitzgerald's characters: " Life is a football game; every one is off-side and the rules abolished and the referee chased off the field." One far-reaching influence has been that our generation has thrown off the restraint and discipline of a moral tradition but has not achieved the resources of a saving self-discipline. It has disobeyed " the first law of the jungle " — " Never let go with your paws before you have caught on with your tail." It has let go of an august authority in morals and religion and has not caught on to a discipline which springs from the freedom of moral maturity. Eugene O'Neill puts that problem in more distinctively religious terms when he says: " The playwright of today must dig at the roots of the sickness of today as he feels it — the death of the old God, and the failure of science and materialism to give a satisfying new one for the religious instincts to find a meaning for life in and to comfort its fears of death with. It seems to me anyone trying to do big work nowadays must have this big subject behind all the little subjects of his plays or novels, or he is simply scribbling around on the surface of things, and has no more real status than a parlor entertainer."

Elmer Davis has put the problem as being that of " build-

ing a stoic ethic on an epicurean metaphysic; " that is, of
deriving a stoic ethic, which rested on an endeavor to achieve
harmony with the universe, from a vague conception of a
possible God indifferent to the fate of man. About this
many will be disposed to comment, " It is a good trick if
you can do it! " This is the theme which appears in a large
amount of the fiction, drama and poetry of the last fifteen years.

V

The great progress of psychology from the turn of the
century to the present time, coupled with enormous popular
interest in both scientific and charlatan brands of psychology,
has been an influence as omnipresent in the life of the period
as salt in the sea. To a real degree the motto " Inward,
Ho! " displaced " Westward, Ho! " The new exploration
of the mind, beginning with William James, had far-
reaching effects on the spirit and temper of the times. It
affected deeply the approach to literature, as it did that to
education, to religion, to ethics. It opened up a new field
of interest, to mention first only one aspect of the development: an interest which came to be substituted for more
strictly moral and religious absorptions. This is not the
place in which to assess the great service of the advance of
psychology to both ethics and religion. Among other things,
it gave to what was often the airy nothing of generalities
in moral theory a local habitation and a name, in tracing the
forces which impel people to action. It gave also an alternate interest for the traditional moralistic black-and-white
schematization of life. It tended to reinterpret the human
search for salvation in terms of personality, in the release

of capacities, the harmonious development of powers, the integration and expression of self. John Bunyan's *Pilgrim's Progress* was rewritten as a search for abundant personal life.

A new chapter in this history was begun with the advent of Freud. Psychoanalysis provided for many a whole new mythology of salvation, thus conceived as release and expression. Its influence in this country dates from about the time of Freud's visit in 1902. From its first discussion in medical journals it was rapidly popularized by dramatists, novelists, poets, critics and teachers, till in 1920 there were more than two hundred books dealing with Freudianism, and since that time it has spread in general knowledge and influence. From these books and writers it has seeped down into the popular mind, affecting multitudes who have never even heard the name of Freud. The Freudian psychology has affected both those who understood it and also the expansive lunatic fringe which gathered around it, as it gathers around any idea.

When we reflect on the wide influence of Freud, Adler and Jung and all the various forms of psychoanalysis, it seems strange to remember that it was only forty years ago, in 1894, that Freud took the first decisive step in opening a new method of interpreting mental life by replacing hypnotism as a means of resuscitating buried memories with his method of probing the mind by questions, a method which came to be called " free association." By this experiment in studying the nature of different kinds of psychoneuroses he made important discoveries and extended them to apply to the normal mind. A glimpse, from the point of view of a very sympathetic or even partisan critic, of what Freud did for psychology is afforded in these words of Stefan Zweig:

" Pre-Freud psychology was an academic specialty, encapsuled in seminaries, lost between the covers of ponderous tomes penned in unintelligible jargon. One who studied it learned no more about himself and his own peculiarities than if he had been studying Sanscrit or astronomy; and a sound instinct led most people to ignore the data turned out from the laboratories as irrelevant because unduly abstract and generalized. By resolutely directing psychological research toward the individual, and by making the crystalization of the personality its central theme, Freud brought the science into touch with realities and thus rendered it vitally important." [10]

First among the effects of Freud on popular thinking, as well as on psychology, has been his demonstration of the existence of the unconscious and the effect of the unconscious on the conscious mind. His work and that of his followers has shown that the conscious conflicts in the mental life, such as everyone feels, are far less than those which go on in the unconscious and which, even though unrecognized, have far-reaching effects on the mind and personality. This unconscious conflict is the real war of life, not a sharp temporary engagement of opposing forces but a " thirty years war," a " hundred years war." This conflict is well pictured in H. G. Wells' description of his hero, Mr. Polly: " He was not so much a human being as a civil war." In that sense there are remarkable parallels between Freud and St. Paul. No one else has so emphasized " the war in the members," which was central in the psychology of Paul. Indeed it is probably not too much to say that Freud is closer to Paul than any other modern writer, including all the theologians. His emphasis of the hidden struggle sapping the strength of the mind and spirit, the revelation of the mental and physical tension due to repression and suppression, have not only furnished fruitful insights into the nature

of mental life and conduct but have had wide and successful therapeutic use, both in mental disorders and in physical
ills. In addition, Freudianism has been a major factor, just
because of its exploration of repression and its resulting
neuroses, in the revolt against Puritanism. It has thus affected powerfully not only psychology but morals and religion as well.

The Freudian psychology brought to fresh attention —
indeed, in many respects, to the first clear attention — the
driving forces of human energy. To Freud this central driving power, the most important factor in personality, is the
sex instinct, including every manifestation of love and af-
fection which the race has known. Adler interprets this
primary motive power in human life as being not sexual
desire but " the will to power." Jung, coming later, combines the two theories in his interpretation. Instead of regarding the *libido* as being either some form of sex drive
or the " will to power," he included under it all instinctive
energy, which flows out through various channels. In all
these variations of theory, there is a recognition of the springs
of human motive and action, and the danger of blocking
instinctive energy without furnishing an alternative outlet.

It was inevitable that this fresh exploration of the rôle
of sex in life should have far-reaching effects both in thinking and in conduct. Sex was interpreted, not as a tree stuck
into the soil of human nature like a flag pole, but a plant of
far-ramifying roots intertwined with the whole of life.

The effects of the Freudian psychology on religion as well
as morals have been indirect but important. One of these
effects has been that already mentioned, in furnishing what
might be called an alternate scheme of salvation, to be sub-

stituted for the search for salvation in the old theological sense or in the strictly ethical sense. The answer to the question " What must I do to be saved? " was here at hand in the terms of the achievement of mental soundness, of freeing the mind from complexes and repressions.

A second effect has been that of the frequent interpretation of religion itself in terms of the Freudian vocabulary. There is nothing in psychoanalysis which logically demands the interpretation, so common among partisan Freudians, of religion as a phantasy or projection of a mother complex or a defense mechanism. But it is an interpretation quite natural to a devotee of a new gospel, anxious to apply it to everything in the heavens above, the earth beneath and the waters under the earth. Freud himself regards religion as an " illusion." He has declared that psychoanalysis " has no advice to offer as to what one shall or shall not do, as for instance, whether or not one should believe in a divine being." But the opportunity to interpret religion in the terms of fantasy lay so temptingly at hand that it was too strong to be resisted by many of Freud's more than twelve disciples. Here, for instance, is the complete settlement of the problem of God, given by one of the inner circle, Fritz Wittels:

" Psychoanalysis has made a thorough study of the phenomenon of transference and we now harbor no doubt that God-in-Heaven is a transference, a projection of the original father-experience beyond the clouds. Man creates his God not so much in the image of his own father but rather in the image of his father-ideal. Hence the Hebrew God, Jehovah, is a formidable, austere judge, while Jesus is the Son of man, who, like the child of a strict father, suffers and atones for us all by his sacrifice.

" The path to faith leads from our parents or their surrogates into our own breast, and thence in a kind of repercussion is projected from the chilly walls of the newly formed ego on to God; introjection and projection, terms commonly used in the psychoanalytic theory." [11]

In quite another direction is the contribution which the Freudian psychology has made to education and social work. It has furnished a new understanding of the hidden motives of conduct, an understanding fruitful in correcting unsocial action and personality. There is also the large service of psychoanalysis in the treatment of mental disorders. In a very real way the rôle of Freud has had parallels to that of Jesus rebuking the demons.

Of far-reaching moral influence has been the effect of Freud on the idea of sin. Freud says that the most bitter blow to human vanity is " the discovery by the psychoanalysists that the ego is not master in his own house." [12] Similar expressions of determinism have led to the substitution, by many, of environmental conditions and influences for moral choices as the source of evil. The result has been the weakening of the sense of moral responsibility and the feeling of guilt. This has filtered down into the thinking of many who have never been directly influenced by the new psychology.

Literature has shown many traces of the effect of the new psychology. In the United States, Eugene O'Neill, Sherwood Anderson, William Faulkner, Ernest Hemingway, Dorothy Canfield, Ellen Glasgow, James Branch Cabell, Robinson Jeffers and many others in varying degree show its influence. It is partially responsible for the almost complete eclipse of Sherwood Anderson as an artist. In England, the work of Brett Young, Clemence Dane, Rose Macaulay, Mrs. Sedgwick, G. B. Stern, the author of *Eliza-*

beth and Her German Garden, and J. D. Beresford, frequently embodies the principles of Freud.

VI

Forces of a different sort have also dominated the popular mood of the boom years, that spiritual elephantiasis, that monstrous expansion of body and smothering of soul, which went on in the late 'twenties. A fit symbol of this malignant disorder was found in the billboards set up over the country when the first tremors of the financial landslide were being recorded, on which a fatuous female figure flaunted a banner which read, " Nothing can stop U. S." It symbolized a mind molded into shape by high pressure salesmen, exerting a pressure far heavier than fifteen pounds to the square inch. Toward the end of the period an increasing characteristic of the national mind was the pressure of worry and fear. All through the era from 1919 to 1933 there was a constant parade of vulgarity and superficiality, a succession of one hysteria after another, a sorry history vividly set forth by Frederick L. Allen in his *Only Yesterday.*

A mood and mark of the early years of the period was what bore the name of " the return to normalcy." It was a reaction from both the high-pitched idealism of the war and the interest in European affairs. Two popular slogans were " Let Europe stew in her own juice " and " Back to business." A misprint almost inspired was that of a North Dakota newspaper which printed a preacher's text as " Righteousness *exhausteth* a nation." A loudly proclaimed, even though illusory, " righteousness " had exhausted the United

States at any rate! And in the slump that followed in the Harding administration, the country struck a new low in political immorality, marking a descent, in the opinion of most judges of such records, even from the achievements of the Grant administrations following the Civil War. Not the soil, surely, out of which a great idealistic literature could be expected to grow.

VII

What might we reasonably expect to find in the literature of an era exposed to such winds? Of course, many looked around after picking themselves up the morning after Armistice Day with a fine sentimental glow and naïvely gazed about for the brave new world promised in all the war advertising. That was hardly a reasonable expectation. Do men gather grapes of thistles? There was just one item in that pathetically optimistic faith which proved substantial. Fifteen years later it does look as though the prophecies of "a new world" may prove true. But as the novel elements painfully appear, their newness does not fit the Utopian pattern which sentimental hope marked out. That pattern was entirely lacking in realistic understanding or historical sense of what fruits grow from war. We find just what, looking back from the vantage ground of today, we can see that it was inevitable that we should find. In other words, literature has been the natural product of a period of deflated idealisms, as well as of the puncturing of pretentious lies. The stick of an extinguished skyrocket came down.

We find, as we might expect to find, disillusionment. Perhaps better than general statements will be one characteristic experience told by a writer demobilized from the army, John V. A. Weaver:

" I found that many of my colleagues shared my anger and disillusionment and my hope of improving matters. What did disturb us deeply was a growing suspicion that everybody, in every land concerned, had lost the war; that we, among millions, had been kidded along, mesmerized and cajoled by older individuals who had used flowery slogans and windy promises to debauch us; that many a face would never laugh among us again because of money interest alone; and that while some of us survivors were fortunate enough not to have lost eyes or legs or pieces of our skulls, all of us had been damaged in spirit, had been boiled more or less hard, had been cheapened and tarnished not for any noble cause, but simply to protect a financial investment.

" We were very angry about it. We did a lot of talking. It appears that the same sort of talk was going on among our contemporaries throughout America. We exhibited dissatisfaction and unrest. When our elders remonstrated and rebuked, we repulsed them with rude noises. When they offered advice, we told them what they could do with it. We began thumbing our noses at rules and regulations, conscientiously defiant. More from a sense of duty than from any real pleasure, we experimented with morals and customs. We behaved badly as a matter of principle. The movement was not in any sense organized. It just seemed to happen. After a while, they began referring to us as the Younger Generation — with the capitals which implied decided disapprobation." [13]

That seems a rather fair illustration of a score of novels and thousands of life experiences. Genuine enough in its origin in the personal experience of many, this mood gained vogue immensely through its establishment as a fashionable rôle. The ranks of the world-weary were increased by battalions who had never held any faith seriously enough to be disillusioned, and whose sharing in it was one of imitative gestures, sighs and pained expressions. An English novelist, one of the bitterest of the " debunkers," Richard Aldington, reveals a specious disillusionment in his story, *Last Straws,* in which satire stumbles unintentionally into burlesque. Three men who had fought together in the war sit around a Paris night club table reviewing their loss of faith and hope. One asks the other, " There's a sort of stink about human life, don't you feel? " And then he elaborates on it for several pages. Allowance for the popularity of the pose must always be made in estimating the importance of the mood of disillusionment for religion. But to put it all down chiefly to pose would be the greatest error possible. If a flood of writers moved from " the best of all possible worlds " to Futility Street, it was because they found the former habitation impossible.

Inevitably the dominant mark of much, probably most, of the significant literature in America since the war was realism, ranging all the way from the naturalism patterned after Zola to the more imaginative realism of such a novel as Ellen Glasgow's *Barren Ground.* The growth of the critical spirit, especially as the regimentation of mind caused by the war relaxed its grip, brought a more skeptical scrutiny to American life and institutions, particularly to middle class ideals and codes, than they had ever received. Novelists used a camera with a sharper lens. This realism was more than a mere continuation of the realism of Howells. It had a much closer relation to the earlier realism of Stephen Crane, and to that of Dreiser in his *Sister Carrie,* published in 1900. This realism bore about the same relation to the flood of costumed historical novels which filled the book stores and libraries from 1900 to 1910, and even up

to the war, as the poetry of Edgar Guest bears to a police
station blotter. An additional influence making for realism
was the fact that emotion was to so large an extent blasted
and withered by the war. The aftermath of the war gave
a new sharpness of line and positiveness of color to the literary painting; it added anger and bitterness plus a certain
" gargoyle " spirit. The very real spiritual values which that
realism holds and the demands which it makes on organized religion will be considered in a later chapter.

Much of the writing of the period furnishes evidence that
it was a sex-excited time. That is by no means peculiar to
America. Bergson writes in his latest book, " Our whole
civilization is sex-excited." In this the war played its part
as war always does. That shift in moral attitude in sex
relations is always a part of the war debt pushed on to the
next and following generations. We are still deeply in the
red. There has been an unflagging persistence of what
Aldous Huxley has so graphically called "the imbecile
earnestness of lust." That shift in attitude, ranging from a
fine sincerity in the search for rationality in sex, down to
the carnival of pornography in which every man, woman
and child in the United States has been provided with more
than his peck of dirt, has come from the various influences
playing upon the period. The undisciplined license is due
in part to the diminution of both faith and authority; to a
juvenile conception of freedom which has resulted in throwing over one convention only to enter the bondage of another, the even more galling bondage of unconventionality;
and also to an inevitable revolt from the pruderies and
hypocrisies of preceding decades.

Much literary production, not vastly important but great

in extent, comes under the head of cleverness, smartness, jauntiness, sophistication. An age when religion and the whole spiritual conception of life is dimmed for multitudes always becomes an age of the wits. A whole school of writers from Carl Van Vechten up or down unintentionally had their portrait drawn by A. A. Milne, who makes a little girl say:

> Now that I'm six I'm as clever as clever
> And I'll go on being six for ever and ever.[14]

And they have. Alfred Noyes in his *New Duckling* has well expressed the spirit of an exhibitionist school of writers:

> I want to be utter other,
> And frightfully modern and mad.

In the midst of these varied types of expression will be found in some quarters the steady continuance of man's immemorial wistfulness, the reaching out for God if haply he may find Him. There is the recognition of spiritual forces, and the picture of the emptiness, the insignificance of life without faith, without God. Much of this is found perhaps most strikingly in poetry, but it appears in drama, novel and short story also.

In this whole outlook, it must not be forgotten that the period is notable for the large number of books definitely on religious questions, not in the field of pure literature but on religion itself. It was a period notable for the extensive publishing and, perhaps, for the reading of religious books. Any estimate of the relative place of religion in public interest must be checked against this feature of the time.

There must be kept in mind also, as a guard against distortion, the remembrance that the most continuous and effective influences on the public mind have not been literary. Sinclair Lewis is no match for Micky Mouse, Willa Cather cannot win against Greta Garbo, in popular suffrage. Mount Parnassus could not compete with Hollywood. What is called "literature" has been of relatively small might compared to the wood pulp of countless forests slaughtered to make a journalistic holiday. As a constant bass accompaniment to the various blends which have gone into the national anthem has been the throaty voice of the salesman, sometimes blaring forth in a Te Deum, latterly sinking to a wail. The mural paintings installed in 1932 in the Whitney Museum of Modern Art in New York City express with at least some approach to accuracy the relative impact of influences in picturing the ballyhoo and slogans of business, the maneuvers of politics, and such arts of the city as cocktail-shaking, movies, radio and racketeering.

Such are a few, at least, of the influences playing on American life during the morning after the earthquake. It is evident that they did much to determine the literature which expressed that life and that, taken together, they created a time of enormous complexity and difficulty for organized religion.

[1] *Twenty-Five Years,* by Edward Grey.   Frederick A. Stokes Company.

[2] Saturday Review of Literature, Nov. 22, 1930.

[3] *The Psychology of the Religious Life,* by G. M. Stratton, p. 343.   The Macmillan Company.

[4] *The Science and Method of Politics,* by G. E. G. Catlin, p. 60.   Alfred A. Knopf.

[5] *Religion and Modern Life,* by W. E. Hocking, p. 358.   Charles Scribner's Sons.

[6] Journal of Religion, vol. III, p. 301.

7 *The Present and Future of Religion*, by C. E. M. Joad.   The Macmillan Company.

8 New York Herald Tribune, The Conning Tower.

9 *The Surge and Thunder*, by Charles G. Shaw.   American Book Company, 1932.

10 *Mental Healers*, by Stefan Zweig.   Viking Press.

11 *Religion Today*, edited by Arthur L. Swift.   McGraw-Hill Book Company.

12 *Freud Collected Papers*, vol. IV, pp. 247–356.   International Psychoanalytic Press, New York.

13 The Forum, September, 1932.

14 *Now We Are Six*, by A. A. Milne.   E. P. Dutton & Company.

CHAPTER TWO

RELIGION IN A DEFLATED WORLD

W HAT of religion amid the years of turmoil that
followed the war?

What of the church, meeting a type of mind
new to it, unfamiliar moods of the spirit, strange tides of
experience, difficult and baffling?

There is a spot in the Black Forest in Germany where
forty-two trails converge. Religion has been on such a spot.
No one adjective can be stretched till it encompasses the
whole religious life of the time. It is bound to crack somewhere. The church and religious thought, as in every age,
have taken the impresses of the time, have reflected, here in
one emphasis, there in another, the widely various stresses
which molded their environment. No evaluation of the life
of organized Christianity in the post-war period could even
approach fairness, in which sympathetic understanding of
the conflicts and tensions which it had to undergo in a time
of confusion did not predominate over the far easier and
simpler, too easy and simple, attitude of lusty condemnation. In a period which has to show in attitudes to social
and political questions both a " new low " of cynical disenchantment and also the peak of the most fatuous optimism,
possibly of all time, when poetry found expression both in
Carl Sandburg and in Elinor Wylie, and fiction both in *An*

American Tragedy and in Elizabeth Maddox Roberts, it is vain to look for any straight trail or undifferentiated pattern in religion. If many of the official interpreters of religion seemed to be bowing down to a Nebuchadnezzar's image of Business, it was also a time when a new ethical realism was developing. If organized religion had to struggle with a revived obscurantism, it also experienced fresh intellectual adjustments and formulations. If the inner life of the church was engulfed by the mechanics of a score of extrovert crusades more distinguished perhaps for motion than for emotion, it was also the time of a fresh emphasis on worship.

That religion occupies a diminished place in the thinking and activity of multitudes of people in the United States today is, of course, not to be questioned. It is the axiom from which discussion starts. A reporter, Morris Markey, in his *This Country of Yours,* published in 1932, makes the assertion that Christianity is hardly to be considered at all as a force in directing the current or objectives of American life. His book records the adventures and conclusions of a 16,000-mile trip undertaken to learn what this country and its inhabitants are really like. His observations were made in too casual and superficial a manner to have any real value except as personal impressions. Nevertheless they are interesting as confirming the impressions of a great many others. Mr. Markey explains that in his travels he asked hundreds of people, " from coal miners who were hungry to bankers and business men and shopgirls and housewives, what they were getting from their religion in these disturbed times." " Only one man said that his church, his God, was a prop to him," the book continues. " He was sincere and I believed him. The others, too, were sincere and I believed them.

Nowhere did I encounter a genuine religious feeling. Everywhere I encountered skepticism, distrust, or amusement at the beliefs of our fathers."

Contrasting with this lack of interest in religion, Mr. Markey found all over the country, even in remote parts, " an intense eagerness to embrace the amenities of art." This he calls not escape mechanism, not an aspect of the " culture craze," but " a definite striving toward the enrichment of life." [1]

On the face of it, such a report and the random manner of its gathering rule it out as convincing evidence concerning the spiritual state of the country. Yet, after large deductions for exaggeration and one-sidedness, it will win the agreement of a large number as giving a substantially fair picture. Whatever its value as observation may be, the thing which cannot be doubted is that its judgment surprisingly coincides with the impression to be gained from a large part of the fiction published in the United States since 1918.

With this preface, several groups of characteristics and influences may rightly receive emphasis. They add up to a peculiar sum and combination of liabilities, internal and external, handicaps which unfitted organized religion for the task of molding and largely influencing the life of its time. These liabilities help to interpret one major mark, already noted, of the literature of the time, the diminished influence and expression of explicit religion.

I

Among such handicaps or liabilities, perhaps the most obvious are the powerful rivals of religion for popular interest and allegiance. Chief among these seem to be science, nationalism, economic absorption and amusement. Five years ago, instead of the phrase, " economic absorption," another word, " prosperity," would doubtless have been used. At that time it was no exaggeration to say that the " religion of prosperity " was one of Christianity's chief rivals in America. Today we have the reverse side of that religion, the economic struggle for existence. It is not as glittering a form of worship, but it makes as strong a demand on the attention. In European countries and in the world generally, communism would appear on any list of the rivals of Christianity. In the United States, however, even at the worst period of the depression, social radicalism has such a relatively slight following that it would be decidedly unrealistic to label communism as a serious rival of Christianity. But the other forces mentioned — nationalism, science, amusement — are formidable rivals of religion. They are accorded by millions the veneration and the devotion usually reserved for some form of religion.

One of the greatest liabilities of organized Christianity was that it was to a real degree bankrupted by the war. It had to confront the need of a battered world in which idealisms were exhausted, the need for moral resources in a spiritual interpretation of reality, with a pathetically emptied treasury. The church had put Jesus into a khaki uniform and experienced insuperable difficulties in demobilizing him. Demobilization is always a difficult social process. Spiritual demobilization, we have learned once more to our grief, is an even more difficult process.

It is no answer to this charge that the church failed in moral leadership to reply that preachers and laymen merely shared in the general attitude of the nation. That simply reiterates the charge in a clarified form. It admits that they were not " the salt of the earth," were not above or ahead of popular emotional mass thinking. The church moved as a captive chained to the conqueror's car.

For this result there were many reasons which need not be explored here. Among them is the fact that neither among religious leaders nor in the rank and file of the churches had there been any clear, thoroughgoing thinking on war. It had never been made a part of the church's major concern. A devotion to peace had come to be accepted " in principle," but no one got really excited about it. Such criticism of war as was made was based not so much on definitely religious grounds as on a more or less sentimental belief in " Progress," a cross between an uncritical trust in evolution and Matthew Arnold's dim " power not ourselves which makes for righteousness."

The weakness of this peace sentiment was clearly indicated in the lack of any vigorous criticism of the Spanish-American War in 1898, and of the launching of American imperialism which followed it. The church by its enthusiastic acceptance of the war, by its adoption of " manifest destiny" and conferring on it a religious sanctity, showed itself a ready instrument to be used by the jingoistic journalism which played so large a part in precipitating the war. The church helped definitely to rationalize the American venture in imperialism. It failed completely to reach or express anything like the moral and spiritual insight of William Vaughn Moody's poems of the period, " Ode in a Time of Hesitation " and " On a Soldier Fallen in the Philippines," or Senator George F. Hoar's spirited leadership of the Anti-Imperialist Society.

An extreme picture of the cautiousness of the peace sentiment of American churches is that of Captain Alfred T. Mahan, a notable churchman, author of a very pious book, *The Harvest Within,* who protested vigorously against the proposal of the Hague Peace conference in 1899 forbidding the use of " asphyxiating deleterious gases." He did so on the high ground of patriotism, declaring that " the United States Government was averse to placing any restriction on the inventive genius of its citizens in inventing and providing weapons of war." To Mahan, the use of poison gas was not at all inconsistent with a life " with Christ at sea." In the same year Theodore Roosevelt, whose lifelong rampant, adolescent militarism did not prevent him from being an idol to large masses of church people, declared in the *Independent* (Dec. 21, 1899): " It is only the warlike power of a civilized people that can give peace to the world."

The World War in 1914 caught religious leaders and churches alike unprepared to act as a critical minority to the emotion and mass suggestion generated by the conflict. It is hardly too much to say that in general after 1917 a moratorium was put on the New Testament, except the passage describing Jesus driving the money changers out of the temple with a whip of small cords. Documented evidence of the support of the war given to the churches, all the way from the paranoiac ravings of a Newell Dwight Hillis down to much more sobered and temperate utterances, private and official, is to be found in *The Churches and War* by Albert R. H. Miller, 1931, in *Religion in Our Times,* by Gaius Glenn Atkins, 1932, in Kirby Page's *National Defense,* 1930, in *Preachers Present Arms,* by Ray W. Abrams, 1933, and in W. E. Garrison's *The March of Faith,* 1933.

Superficially, the church thrived during the war. But in

most sensitive quarters apprehension was felt for the aftermath. Early in 1918 one thoughtful preacher prophesied,
" The soldiers will come back like the day of judgment."
That prophecy was not literally fulfilled. The expectation
was that the men in uniform would come back filled with
vehement criticism of the church. The Day of Judgment
came, but in a different and more deadly form; not in loud
recriminations but in apathy and silence. Organized religion
simply did not register as a field of interest. It had wasted
its substance in riotous living in a far country, and by an inevitable spiritual law which no man can abolish, it began to
be in want. That want is inseparably related to the whole
literature of futility, which flourished in the post-war years.

II

From another point of view, a major liability of organized
Christianity has been the dominance of a traditional mood
of romantic optimism, which has unfitted it to function in
a world turning increasingly to realism. Even where this
mood has not found expression in the worship of Saint
Pollyanna, it has been felt in a complacency kept alive by
restricted attention to a partial view of its world, well
screened from the ugly realities which do not fit in with its
romantic view of life.

The Commission on Social Trends in the United States,
which published its voluminous report in December 1932,
might well have included among its illustrations of the
tragic " lags " which exist between the social sciences and
social practices and the mechanical sciences, with the resulting changed situations, many striking instances from the

field of religion. The social and economic outlook characterizing much of the religious mind of the day of Henry Ford and J. P. Morgan was that of the naïve idyllic optimism of Ralph Waldo Emerson and Theodore Parker. In his essay, " Emerson Re-read," [2] James Truslow Adams has given unintendingly a penetrating criticism of this romanticism so prominent in the mental world of the churches. Mr. Adams describes with sympathy the stimulating and inspiring effect which in his youth the reading of Emerson had upon him. In middle age Mr. Adams went back to Emerson to see whether the same effect would be produced. He says that the old spell was broken, the old magic gone; and in analyzing it, he ascribes the failure to Emerson's lack of " a sense of the tragedy of life." It is just that lack of a painful " sense of the tragedy of life " which makes the whole message of the average pulpit seem so unreal and irrelevant in today's world, in the minds of multitudes of people. Boy Scouts in the pulpit are not enough to challenge their attention or serious consideration.

A new test of the pronunciation of "shibboleth " had been set up for accepted orthodoxy. The shibboleth for the past forty years has been the belief that " the world is growing better." Parrot-like repetition of this slogan has been made almost a passport to good standing in religious circles. Realistic understanding of economic and political actualities, insights into social conditions, which might have given real power and moral leadership to the churches, have been again and again banned and damned as destructive and pessimistic.

In the little village of Selborne, in England, the visitor is shown the row of trees which Gilbert White, the author of *The Natural History of Selbourne,* planted around his parsonage to shut out the view of the slaughter house. That beautiful row of trees may well stand as a symbol of the various other screens with which other occupants of parsonages and churches in our time have shut out from their view the disturbing vision of the brutalities and cruelties of civilization. In an age marked, outside the church, by an increasingly piercing sight of ethical conflicts, of the powerful and sinister forces which control and condition the life of millions, a large part of the church has continued to look out on the world, when it has really looked at all, through the rosy glasses either of a mild sentimental liberalism, or through the full pink of nineteenth century optimism. Sure judgment on that condition is passed in one sentence, the observation of Karl Barth: "The age which has no great anguish on its heart will have no great music on its lips." Christianity has not been singing in great music. Above the din of jazz which has split the ear drums, there has not sounded in sufficiently stirring volume a song of redemption of this "sorry scheme of things entire." The lack has not been so much in the throat as in the heart; it is not a lack of vocal chords so much as of an anguish which might set them vibrating with great music.

III

An additional liability of the church has been its seduction by the contemporary worship of success. There is a sharp painful picture, which we cannot dismiss as an unfounded libel, in a bit of stage direction in O'Neill's *Mourning Becomes Electra,* describing a minister: "Hills is a type of well fed minister of a prosperous, small town congregation, stout and unctuous, snobbish and ingratiating, conscious of godliness, but timid and always feeling his way." Hills is not the whole ministerial train, by any means; but he has been in the procession. Much preaching has no more relation to life than the romantic novels of George Barr McCutcheon or Jeffery Farnol. It has offered an escape, an evasion of the real world, just about on a par in relevance to present life with the costumed stories of Sabatini.

In many a Protestant cathedral, far more fitting than statues of Jeremiah, Amos and St. Peter, which are often found, would be a statue to a figure who has actually been a patron saint of many of the worshipers — Horatio Alger. He was the author of the stories of poor boys who " made good," on which a generation fed their souls in youth. His philosophy of the primacy of success formed an uncanonical Epistle to the Americans. In an adjoining niche might well be a statue of Herbert Spencer, whose doctrine of inevitable progress was far more influential on a generation than that of original sin. Whatever might be sung by the choir, a favorite anthem of the pulpit was:

> Out of the darkness of the night
> The world rolls into light,
>   It is morning everywhere.

Spencer's philosophy was a doctrine of Irresistible Grace interpreted in social and economic terms.

To a degree painful to contemplate, organized religion, owing largely to its lack of equipment for clear thinking in the realm where ethics and economics mingle and to the befuddling of its moral sense by the seduction of wealth, ac-

cepted the rôle of Court Chaplain to the financial nobility.
In their uncritical sprinkling of incense on the status quo, the
churches have often verged perilously near the apex of complacency reached by Edward Everett in his immortal words
on American government: " Our government is in its theory
perfect, and in its operation perfect also. Thus we have
solved the great problem of human affairs."

One minor reason for this has been unquestionably the
increasing separation of many of the city churches from poor
neighborhoods. As the district around the church grew
crowded, as the character of the neighborhood "went
down," as it was phrased — in other words, as the need for
ministry was intensified — the churches followed their membership out to more pleasant prospects. It made a physical
gulf much wider than that which separated Dives from
Lazarus. Indeed, without any cynicism it may be said that,
as many " downtown " churches saw their members moving
out to the residential hills surrounding a typical city, they
took to heart the words of the psalmist, " I will lift mine eyes
unto the hills whence cometh my help."

There can be no doubt that the service which might have
been rendered by a critical Christian minority, in an age
when success was indeed the " bitch goddess " which William James called it, was not performed. In 1932 a curious
law case came before a New York court. On the death of
the Shah of Persia one of the largest New York city banks
was appointed executor of his estate in the United States.
Objection was raised in Persia that the New York bank was
not qualified to administer the estate, since the Shah was a
Mohammedan and the bank was a " Christian institution."
So the bank was forced to go solemnly to court and adduce

legal proof that it was not a Christian institution. Needless to say, it made its case easily and completely! There are a great many revered institutions which could easily prove their non-Christian character, or to put it more strongly, their anti-Christian character. But that character has not been discerned by eyes blinded by the glamour of " success."

Some observers have found in the character of religious architecture of the last generation, aside from Gothic architecture, a clue to the comparative impotence of religion, its lack of coercive quality and commanding significance. Dean William P. Ladd of the Berkeley Divinity School has put this feeling cogently: " The art of any period expresses its true character. It tells no lies. If we stand inside one of the Gothic cathedrals of the middle ages, who can but feel that the men who thus built, whatever else they may have been, were men of a high and serious purpose? Their religion must have been characterized as is their building by reality, conviction, clarity, poise, solidity, purpose. Today there is no religious art. Artists generally seem to find little in the church with which they can make contact, and are skeptical that the church can go along with them in any adventurous and original creative work. I have enumerated certain words which naturally come to one's mind within a great medieval cathedral. If we enter one of our present-day churches, what words would come with similar inevitability to our minds? Would it not be some such list as this: conventionality, frivolity, restlessness, pretentiousness, sentimentality, futility, jangling discord? Even in the best of our present-day church edifices there is a timid imitation of the past, a servile spirit which hardly does justice to Jesus or St. Paul. And as in our church buildings, so in all our so-called religious art there is a sad vacuity, an absence of any seriousness of conviction and of purpose."

Another handicap which crippled organized Christianity in its ministry to the post-war period was the fact that the so-called social gospel was a war casualty. This does not mean that passionate interest in the social implications of the Christian gospel was everywhere swept away. But as a dominant note, as the central emphasis of the church, it was lost. It sank with other deflated idealisms. The war marked the end of a chapter in the reform movement, in political progressivism, a chapter recently traced by John Chamberlain's *Farewell to Reform.* The " social gospel " shared its fate. No doubt partially from compensation, perhaps also as many feel as an evasion, new emphases notably on theology and worship have displaced the social gospel which had been gaining since the publication of Walter Rauschenbusch's *Christianity and the Social Crisis* in 1907. That freezing of every social movement is, in the long run, always one of the worst legacies of war, a supreme example of the sins of the fathers visited on the children of oncoming generations.

This judgment must, of course, be qualified by the recognition of the increase in force and sharpness in the church's witness against war — though of how stout a fiber that witness is made is yet to be tested. There is also the evident fresh concern of ministers with the question of a new social order. That concern is one real spiritual gift of the depression. Here again, however, we have yet to see what effect any first indications of the long awaited " upturn " may have on the chorus of voices in the church now calling for a new order. Will it be another case of " the river past and God forgotten"? Will the fervor of the voices be muted and the churches turn back with relief to interrupted building projects and a contented normalcy? Will the churches reveal that what in this critical mood of social discontent they were most fervently interested in was not the coming of an order of love, a Kingdom of God, but merely the return of prosperity? The answer to that question lies in the years ahead.

Doctrinal controversy of varying degrees of acrimony loomed large in the period. Whatever ultimate results history may assign to that chapter of warfare, it is surely to be listed as among the chief liabilities to the Christian religion as a molding influence on the national mind. Distorted as that controversy was through the public press, it resulted in a caricature of religion which found a sure lodgment in the minds of multitudes. The effect of such controversy fits very well Macaulay's rhetorical question, " What army commanded by a debating society ever achieved anything but disgrace?" In large parts of the country, during the years of the fundamentalist warfare, the hymn, " Onward, Christian Soldiers," to be fairly descriptive of the situation, should have been amended to read,

> Like an angry debating society
> Stands the church of God.

In an age of confusion, the church itself was confused. The first Anglican Bishop of Calcutta died lamenting two things — prickly heat and Presbyterianism. To think of anyone confronted with the appalling spectacle of India wasting his emotional energy on such cosmic issues, seems, from this distance, to indicate a mind slightly out of focus. Such is the impression which the fundamentalist controversy has given to large numbers of people, particularly those whose minds and experience have found expression in the literature of the period.

To sum up in a sentence, then: With such a background, with the resources and energies of religion hobbled in different ways, it is not surprising that we find the relation of post-war literature to religion more evidently that of the indication of spiritual need and challenge to religion than of any mounting ascendency of faith.

[1] *This Country of Yours,* by Morris Markey.   Little, Brown & Company, 1932.
[2] Atlantic Monthly, October, 1930.

CHAPTER THREE

POST-WAR REALISM

A FEW years after the war Witter Bynner wrote a little poem of three verses which might well serve as a text for the most characteristic literature of the decade following.

> The old men said to the young men,
> " Who will fight to be free? "
> The young men said to the old men,
> " We."
>
> The old men said to the young men,
> " It is over now, you can go."
> The young men said to the old men,
> " No! "
>
> The old men said to the young men,
> " What is there left to do? "
> The young men said to the old men,
> " You! " [1]

That accusing word, " you," has been flung all over the landscape. The accent has varied from serious, searching criticism to gleeful, savage onslaught. The mood has, in some authors, been that of a thoughtful pessimism, in others that of a noisy, adolescent revolt, conscious of being terribly shocking and having a lovely time throwing rocks through the court house windows. But in all the voices the constant note of a fresh appraisal, a skeptical questioning of American life and its assumptions, has been heard.

This mood has found expression in all varieties of writing, in criticism, history and biography as well as in poetry and fiction. In the field of criticism, both literary and social, the post-war years are marked by what is almost the first flowering of thoroughgoing critical evaluation of American literature, life and institutions. In novels and poetry, however, and to a real extent in other fields of literature also, the war did not so much create a new mood as give an acceleration to attitudes which had been developing both in Great Britain and America for a generation. It brought a revelation like that of a star shell bursting over the trenches, showing many a dim mass which had generally been regarded as a rose garden to be in reality a barbed wire entanglement.

Stout certainties increasingly gave way to question marks. "The war startled us out of pleasant places of thought into horrified awareness of the maladjustments of political society, and the peace thrust us into an era of rebellion against the smugness which had accepted the pre-war world as something to rejoice in." [2]

The end of the war was, for many, an hour in America's life like the fatal twelve o'clock in the story of Cinderella, when the spell of illusion was snapped, when the cloth of gold turned into rags, when the stately coach became a pumpkin shell and the horses scampered off in the form of mice. Central in the mood was the realization that the preceding age had, in the words of George Eliot, "bequeathed to the young generation a tumbled house." The uncritical acceptance of Victorian stabilities had passed almost as completely as the mutton-chop whiskers of William K. Vanderbilt.

This critical spirit found inevitable expression in the notes marking the literature of the time: *realism* of various sorts, *disillusionment* and *the sense of futility*. If this was not a soil from which we might reasonably expect great literature, in the sense of interpreting the timeless history of the human spirit, it has enormous importance for religion in its expression of the mind of the time. Under these three closely related aspects of the writing of these post-war years, may be grouped three characteristic revolts of the '20's: the "revolt from the village," of which *Main Street* was the shining banner; the revolt from Puritanism, in which cause a noble army, men and boys, the matron and the maid, marched under the aegis of H. L. Mencken; and the revolt from sanctified optimisms in the economic world. The bogey of Puritanism proved a veritable godsend to many writers, and to a large company who did not express their glee through the linotype. For it filled a great need — that of a new devil. The old theological devil had expired, and his passing left a lonesome place against the sky. In "Puritanism" a new devil was discovered, a fixed point against which all one's rage could be discharged, a new root of all evil. Through scores of books and piles of articles as thick as the leaves of autumn, the castigation of the devil went on. Like the reiteration of the old sailor in O'Neill's play, *Anna Christie,* "dat ole devil, sea," was heard the lament, "dat ole devil, Puritanism." The fact that most of the devotees of this New Orthodoxy, like their High Priest, Ludwig Lewisohn, had but the slightest understanding of what Puritanism really was and is historically, and that from this

abundant ignorance they confused Puritanism with their
version of the conventions and restraints of present-day life
in a small town, did not in the least abate their zeal or spoil
the gaiety of the party.

The third revolt is connected with the death of Pollyanna.
For the report of her passing seems not to be exaggerated.
The nineteenth century faith in automatic progress has
turned to ashes. The descent from the peak of rosy hopes
of the beneficent results of the unimpeded freedom of self-
interest has been sharp and steep. The smoke of factory
chimneys is no longer hailed with trusting faith as a pillar
of smoke by day sure to lead the chosen people out of the
wilderness into the promised land.

I

In any effort to evaluate the service of realistic fiction to
the understanding of American life, it is necessary to dis-
entangle what is essential realism from the various accumu-
lations which have so frequently appeared with it that they
have been judged to be inseparable parts of it. The simple
definition by Howells expresses the essential thing: " Realism is nothing more nor less than the truthful presentation
of material." That makes clear, what is often obscured, that
realism is a method, a spirit, not a philosophy.

Two things may well be kept in mind. The first is that
so many sideshows have been set up around realism that
they have obscured the main tent. The most frequent and
confusing of these is the ponderous philosophy which calls
itself " naturalism," which is a pessimistic philosophy of
determinism using for the most part the method of photo-

graphic detail. Naturalism may roughly be called a theory of fiction which aims to include "nothing but nature." It was inevitable that the scientific movement of the latter part of the nineteenth century, especially that reverential awe of science which elevates it to a philosophy, should reach over into the field of fiction. The term was first used by Zola in France, and its accepted meaning was largely defined by Zola's practice in fiction. Man was both the creature and victim of "nature," taking that term as the sum of physical influences affecting man. Naturalism dethrones man from his traditional seat "a little lower than the angels," and gives him a place with his relatives in the zoo. "We naturalists, we men of science," wrote Zola, "we must admit nothing occult; men are but phenomena and the conditions of phenomena."

The naturalistic canons of fiction were employed in America by Stephen Crane and Frank Norris in the 1890's. The most thoroughgoing and consistent practitioner of the twentieth century in America is Dreiser, with Sherwood Anderson, Jack London, Hemingway, Masters, Faulkner and others showing its influence.

Naturalism claims to approach life in a scientific spirit, to deal with nothing but facts, to observe from the outside. This intention has very often been violated, as frequently in Dreiser. In the analysis and description of personalities and their action there is often pressed into service a philosophy imported from cloudland, one which has no more foundation in demonstrated fact than the medieval castles suspended in pink clouds in Maxfield Parrish's pictures. Naturalism has brought the liberty of an enlarged and unexpurgated dictionary. It has made an almost religious

principle of " frankness." Vital areas which had been regarded as a forbidden zone by " genteel " literature were
dealt with in the endeavor to study and portray the whole
personality. It was natural that, inasmuch as sex had been
the most interdicted topic, it should receive a major portion of attention. This fitted in very well with the new
Freudian emphasis on the rôle of sex in life, though the
emphasis on sex relations by many novelists, following the
lead of Zola and Flaubert, preceded any wide influence
of Freud.

Naturalism brought a new doctrine of determinism.
John Calvin came back to earth in a new incarnation. The
determinism of the twentieth century was not theological
but physical. It was also, in many writers, social and
economic. Man was a marionette in whom free will was a
mocking delusion. This view did not ordinarily involve
belief in fatalism in the sense in which it appeared, either by
design or by malignant chance, in Hardy. It is rather the
blind action of physical forces. A new type of determinism
came also from looking at the spectacle of man helpless
against the social forces of his environment or the vast im-
personal processes of modern industry.

Not necessarily a part of any theory of naturalism, but a
frequent feature of its practice by naturalistic writers, was
the selection of abnormal, queer, often grotesque types of
persons as characters in novels. These illustrated the theory
better than more normal, vigorous characters would. That
is doubtless why most post-war fiction has had such a large
gallery of halfwits, neurotics, morons, and psychopathic
cases. These range from the bulky dentist, *McTeague,* in
Norris's novel, 1899, the big giant with the low I.Q., to

caricatures like Elmer Gantry, and the derelicts who swarm in the work of William Faulkner and Erskine Caldwell. The philosophy of naturalism and the method of realism are two separate things. They have frequently, however, been confused. One result has been that people who reject such an outmoded dogmatic philosophy as that which Theodore Dreiser drags along with him have rejected as well the real values in his reporting, and in that of a score of others. Again, the word " realism " has been associated with those literary steam dredges whose one aim and accomplishment has been to churn up the mud at the bottom of life. The working motto of a good many journeymen of fiction has been, " There is no truth but Mud and I am its prophet! " Realism is not a gospel of mud; it is simply a method which sculptors in mud have frequently used. There is the realism of Dorothy Canfield as well as that of William Faulkner's clinical case studies of Mississippi degenerates; the realism of Willa Cather's Nebraska, as well as that of Ernest Hemingway's prize fighters and dipsomaniacs.

Around the subject of realism, a sort of theology has begun to cluster. Professor Walter B. Pitkin has become the Thomas Aquinas of the faith, having listed and described no less than nine " elemental kinds of realism," with such formidable identification tags as " presentative physical realism " and " interpretative biological realism." But one need not wander off into such a Ph.D. wilderness in order to understand the general meaning of realism in literature. The judgment of Rolvaag indicates it: " The unforgivable sin is to write about life untruthfully." The meaning is equally clear in Dreiser's description of his doubt and confusion, on his going to New York to practice journalism;

" In a kind of ferment or fever due to my necessities and desperation, I set to examining the current magazines and fiction and articles to be found therein — Century, Scribner's, Harper's. I was never more confounded than by the discrepancy existing between my own observations and those displayed here, the beauty and peace and charm to be found in everything, the complete absence of any reference to the coarse and the cruel and the terrible. How did it happen that these remarkable persons, geniuses of course, one and all, saw life in this happy roseate? Was it so and was I all wrong? . . . They seemed to deal with phases of sweetness and beauty and success and goodness such as I rarely encountered." [3]

" The purpose of writing," says Conrad, " is, above all, to make you see." That has been achieved, of course, by the great romanticists, as well as by realists. It is distinctly an achievement of a large company of writers in the past fifteen years, many of whom will look, no doubt, as out of place in the list of the spiritual assets of the time as the village atheist in a church choir: Dreiser, Sherwood Anderson, John Dos Passos, Ernest Hemingway, Zona Gale, Sinclair Lewis, Ellen Glasgow, Carl Sandburg, T. S. Stribling, Willa Cather, Robert Herrick, Eugene O'Neill.

In this connection one point concerning the prolonged discussion over literary " humanism " which marked the years 1929 and 1930 may well be noted. Professor Irving Babbitt and many in the camp of the humanists pleaded vigorously for " the literature which combines excellence of form and soundness of substance " and which includes " the humanistic virtues of moderation, common sense and decency." [4] The words have a fine ring about them. From that position many volleys have been fired into the ranks of the despised naturalists and realists during the course of the paper battle. What the humanists either forget or disregard is the fact that much of the literature which has embodied those qualities has been painfully lacking in other qualities very necessary for the preservation of real values of human dignity and worth, namely, eyesight and insight, the power of seeing and understanding the manner in which the social and economic powers of our day are mangling, maiming, despoiling human life for millions. So many of the approved "humanists" have been deaf, dumb and blind to the actual tragedies of life. They have been meditating on an ivory tower. For that reason the product of "humanism" has been weighed and found wanting. It has failed to bring into being an effective criticism of some of the most powerful inhuman forces of our time. The disintegration in literature, which so pains Mr. Babbitt and Mr. Paul Elmer More, is not primarily in literature but in life itself.

The achievement of realistic fiction is a service of great importance and significance to religion, for in that group and in others we have a report of people who have cut their eye teeth. They have played the part of a clear-eyed Little Red Riding Hood. Undeceived by the beautiful lace cap over the wolf's ears, they have blurted out, "What big teeth you've got, grandma." They have exclaimed on the big dangerous teeth of many a masquerading grandma in our modern life, knocked down many a beautiful screen hiding a dirty corner, punctured many a sham, shown beauty in unlikely and unexpected places. They have justified the thanksgiving of Stuart Sherman, uttered just a few

months before his death in 1928: " The age in which we
now live appears to me to be a great and fascinating period
in the emotional and literary discovery of America, because
the woods are full of lighted torches, are full of men and
women bent on exploring and reporting the truth as they
see it and nothing but the truth, and great areas of repressed truth about their own lives and the lives of the
American people. One feels the quickening breath of this
spirit in many places; in history, in biography, in criticism,
in poetry, in our so-called fiction, which becomes more and
more a peculiarly intimate and veracious form of contemporary history." [5]

Not only are we indebted to " lighted torches," but to
unbent knees and unbowed backs. For this group, in their
frequent reporting of things as they are, have again and
again played the part of those three Hebrews who refused
to bow down to Nebuchadnezzar's image. To the mon-
archs of our industrial world, who have set up a golden idol
to be worshiped, standards to be accepted, ugliness to be
acclaimed as beautiful, cruelties and frustrations to be endured, many who deal in facts rather than fairy tales, have
said: " Be it known unto thee, O King, that we will not
serve thy gods nor worship the golden image which thou
hast set up." That is no inconsiderable service to a spiritual
conception of the purpose of life, particularly when it was
rendered, in many cases, ten to twenty years ahead of the
time in which any considerable section of the church had
begun seriously to question the beneficent human results of
an enthroned business philosophy of life.

Let us not make the tribute too uncritical. Mr. Chesterton
says of Macaulay's style that some of the time it was steel;

some of the time it was tin. Steel and tin are well mixed in post-war novelists. Let us look first for some steel.

II

Here is one usually regarded, by those with a faith in moral and spiritual realities, as having much more tin than steel — Theodore Dreiser. " Can any good come out of Dreiser? " has been a frequent question. Much of his characteristic work had already been done by the end of the war, including those novels which really opened the present era in realistic fiction, *Sister Carrie* and *Jennie Gerhardt,* the first of which so scandalized the public that it was withdrawn from publication for several years. Also belonging in the pre-war years are the two novels, voluminous mountains of words, on an American superman, *The Titan,* and *The Financier,* based on the career of Charles T. Yerkes. Since then he has written the novel which made his greatest success, *An American Tragedy,* four books of short stories, three books of autobiography, *A Book About Myself, Dawn* and *A Traveler at Forty,* and a book of philosophical essays, *Hey, Rub-a-Dub-Dub.*

Dreiser came into the literary world like a barbarian invasion. He was at first regarded much as the genteel of Rome must have looked on the blond gigantic Goths who poured in on their classic city. And his whole personality, philosophy and technique were just as destructive to the cozy and trim world of the genteel novel as were the Vandals to the beauty of Mediterranean cities. There is much about him that suggests the Goth or Vandal, in both strength and crudeness. Even in his style there is a massive heavyfootedness. Dreiser lumbered into the field of literature more heavily handicapped than any modern writer who has gained a place of first importance. He is the victim of an endlessly verbose style, undistinguished and often ungrammatical, as full of irrelevant detail as a five and ten cent store. Yet this very handicap makes his achievement all the more significant.

Three aspects of Dreiser may be selected as having particular importance for the religious and moral thinking and life of our day.

The first is found in the underlying philosophy which pervades the whole of his work. He presents probably the most thoroughgoing mechanistic, naturalistic point of view of any modern American writer. A widely read author with so definitely an anti-religious, anti-christian, a-moral outlook is one who cannot be ignored by those committed to a spiritual interpretation of life. It is of course easy to show that Dreiser's pretensions to a really scientific basis for his so-called philosophy is the most fictitious part of his fiction. His elaborate theory of " chemisms " in the blood, as the determining source of conduct, would make any competent psychologist or authority in physiological chemistry imagine he was reading in the more fantastic portions of the works of the brothers Grimm. Dreiser had the misfortune to become soundly converted to the materialism of Tyndall just about the time it was being laid away in moth balls by both scientists and philosophers.

But pointing that out by no means disposes of Dreiser as an influence. Aside from his own personal ideas, his brooding and groping, now dogmatic in the extreme and now quite humble and tentative in the presence of mystery, his work expresses tendencies of view and mood rather widely held. They represent attitudes which present a strong challenge to organized religion.

Dreiser expresses two types of determinism, that of nature and that of economic forces. He sees life directed by chance.

"We are all such pathetic victims of chance, anyhow. We are born, we struggle, we plan, and chance blows all our dreams away. If, therefore, one country, one state dares to dream the impossible, why cast it down before its ultimate hour? Why not dream with it? It is so gloriously, so truly a poetic land. We were conceived in ecstasy and born in dreams. And so, were I one of sufficient import to be able to speak to my native land, the galaxy of States of which it is composed, I would say: Dream on. Believe. Perhaps it is unwise, foolish, childlike, but dream anyhow. Disillusionment is destined to appear. You may vanish as have other great dreams, but even so, what a glorious, an imperishable memory!" [6]

In the thirty years of his writing there has been no perceptible progress, growth or change in Dreiser's philosophy, with the notable exception of his profession of conversion to communism in recent years. His statement in 1931 might be made to cover all his work since *Sister Carrie,* published in 1900:

"Life is to me too much of a welter and play of inscrutable forces to permit of any significant comment. One may paint for one's own entertainment, and that of others perhaps.

"As I see him, the unutterably infinitesimal individual weaves among the mysteries a floss-like and wholly meaningless course — if course it be. In short, I catch no meaning from all I have seen, and pass quite as I came, confused and dismayed.

"I find life to be not only a complete illusion or mirage which changes and so escapes or eludes one at every point, but the most

amazing fanfare of purely temporary and always changing and ever
vanishing and, in the main, clownish and ever ridiculous interests
that it has ever been my lot to witness — interests which concern at
best the maintenance here of innumerable selfish, self-centered, and
cruel organisms whose single and especial business it is to exist each
at the expense of the other." [7]

A great deal of the philosophy underlying the massive
American Tragedy is to be found in one paragraph in that
book:

" It is a question whether the human will, of itself alone, ever has
cured or ever can cure any human weakness. Tendencies are subtle
things. They are involved in the chemistry of one's being, and those
who delve in the mysteries of biology frequently find that curious
anomaly, a form of minute animal life — chemically and physically
attracted to its own disaster." [8]

In the long analysis of the motives which led Clyde Grif-
fiths to the killing of Roberta ~~Arnold~~ Alden, in *An American
Tragedy,* any deliberate intention is almost completely ana-
lyzed into " tendencies " which are physiological rather than
psychological. The question of guilt is really irrelevant. It
is not Clyde's conscience which is studied but his nervous
system. It is not a problem in morals but in what Dreiser
calls " bio-chemistry." The whole tragedy is depicted as
moving almost automatically like a set piece of fireworks
after the fuse has been lighted.

The second aspect of Dreiser considered here, his great
mass of description of the effects of the industrial system on
human life, has far more of a positive value for religion and
morals. His refusal to turn away from the ugly searing
marks on humanity made by the steam roller of a rampant
industrialism has been a genuine and great moral asset of

the twentieth century in America. For the whole school of polite fiction had been guilty of gross immorality in averting its eyes from that type of reality. In a notable passage in his autobiography Dreiser describes his perception of that immorality of conventional popular fiction:

" You could not write about life as it was; you had to write about it as somebody else thought it was, the ministers and farmers and dullards of the home. Yet here I was in a profession (journalism) that was hourly revealing the fact that this sweetness-and-light code, this idea of a perfect world which contained neither sin nor shame for any save vile outcasts, criminals and vagrants, was the trashiest lie ever foisted upon an all too human world. Not a day, not an hour, but the pages of the very newspaper we were helping to fill with our scribbled observations were full of the most incisive pictures of the lack of virtue, honesty, kindness, even average human intelligence, not on the part of a few but of nearly everybody." [9]

It was the " age of dinosaurs " of which Dreiser wrote, vast combinations of industrial and financial power which were changing the pattern of life for millions of Americans. It is the victims of this dinosaur era of life which he sees and portrays, not as a rebel or propagandist but just as a spectator. His great service lies in his detailed pictures of the defeat, the harrowing, the frustration which our civilization brings to multitudes of people. His whole written work might be summed up in Mark Twain's direction: " Get the facts first. Then you can distort them as you will." Dreiser has distorted his facts, but he has had facts, tragic facts, heartbreaking facts. Life was doing ugly and cruel things to people. The confusion and suffering, spreading chaos and stark tragedy which mark the outworking of the scramble of greed, when the hands of greed control such power as an industrial age puts in its hands, are drawn in painful detail. The beaten, the weak, the bewildered limp across the pages. Dreiser was one of the first to disclose forcibly this human parade.

In place of the Horatio Alger story of the poor boy who goes up to the city to emulate the romance of Dick Whittington's conquest of London, he showed, as he knew from experience, what happened to boys in cities. A lasting value of *An American Tragedy* is the picture of the forces playing on millions of boys, the mangling and misshaping of life, the degeneration and decay that result. For these victims he has a deep and wondering pity.

Dreiser does not know what his facts mean. He tries to press them all into the inadequate mold of a pessimistic determinism. He is neither a philosopher nor a social critic. Indeed, one may truthfully say of him what was said of Lord Byron, " When he tries to think he is a child." But he does see and report, and his facts constitute a major item of business for religion.

A third aspect of Dreiser's work which relates it to religion is his deeply felt pity. He is, as has been said, *a-moral*. He does not affix guilt. He does not condemn. The sense of moral responsibility is absent, almost entirely. Yet there is a real pity for many of his characters — a pity, be it noted, for which there is no logical place in his deterministic philosophy. " Nigger Jeff," in *Free and Other Stories,* is a vivid example of this pity. It is one of the most moving descriptions of a lynching which has ever been written. *The Lost Phoebe,* in the same volume, the story of an aged man's losing his mind on the death of his wife, is another instance.

III

Sherwood Anderson does not today occupy the place of importance in American literature which he had fifteen years ago, nor that which many critics and readers expected him to hold. Very little of his recent work has been comparable to the achievement and promise of his earlier books. His mannerisms have seemed to harden on him like a shell; repetition has been more characteristic of his work than growth and progress. Yet that does not rob him of historical importance. He was one of the major literary figures of the turbulent 1920's. He is, at least, of first importance for memorable picturing of some of the chief forces and influences playing upon American life in the decade following the war.

It may seem strange to include Sherwood Anderson among those writers regarded as predominantly realists. He has so much of the fantastic, the psychopathic, in his gallery of portraits. His obsession with sex has resulted in an obvious warping and unbalance in his outlook and treatment of character, and his selection of theme. Yet with these characteristics there have been joined others which give him a place among those who have looked with clear, seeing eyes at the world in front of them and presented disturbing and challenging pictures of it. The qualities which entitle Anderson to a place among realistic writers are the very ones which make him and his work of significance and importance for religion.

First, perhaps, among these are what Lewis Gannett calls "his uncanny awareness of human beings as individuals." Anderson's philosophy is a blur, but his portraiture is often of shocking clearness. He is at his best in the short story, etching an individual. His great preoccupation has been the endeavor to " crawl under the skins of people," to find inner secrets of life. He is not loaded with philosophical impedimenta as Dreiser is; he is not so confined to the reporting of external facts. Nor is he a satirist and caricaturist as Lewis is. When Anderson escapes from theory and the cloudy soliloquy which doth so easily beset him, and writes objectively, with patient and revealing detail, he creates memorable pictures of individual people, lifelike, often tragic. They are pictures of real significance to an understanding of various phases of American life.

His description of the effects of an industrial civilization on life is what undoubtedly gives him his most permanent importance. In his particular flair for the portrayal of baffled and frustrated lives, he has recorded again and again his sense of the crushing of something beautiful by a mechanized, standardized, greed-driven order of life. A characteristic sentence is, " The living force within could not find expression." His pages are filled with people who " die with all their music in them." In that strange gallery of mangled souls, " grotesques " as he calls them, *Winesburg, Ohio,* there are many who resemble the demon-possessed in the New Testament. There are the misshapen, run over by environment which has defeated them. In his novel *Poor White,* and to a smaller extent in *Marching Men,* and in his autobiography *A Story Teller's Tale,* which may very possibly be his lasting book, he chronicles the movement of a midwestern juggernaut with the human wreckage it leaves in its trail. Two chants in his *Song of Industrial America* give a characteristic theme:

" First there are the broken things, myself and the others. I don't mind that — I'm gone, shot to pieces. I'm part of the scheme — I'm the broken end of a song myself. We are all that, here in the West, here in Chicago. Tongues clatter against the teeth. There's nothing but shrill screams and a rattle. That had to be — it's part of the scheme."

" You know my city, Chicago triumphant — factories and marts and the roar of machines — horrible, terrible, ugly and brutal. It crushed things down and down. Nobody wanted to hurt. They didn't want to hurt me or you. They were caught themselves." [10]

In his *Notebook* he says: " The dominant note in American life today is the factory hand. When we have digested that fact, we can begin to approach the task of the present-day novelist with a new point of view." It is that point of view, of an America in which the factory hand is the dominant figure, which appears in much of Anderson's work.

To this midwestern America, pictured often as " an unbearable commonplace tempered by lunacy," he brings a critical spirit and evaluation that give him significance as a moral force. There is probably no passage in his work more revealing of this aspect of Anderson than the following from the *Notebook:*

" When one thinks of America as it was, but a few generations ago, a vast wilderness across which railroads had to be laid, whose forests had to be cut away and whose cities were yet to be built, one can understand that there was a time in America when to be perpetually on the go, to be a hustler and a go-getter, was a kind of moral duty.

" Then, perhaps there was no time to be wasted in this foolishness of trying to understand each other, of trying to really call up before ourselves, through the world of our artists, something of the inner quality of lives. To be a go-getter was then perhaps a moral duty.

A tree might have fallen on the head of the pioneer who for a moment lost himself in the effort to understand his neighbor. Alertness was the mood of the times.

" It may now be that a time has come to ask ourselves questions:
" Are our lives worth living? " [11]

His best work in fiction is undoubtedly in the volumes of short stories, *Winesburg, Ohio,* and *The Triumph of the Egg* and *Poor White,* a novel dealing with the coming of machinery to a midwestern town. He has shown the same predilection for autobiography that Dreiser has and has produced three autobiographical works: *A Story Teller's Tale,* an important book for picturing the social effects of industrialization; *Tar,* a story of his boyhood; and *Sherwood Anderson's Notebook.* To this task of picturing his time and environment he brought an early experience of the widest variety, having worked in all sorts of jobs which brought first-hand acquaintance with people, with poverty, with suffering. He worked in a stable, was a tramp at seventeen years of age, a factory hand, a mechanic's apprentice, worked in a bicycle manufacturing establishment, was manager of a factory. Indeed, there is no group of facts which reveals more of the difference between most of the genteel literature so characteristic of the 1880's and 1890's and that of the realistic writing since the war than the education and experience of the writers. Dreiser, Anderson, Carl Sandburg, Eugene O'Neill, Dos Passos, Hemingway, were equipped for writing about life by an apprenticeship of every variety of job and experience. That education forms a striking contrast to the usual conventional restricted apprenticeship of most American writers, with such outstanding exceptions as Whitman and Jack London. That difference in experience reflects rather accurately the difference in product, and is one of the reasons for it.

IV

Sinclair Lewis has reached such a height of fame that he is, according to Bernard de Voto, in imminent danger of becoming a sun myth. Both the uncritical praise of many who might not be unfairly called worshipers, and the equally uncritical damnation of many others who have never sufficiently overcome their prejudices to do him even the justice of an unbiased reading, have made Lewis's worth and significance hard to evaluate. Certainly no writer of this generation in America has received greater attention or been given wider reading. The fact that the names of two of his novels, *Main Street* and *Babbitt,* have passed into the language as common nouns, is a fair measure of his importance. Lewis is significant both for his expression of common attitudes and moods, and for his influence on the popular mind.

Lewis is a very different type of realist from Anderson. He is primarily an adept at delineating exteriors. Early in life Lewis must have seen and taken to heart the advertising slogan, " Take along a Kodak." He has been the literary Eastman of his time. Yet he is really more of a cartoonist than a photographer, with a satirical gift for caricature, a gift like that of Hogarth. It is easy to point out the one-sidedness of Lewis's pictures of life in *Main Street,* in *Babbitt,* in *Arrowsmith.* That has been done a thousand times, notably by Sherwood Anderson in these words: " For some reason Mr. Lewis has himself found but little joy either in life among us or in his own effort to channel his reactions to our life into prose. I am very sure that in the life of every man, woman and child in the country there are forces at work that seem to have escaped the notice of Mr. Lewis." [12] Many have, however, been so satisfied with their demonstration that *Main Street* and *Babbitt* are not balanced, rounded pictures of American life, that they have rendered themselves insensible to the stinging truth that Mr. Lewis's snapshots on Main Street revealed.

The perfect tribute, however, to the amount of essential truth in *Main Street,* is to be found in the publication, eight years after its appearance, of *Middletown* by Robert and Helen Lynd. Few books have ever been given such a tremendous documentation as *Middletown* gave to *Main Street. Middletown* is the most extensive and thorough-going analysis an American town has ever received. It might well be considered a gigantic footnote to *Main Street.* In patiently gathered and honestly recorded detail Lewis's indictment of the thing-full emptiness of a middle western town is sustained. In both fiction and fact there is recorded the irony that after the wilderness was made into civilization, civilization had made it into a new and bleaker type of wilderness. The Lynds' chapters on the cultural life, religion, business and the dominant codes and ideas of a typical product of an industrial civilization give evidence for the plaintiff Lewis, in *Babbitt* and *Main Street,* and large parts of *Elmer Gantry,* against the emptiness, the dullness, the standardization on a low cultural and spiritual level. In his picture Lewis was on the side of the angels.

An audit of Lewis's service to social criticism reveals an

impressive total of contribution to a fresh esthetic, moral
and spiritual evaluation of many phases of American life.
It is that critical appraisal which makes it no exaggeration
to recognize in his fiction a definitely religious asset if we
consider, as we should, religion as including devotion to definite and concrete spiritual values, such as beauty, truth, love
and righteousness. This is made clear when some of
the chief targets of Lewis's concentrated and passionate attack in *Main Street, Babbitt* and *Arrowsmith* are recalled.
He has ridden in onslaught against sheer ugliness, the random unconsidered ugliness of American small towns and
cities; against hypocrisy, both that type represented in business selfishness and corruption masquerading as " service,"
and that empty pretense which attempts to use so-called
" culture" for the purpose of window-dressing. He has
tilted like an infuriated Don Quixote against the blind worship of bigness and the cult of boosting, blind to the moral
qualities of the thing boosted; against an official patriotism
which is made a cover under which all sorts of ugly crawl-
ing things find protection; against cruelty and inhumanity;
against a traditional Puritanism that often set like a straight-
jacket on the human spirit; against a provinciality of outlook that acted like a prison for the mind.

The above paragraph may look to some like an unjusti-
fied award of a distinguished service medal for meritorious
conduct in moral warfare. But each citation can be amply
documented. Run through *Main Street,* for instance, and
pick out a very few thrusts at public enemies. Take the
opening pages of *Main Street,* which in a way set the theme,
the thoughts of Carol Kennicott as she looks out on the
Middle West through a railway car window:

" What is its future? she wondered. A future of cities and factory smut, where now are loping empty fields? Homes universal and secure? Or placid chateaux ringed with sullen huts? Youth free to find knowledge and laughter? Willingness to sift the sanctified lies?

" Or creamy-skinned fat women, smeared with grease and chalk, gorgeous in the skins of beasts and the bloody feathers of slain birds, playing bridge with puffy, pink-nailed, jeweled fingers, women who after much expenditure of labor and bad temper still grotesquely resemble their own flatulent lap-dogs?

" The ancient stale inequalities, or something different in history, unlike the tedious maturity of other empires? " [13]

Into Carol's mind also is put Lewis's criticism of the parasitic nature of many prairie towns:

" The fact is that they no more exist to serve the farmers who are their reason of existence than do the great capitals; they exist to fatten on the farmers, to provide for the townsmen large motors and social preferment; and, unlike the capitals, they do not give to the district in return for usury a stately and permanent center, but only this ragged camp. It is a ' parasitic Greek civilization ' — minus the civilization." [14]

Again and again there is crushing satire on the cheap devices by which a small town tries to put itself " on the map." Toward the end of the novel, is given a picture of the chief hustler, promoter, go-getter, of such a campaign, one James Blausser. Allegedly in his honor, the Commercial Club of Gopher Prairie gives a banquet, at which the atmosphere is highly charged with " oratorical references to Pep, Punch, Go, Vigor, Enterprise, Red Blood, He-Men, Fair Women, God's Country, James J. Hill, the Blue Sky, the Green Fields, the Bountiful Harvest, Increasing Population, Fair Return on Investments, Alien Agitators Who Threaten the Security of Our Institutions, the Hearthstone the Foundation of the State, Senator Knute Nelson, One Hundred Per Cent Americanism, and Pointing With Pride." [15]

Typical of his economic criticism is his phrase, " the secret trails that lead to scared pocket books." He thus exposes the financial reasons which prompt opposition to " radicals ":

" Why can't you Tories declare war honestly? You don't oppose this organizer because you think he's seditious, but because you're afraid that the farmers he's organizing will deprive you townsmen of the money you make out of mortgages and wheat and shops.

" Of course, since we're at war with Germany, anything that anyone of us doesn't like is ' pro-German,' whether it's business competition or bad music. If we were fighting England, you'd call the radicals ' pro-English.' When this war is over, I suppose you'll be calling them ' red anarchists.'

" What an eternal art it is — such a glittery delightful art — finding hard names for our opponents! How we do sanctify our efforts to keep them from getting the holy dollars we want for ourselves! " [16]

It should be remembered that these satires on the injustices and cruelties of rampant patriotism and " 100% Americanism," came in 1920, when the war psychology was still so largely dominant.

The results in warped personality, immoral character and social maladjustment of mind of the official religious orthodoxy of Gopher Prairie are depicted both with skill and with the heat of hatred. What the hard loveless religion of Main Street did to Lewis's favorite character, Miles Bjornstam, a non-conformist to the economic gods of the village, is graphically portrayed. Because a neighbor didn't like Miles's using his water, he carried it from another well. Miles's wife and child contract typhoid as a result. No one even called on them but Carol Kennicott and she became

their nurse. To a committee from the church which made
a belated call Miles says:

" ' You're too late. You can do nothing now. Bea's always kind of
hoped that you folks would come to see her. She wanted to have a
chance and be friends. She used to sit waiting for somebody to
knock. I've seen her sitting here, waiting. Now — Oh, you ain't
worth God-damning.' He shut the door. She died and the boy.
Miles said to Carol, ' I can't ever pay you back for what you've done.'
Miles' rebuff spread and no one came to the funeral. That afternoon
Juanita Haycock dropped in to brighten Carol. She said, ' Too bad
about this Bea. But I don't waste any sympathy on that man of hers.
Everybody says he drank too much, and treated his family awful,
and that's how they got sick.' " [17]

Miles sold his dairy and bade Carol goodbye — a broken
man. It was said that before he went he cursed the town.
There was talk of arresting him, of riding him on a rail. It
was rumored that at the station old Champ Perry rebuked
him: " You better not come back here. We've got respect
for your dead, but we haven't got any for a blasphemer and
a traitor that won't do anything for his country and only
bought one Liberty Bond." Some of the people who had
been at the station declared that Miles had made some seditious retort: something about loving German workmen
more than American bankers; but others asserted that he
couldn't find one word with which to answer the veteran.
Kennicott commented: " From what Champ says, I guess
Bjornstam was a bad egg, after all. In spite of Bea, don't
know but what the citizens committee ought to have forced
him to be patriotic — let on like they could send him to
jail if he didn't volunteer and come through for bonds and
the Y.M.C.A. They've worked that stunt fine with all these
German farmers." [18]

Who can doubt that Miles's profanity is quite in the spirit of the Jesus of the 25th chapter of Matthew?

Lewis's criticism of the perverted religion of Main Street seems to be summed up in the remark of Fern Mullins, the expelled high school teacher: " My dear, Mrs. Bogart's god may be — Main Street's god, but all the courageous, intelligent people are fighting him — though he slay us."

Of the results in character education of the type of orthodoxy represented by Mrs. Bogart, the town gossip and persecutor, Lewis gives this picture. First in the words of Cy's self-righteous mother:

> " ' I just don't see how folks can talk and act like they do. You don't know the things that go on under cover. This town — why it's only the religious training I've given Cy that's kept him so innocent of — things. . . .
>
> " ' If I had my way there wouldn't be none of them, not boys nor girls neither, allowed to know anything about — about things till they was married.
>
> " ' It's terrible the bald way that some folks talk. It just shows and gives away what awful thoughts they got inside them.' " [19]

But in four months, Doctor Kennicott's wife Carol

> " had beheld Cy hanging a cat, stealing melons, throwing tomatoes at the Kennicott house, and making ski-tracks across the lawn, and had heard him explaining the mysteries of generation, with great audibility and dismaying knowledge.
>
> " He was, in fact, a museum specimen of what a small town, a well disciplined public school, a tradition of hearty humour, and a pious mother could produce from the material of a courageous and ingenious mind." [20]

There is permanent value to *Babbitt* as a picture of what might be called the " frozen assets " of civilization — its spiritual possibilities frozen by fear, in a mass-minded, stand-ardized order of life. There is hustle and glare, but con-fusion, confusion of aim and a heavy fog obscuring values. Babbitt blusters because he is afraid, afraid of the ostracism which is visited on any deviation from the Nicene creed of regularity, of prosperity and conformity. That cowed fig-ure, driven back at last from tentative efforts to find and save its soul, a picture not only of an individual but of cities also which he and his like have made in their own image, makes a permanent rebuke and challenge to religious institutions which have failed to fulfill their function as redeeming agencies of a critical minority.

The technique is largely that of the cumulative effect of the piling up of photographic detail. This is seen in its clearest form in the first seven chapters which are devoted to the chronicle of one day of George F. Babbitt's life. By the end of a day we have assembled a case study for an indictment of business, political, social and family life.

It should be noted, in any attempt to assay the services of not only Lewis but a group of other novelists of the 1920's to American criticism, that in general the novelists preceded the critics in making articulate the newer spirit of post-war economic and social and political criticism. Much of the criticism represented by such figures as Van Wyck Brooks, Mencken, Lewis Mumford, Parrington and others was con-temporaneous with that of the fiction writers. But the novelists got through to the public mind first, and did a trail-blazing service. To use a football analogy, they were the " interference " which opened up a hole in the solid line of tradition and convention, through which later criticism in non-fiction form could effectively go. And that in itself is no small service. The critics of the early 1930's may well say of many of the novelists of the 1920's, "Others have labored and we have entered into their labors."

There is, of course, a reverse side to the medal presented to Lewis for distinguished public service. His deficiencies as a critic lie in the same sources as do his failures as a novelist. They lie in the fact that Lewis is primarily a great satirist rather than a novelist. His intense hatreds, his red-headed rage, spoil his hand as an artist. It is that for instance which makes his pictures so one-sided, which makes *Elmer Gantry* much more of a comic strip, a cartoon, than a study of religion. The most formidable criticisms of *Elmer Gantry* as a serious dealing with religion in America have come, not from the inside of the church, but from dispassionate literary critics. A great deal of the foaming rage and contempt which most church people poured upon that novel of a renegade preacher may be largely discounted. What cannot be discounted, however, is the judgment of such a critic as Bernard de Voto:

" As a novel about a false priest, it is intolerably deficient in understanding, intolerably naïve in its consideration of spiritual affairs, intolerably faulty as a presentation of experience. But considered as the work of a sociologist in fiction, a headlong satire of religious hypocrisy and commercialism written by a man who furiously hates them, it is one of the most invigorating books of our time. Similarly with *Arrowsmith,* a study which was also directed by an expert — one who happens to dislike the Rockefeller Foundation. A realistic novel about a bacteriologist would require more subtlety and intricacy of understanding than is ever expended on Martin. But it is a novel of great power and great charm, and those qualities proceed from the satirist's fervor — his hatred of stupidity, his scorn of frailty and time-serving and injustice, and his admiration of heroism and determination. And *Babbitt*. It has made a mould; it has worked its way into the possession of everyone, a complete expression of our time. But not as an expression of the truth about business men, or even about George F. Babbitt, but as an expression of our sentiments in this generation about them." [21]

The same general criticism is made by T. K. Whipple, when he says in *Spokesmen* that " nothing is missing in *Elmer Gantry* except religion."

Much of Lewis's force comes from brightly burning hatred; but it deflects his aim, like the berserker rage of an infuriated pugilist. It makes a lively spectacle, but leaves much to be desired as an honest portrait. He is too much in love with sharp black and white to render life truthfully. His villains are solid black; his favored characters often approach sainthood. The effect, for instance, of his terrific indictment of the Cumberland Gap penitentiary, in *Ann Vickers,* a picture revealing a sustained glow of moral indignation, is heightened by the fact that the warders are villains and the prisoners all, or nearly all, heroes and heroines. This domination of the mind by rage, the overshadowing of the novelist by the satirist, has resulted in so much of his writing, which might have been devoted to legitimate drama, being occupied with the repetition of slapstick performances more suited to a burlesque show. More seriously, it has had the ironical result that Lewis, the arch-enemy of provincialism, is himself a provincial in many of the most important countries of the mind and spirit of man.

V

In the work of more than a score of other novelists, various types and degrees of realism are to be found. Separated by great divergencies in point of view, subject matter and method, they are yet more or less united by a common concern for honest drawing, for integrity of portraiture; they share an aversion for curtains and for mists of sentimentalism. It is this approach to life and the representation of experience which marked off the group of fiction writers discussed in this chapter and the next both from such typical romantics as Booth Tarkington and from the earlier realism of Howells. Howells was unquestionably a pioneer and exponent of realism. By many he was considered, in his time, as the " bold, bad man " of things as they are. To many readers whose nerves demanded excitement and the breathless unwinding of plot, he was incomparably dull. Yet Howells, in comparison with post-war realism, had a very rosy and restricted vision of life in America.

In the remainder of this chapter a group of seven or eight novelists are to be considered who may profitably be discussed together, not only on the basis of a somewhat common realism but also in that they deal particularly with rural and small town life. In varying manner, they all contributed to that fresh scrutiny and appraisal of country and village life which was so strong a mark of the fifteen years from 1915 to 1930. They reflect neither the naturalism of Dreiser nor the satire of Lewis; yet they all do exhibit the untraditional and unconventional dealing with the small town world which was ushered in by the publication of Edgar Lee Masters' *Spoon River Anthology* in 1914.

When Masters made his tour of observation in the Spoon River cemetery, lifting up the grave stones and trying to peer into what realities of life had been covered up under the customary epitaphs, he was the first of a long parade of

writers which wound its way through the highways and
back alleys, the open fields and villages of the Middle West
and other sections, and brought in a startling minority report. Masters brought a great shock to people, because a
sentimental lyricism, such as found emotional expression in
" The Old Oaken Bucket," had been the dominant attitude
of the great majority. Masters put arsenic in the " Old
Oaken Bucket." To a generation which had accepted without examination the *cliché* that " God made the country and
the devil made the town," and which had come to regard
with a sentimental piety the rural regions as the home of
whatsoever things are pure, lovely and of good report,
Spoon River was a blasphemy. The continued examination
and report which novelists made, not certainly in the spirit
of Masters but with unbandaged eyes, did much to estab-
lish new standards of judgment and the revision of accepted attitudes. It helped to make a new national mind
on the subject of American town life.

In this connection, the question already glanced at may
well arise: All this is granted, as a matter of literary criticism, but what has it all to do with religion and ethics?
It is a fair and obvious question. The answer, to the support of which the present volume is largely devoted, is short
and simple. The answer is that honesty is a fundamental
virtue and an essential prerequisite to a genuinely religious
interpretation of life. If religion is concerned with an interpretation of life in the light of absolute values, it is of
primary importance that it have a truthful picture of life
as a basis of interpretation. Otherwise it can never escape
the distortions and refractions of a false and fanciful view
of its subject matter. The most fundamentally immoral

books and plays are not those in which obscenities and crime occur, but those which present a misleading and unreal picture and interpretation of life. The most thoroughgoing criticism of the immorality of a romantic optimism, false to the facts of life and the forces acting on it, is that of Jesus when he said to some complacent interpreters of his times: " Ye know how to discern the face of the heaven, but ye cannot discern the signs of the times."

Willa Cather owes her high place in contemporary fiction partly to her style; her significance for our present interest lies in what might be called her combination of realistic picturing of frontier and rural life with an idealism which recognizes and portrays the force and beauty of character and personality. Thus there are two great values for religion and morals, the truthful representation of the struggle with nature and environment, and the real " success " of character triumphing over frustration. To her work she brought the intimate knowledge of early experience and also that gift which Arnold Bennett has called a novelist's greatest need — " an all-embracing Christlike sympathy." Miss Cather's recording of a characteristic employment of childhood days shows clearly this gift of the imaginative entering into the experience of people. She would ride her pony to visit the neighbors, immigrants from various parts of Europe. " I used to ride home," she says, " in the most unreasonable state of excitement. I always felt as if they told me so much more than they said, as if I had actually got inside another person's skin." Her most important novels are those dealing with Nebraska: *O Pioneers,* 1913, *The Song of the Lark,* 1915, *My Antonia,* 1918, *One of Ours,* 1922, and *The Professor's House,* 1925. In the first four of these novels there is the theme of the struggle of character and will against the impending frustration of environment. Alexandra Bergson, in *O Pioneers,* Thea Kronberg in *The Song of the Lark* and Antonia Shimerda in *My Antonia* are spiritual sisters. Each lives out an Odyssey of the soul, rising to triumphs of different sorts by sheer tenacity of will, by unyielding energy, by character which transcends the slings and arrows of fortune. These three books are " success stories," but of a very different type from the traditional pattern. They are inward successes, the success of courage and self-giving. Willa Cather is no more afraid of what seems an endorsement of revered morals than she is afraid of endorsing gravitation. Thus at the end of *My Antonia,* when Antonia comes to harbor after a tumultuous voyage in what seems an old-fashioned completion of life, we read, " That is happiness — to be dissolved in something complete and great." The finding of happiness and an unassailable " success " in complete dedication to a task — that to Miss Cather is as much reality as the ugly mud houses of the prairie or the provinciality of small towns. Her three notable women heroines have a spiritual kinship to that pride of a pioneering race, Lucinda Matlock, depicted in Masters' *Spoon River Anthology.*

Yet Willa Cather is no more blind to the pettiness and repression of village life than is Sinclair Lewis in his pitiless exposure of the spiritual tyranny of Main Street. She says of it:

" The life that went on in them seemed to me made up of evasions and negations; shifts to save washings and cleaning, devices to propitiate the tongue of gossip. This guarded mode of existence was like living under a tyranny. People's speech, their voices, their very glances, became furtive and repressed. Every individual taste, every natural appetite, was bridled by caution. The people asleep in their houses, I thought, tried to live like the mice in their own kitchens; to make no noise, to leave no trace, to slip over the surface of things in the dark. The growing piles of ashes and cinders in the backyards were the only evidence that the wasteful, consuming process of life went on at all." [22]

In *My Antonia* the story is put in the form of the recollections of early days on the Nebraska and Kansas prairies by a railroad builder and lawyer. Into the space of a lifetime there is crowded the process of transforming a primitive region into a standardized portion of the modern world. Antonia, a young girl of immense vitality and courage and love of life, meets adversities which would have swamped a nature of less ardor and fortitude. She falls in love with a cheap vulgar cad, is tricked into a pretended marriage and achieves the inglorious role of an unmarried mother. That for a start. The stage is all set for a second defeat of life in a marriage to a good, dull man and her immersion in the cares of a large family. But she illustrates what has been said to be the author's achievement, " the triumph of mind over Nebraska," and finds satisfactory fulfillment of life in the preservation of her own unconquered spirit and devotion to her family.

In *One of Ours,* her Pulitzer prize novel, Miss Cather shows defeat rather than the triumph which was the theme of her three epics of women. Claude Wheeler, the hero, never broke through the cramping limitations of environment which frustrated his sensitive nature and chaotic aspirations. We have the story of his early life on a farm, his education, the flowering of his nature under the stimulation of a college town family which has achieved freedom and independence of spirit. Then his life goes under a cloud through a tragic mismating with a frigid, self-centered, ultra-pious type of religiously warped girl, Enid Royce. Claude has failed to recognize the greatness and love of another girl, Gladys Farmer, a woman fit to stand with other Cather heroines. The war comes as a convenient way of escape for Claude. After a career of " glory " he dies on the battlefield and thus escapes the defeat of life in Nebraska. Claude thus writes his own epitaph in his words to his wife:

" ' You see, Enid, I've never yet done anything that gave me any satisfaction. I must be good for something. When I lie still and think I wonder whether my life has been happening to me, or to somebody else. It doesn't seem to have much connection with me.' " [23]

The heart of the author's sympathy and philosophy seem to be expressed in the thoughts of Gladys Farmer:

" She believed that all things which might make the world beautiful — love and kindness, leisure and art — were shut in prison and that successful men like Bayliss Wheeler held the keys. The generous ones were somehow weak and could not break the bars. . . .

" There were people, even in Frankfort, who had imagination and generous impulses, but they were all, she had to admit, inefficient — failures. There was Miss Livingstone, the fiery emotional old maid who couldn't tell the truth; old Mr. Smith, a lawyer without clients, who read Shakespeare and Dryden all day long in his dusty office; Bobbie Jones, the effeminate drug clerk who wrote free verse and ' movie ' scenarios, and tended the soda water fountain." [24]

In *One of Ours* there is a passage describing Claude's mother reading to him from Paradise Lost which serves as a window for the religious conflict of a whole generation. His mother's religion of dogma and tradition comes into conflict with a disturbing challenge in a more human and untrammeled outlook, as represented by Claude:

" Her voice groped as if she were trying to realize something. The room grew greyer as she read on through the turgid catalogue of heathen gods, so packed with stories and pictures, so unaccountably glorious. At last the light failed and Mrs. Wheeler closed the book.

" ' That's fine,' commented Claude from the couch.

" ' But Milton couldn't have got along without the wicked, could he? '

" Mrs. Wheeler looked up. ' Is that a joke? ' she asked slyly.

" ' Oh, no, not at all! It just struck me that this part is so much more interesting than the books about perfect innocence in Eden.'

" ' And yet I suppose it shouldn't be so,' Mrs. Wheeler said slowly, as if in doubt.

" Her son laughed and sat up, smoothing his rumpled hair. ' The fact remains that it is, dear mother. And if you took all the great sinners out of the Bible, you'd take out all the interesting characters, wouldn't you? '

" ' Except Christ,' she murmured.

" ' Yes, except Christ. But I suppose the Jews were honest when they thought him the most dangerous type of criminal.'

" ' Are you trying to tangle me up? ' his mother inquired, with both reproach and amusement in her voice.

" Claude went to the window where she was sitting and looked out at the snowy fields, now becoming blue and desolate as the shadows deepened, ' I only mean that even in the Bible the people who were merely free from blame don't amount to much.'

" ' Ah, I see! ' Mrs. Wheeler chuckled softly. ' You are trying to get me back to Faith and Works. This is where you always balked when you were a little fellow. Well, Claude, I don't know as much about it as I did then. As I get older I leave a good deal more to God. I believe He wants to save whatever is noble in this world, and that He knows more ways of doing it than I.' She rose like a gentle shadow and rubbed her cheek against his flannel shirt sleeve, murmuring, ' I believe He is sometimes where we would least expect to find Him — even in proud rebellious hearts.' " [25]

Willa Cather does not tilt at windmills; she enlists in no crusades; she is not concerned in problems as such. Yet her objective descriptions contain a steady indictment of the repressive provincialities which often dominate the town and country. She makes clear the tragedy inherent when in the name of a vulgar Americanism the colorful variation and spiritual inheritance of immigrant races is flattened out. Once, in the story, " The Sculptor's Funeral," in her early book of short stories, *The Troll Garden,* she writes vehemently of the ugliness and petty vindictiveness of the small western village. A sculptor is brought home for burial to a little Kansas town, and the condemnation visited on him in death as in life by his mean-minded neighbors makes a stinging indictment. In the story " Paul's Case," in *Youth and the Bright Medusa,* 1920, there is a vivid portrayal of the suffering of soul endured by a boy in a middle western town, a sense of frustration so strong that to relieve it he steals a thousand dollars, lives like a millionaire for a week and then jumps under a train. In *The Professor's House* there is an undertone of criticism of the commercial idol of success in the description of the sense of defeat which wealth brought to a college teacher and his nostalgia for the earlier, simpler house of his days of comparative poverty where he had been happy.

Something of the same mixture of descriptive realism with an idealistic appreciation of some moral values ordinarily associated with traditional religion is found in Dorothy Canfield Fisher. If Lewis and Dreiser and Masters may be said to have led the revolt against the village, Dorothy Canfield may be regarded as probably the most effective attorney for the defense. Yet she is by no means a blind defender.

A wealth of observant detail in her novels and short stories proclaims a knowledge of the small town as intimate as that of Lewis, Glenway Westcott, or Ruth Suckow. In addition she has that considerable fund of peculiar knowledge which only love can give. Thomas Carlyle unintentionally made an acute bit of literary criticism when he said, " A loving heart is the beginning of all knowledge." The village has yielded to Dorothy Canfield many secrets which were denied to Lewis, just as sympathy always sees more and farther than satire. Yet she has not been blinded by that romantic theory of the beautiful life of small towns that has vitiated so much of the work of William Allen White and made almost a total loss of Booth Tarkington as an unsophisticated juvenile. In her work done before the war, particularly the two novels, *The Squirrel Cage,* 1912, and *The Bent Twig,* 1915, she brought vigorous criticism against two powerful tendencies of her time, the soul-stifling exactions of " society " and the domination of financial success over the life of the mind. *The Squirrel Cage* is a " problem novel " of the type which flourished before the war, dealing with the warping of spirit and mind by the squirrel cage of meaningless motion demanded to keep up with society, with the resulting crime against childhood and youth.

In *The Bent Twig* there is a fine example of what is perhaps Dorothy Canfield's outstanding service, the recognition and portrayal of the spiritual values and possibilities of family life. The struggle between plain living and high thinking is vividly drawn. *Her Son's Wife,* 1920, is a memorable story of growth in personality, of the development of character under the challenge of what seems to be disaster.

The story is a strong piece of character creation and human drama. Mrs. Mary Branscomb, a widow with a passion for ordering other people's lives for them, faces a shock which threatens to leave her life in ruins. When her son, whom she idolizes and whose decisions she has always tried to make, marries a girl far beneath him in the social and intellectual scale, ignorant, with poor taste, vulgar, it is hard for her to adjust herself to the situation. The theme of the novel is the courage which Mrs. Branscomb brings to that challenging situation. In meeting the emergency her character undergoes a transformation. She determines that when her granddaughter is born she shall be enabled to overcome her inheritance. Mrs. Branscomb makes a winning fight, both for herself and for the granddaughter. In her other novels, *The Brimming Cup, Rough Hewn* and *The Deepening Stream,* Mrs. Fisher treats the themes of adjustment in marriage and the bringing up of children with a firm grasp of lasting spiritual values. Her novels present a strong case for the monogamous family in which there is a primary recognition of the spiritual elements in personality. Lest this tribute may seem to condemn her novels to the limits of Sunday school fiction, let it be said that much of her fiction of family life represents just that conception of the values in marriage found in a writer quite outside the ranks of Sunday schools — Walter Lippmann in his chapter on " Love in the Great Society " in *A Preface to Morals.*

Zona Gale's literary progress may fairly be made to serve as a chart of the movement of the popular mind in regard to the small town between 1907 and 1920. She traveled from farthest east to farthest west; if not perhaps quite farthest west in critical realism, at least west. In 1907 and 1908 she published two volumes of short stories of village life, *The Loves of Pelleas and Etarre* and *Friendship Village*. No more lyrical, saccharine fairy tales of village life as it never was have ever been contributed to the American library of perfumed romance. Each story dripped with the inherent good and love in the human heart and sweetness triumphed with what got to be, even to sentimental readers, a tiresome regularity. Even the rocking-chair public sometimes thought that the devil ought to be given a fairer " break." Then in 1918, two years before the publication of *Main Street,* she published *Birth,* a novel which never achieved the notice it richly deserved. The lens was focused on the same middle western village but out of the developing room was brought a startlingly different photograph. For the village pictured was a lifelike predecessor of Gopher Prairie. Miss Gale had laid aside her collection of God's noblemen in homespun and presented people. Marshall Pitt, an ineffectual, bungling traveling man for some kind of apple product gets stranded in a little town and married one of its misshapen products, Barbara Ellsworth. After her father's death, he takes over, with indifferent success, the newspaper business in which her father had been engaged. Pitt discovered that his wife was a scatter-brained creature with not even the compensating virtue of loyalty. The son, Jeffery Pitt, is a strange mixture of weakness and ineptness like his father, but at Malcolm's death he comes to life with unsuspected vigor. *Birth* marks a real stage in the emancipation of fiction from the blight of unreality in its treatment of the American village.

Miss Lulu Bett, published in 1920, and made into a play which took the Pulitzer prize, went even farther into realistic scrutiny and portrayal of the village and the people. The novel is really a study in torture. Lulu Bett, the maid of all work to her sister and her sister's husband, is made the butt of all the cheap horseplay and practical jokes that a loud moronic go-getter, Dracon Dwight, can devise. The worm finally turned and Lulu Bett declared a revolution. It was an inglorious affair, a trick pretense of marriage and a pathetic caricature of a wedding trip from which she returned unwed. But her declaration of independence had done something for her soul; she was no longer the mute slave she had been. The book contains some devastating pictures of the unlovely, shoddy types to be found in a small town, and of the mean ideals of life which often prevail. Similar sharp biting etchings which carry their own social criticism are found in her novel *Preface to a Life*, 1926, and the volume of short stories, *Yellow Gentians and Blue*, 1927.

Let us turn, in conclusion, to the farm. The same change that we have noted in the literary treatment of the small town is paralleled in the literary fortunes of the farm. The stock attitude of homesick piety, indicated by the enormous and tearful success of Denman Thompson's *Old Homestead* on the stage, prevailed for fifty years. Such excursions into realities as that of Hamlin Garland in his realistic period, in *Main Travelled Roads* and *Rose of Dutcher's Coolly,* did not seriously upset the accepted convention. It was not until after the war that the farm novel went " stark." To be sure, there was a mixture of realism in such glorifications of the pioneer as *Vandermark's Folly*, 1922, by Herbert Quick, but Quick's work was largely in the romantic tradition.

Typical of the extreme somberness of the post-war realism as applied to farm life are two women novelists, Martha

Ostenso and Ruth Suckow. In these two writers the pendulum went far to the other extreme. The gaunt farmers who stump their way through their stories are figures of almost unadulterated gloom; they seem to be ruined morally as well as economically; they represent rural America in decay. And many residents of Iowa may be pardoned for vigorously proclaiming that they never knew such neighbors in the flesh. However, the works of these two women have a genuine historical interest in view of the plight of the farmers of the Middle West in the hungry years 1930–1933. For the novels preceded by several years any genuine national recognition of the desperate plight to which the era of " prosperity," to say nothing of the depression, had reduced the farmer. It is easy to say that such novels as Martha Ostenso's *Wild Geese* and Ruth Suckow's stories, *Iowa Interiors,* are overdrawn, unbalanced, pathological studies. Even if that were granted, they have done an immense service in drawing aside the curtains that helped to hide a tragic social and economic maladjustment. Whatever may be the defects of exaggeration as a literary technique, there are times when it is a far more effective social force than balanced rational statement.

Miss Ostenso's *Wild Geese* gives the history of the family of Caleb Gore in a Scandinavian farming community in the Northwest. The father strides through the pages like an ogre from a cave, covered with Scandinavian gloom. He rules his wife by blackmail, by the intimidation of a secret which he knows and holds over her. Tyranny and greed dominate his actions. One rebel alone encounters him, his daughter Judith. Murder is in her eyes and heart and once takes possession of her hands in an unsuccessful attempt to kill her father. There is a grim ending to the story in the retribution which overtakes the father in the burning of his acres of flax. There is power in the recital, supplemented by detail of the rural background. Similar in tone is Miss Ostenso's later novel, *The Waters Under the Earth*, 1930. There is the same repressive domination of a family, the Vreland family of four children, by a puritanical tyrant of a father. The children both fear and love him, and are thus frustrated in their attempt to achieve any life of their own — all except one, Carlotta, who does break jail and find a life of her own.

Ruth Suckow's work presents much more normal people — hard, many of them, as unbroken soil, shaped and conditioned by the rigors of pioneer life. *Country People*, 1924, is a farm ledger, with emphasis on the bleak spiritual side of Iowa farming. The history of the Kaetterhenry family is traced for three generations following their settling in Iowa in 1850. They were hard working, money-saving and achieved material prosperity and cultural and spiritual bankruptcy. The picture corresponds closely with the early portions of *So Big* by Edna Ferber, save that there is no figure to match in vigor or character Miss Ferber's heroine and no comparable recognition of the positive values of farm life for personality development. Miss Suckow's work is faithful to the point of dullness. If she set out to convey a sense of unrelieved monotony in farming, she succeeds. In *The Odyssey of a Nice Girl*, 1925, there is the same sincere attempt to deal realistically with the soil and its cultivators. The novel gives a girl's life up to the time of her marriage. It depicts the struggles of a young girl " put in a pocket " by parental and family love, balked in her efforts to achieve a

life of her own by the thwartings of family " concern." We
follow her through high school, through her early endeavors
in music and elocution. She does make one sortie out into
the world in a year at a Boston academy of expression.
Then the shades of the prison house descend, only to be escaped by a flight to an uncle and a marriage with a garage
mechanic. It is a somber chronicle, compounded of dullness,
sincerity and strength, with the theme of the repression and
frustration of young life, and the mean unimaginative type
of mind, affected by the long hard struggle with the soil.

This dour and stark interpretation of the rural Middle
West finds formulation in an essay written by Glenway
Westcott as an introduction to his book of short stories,
Good Bye, Wisconsin, 1928. The Middle West is:

". . . a place which has no fixed boundaries, no particular history;
inhabited by no one race; always exhausted by its rich output of food,
men and manufactured articles; loyal to none of its many creeds, pro-
hibitions, fads, hypocrisies, now letting itself be governed, now un-
governable. There is no Middle West. It is a certain climate, a certain landscape; and beyond that, a state of mind of people born where
they do not like to live." [26]

In striking contrast to these fugues on one note, are the
novels of Ole Rolvaag, *Giants in the Earth* and *Peder Vic-
torious,* veritable epics of the pioneer, true sagas of the soil
in the grand tradition. Rolvaag was an immigrant born in
Norway almost within the Arctic Circle, landed in America
in 1896 with nothing but a railway ticket to South Dakota.
He worked at farming and other jobs, turned to school and
college, and in 1906 became professor of Norwegian literature at St. Olaf College, Northfield, Minn. Written originally in Norwegian, *Giants in the Earth* was published in
English in 1927. Its interest is not primarily sociological; it

cannot be fairly included in revolt literature. It centers in the field of psychology rather than that of agricultural economics. It portrays in powerful objective detail the pioneer's struggle with the soil, with nature at times malignant. But its greatest significance is in the delineation of the inward drama — what Professor Parrington calls the first adequate evaluation in fiction of the Western settlement "in terms of emotions; it penetrates to the secret inner life of men and women who undertook the heavy work of subduing the wilderness." As in Willa Cather's *My Antonia,* there is a strong sympathy and appreciation for the life of pioneer women, for its heroism and bleakness. His novels are a voyage of hardy Norsemen transferred to the land, a saga of Eric the Red on the billowing prairies of the Northwest. Rolvaag writes an epic of courage, shadowed by a tragic sense of futility and an overtone of determinism, as though man, represented by the dauntless Per Hansa, were cast for a struggle with powers overwhelming for him. Yet in spite of the tragic ending, with Per Hansa meeting his death in a snowdrift, the feeling is conveyed that there is an absolute greatness and value in the heroism and endurance from which no defeat can subtract. In spite of the cruel fatigue and anguish, there is a recurring note not far from Clough's "Say not the struggle naught availeth." For Per Hansa and the other pioneers are part of something bigger than an individual pilgrim's progress; they are the spearhead of the human trek; they are the future.

In the inner drama religion is central. Indeed, the chief theme is not local or dated; it is universal. The breaking down of the mind of the wife of Per Hansa, Beret, is a powerful tracing of the combined effect of conscience, the loneliness and homesickness of an immigrant and the haunting effect of a rigid creed into which have been incorporated the survivals of paganism earlier than Christianity. For these reasons Rolvaag has contributed not only to fiction but to American history and to the study of religion — an historical traditional type of religion which is related both to the fortification of life and to its damnation.

[1] Used by permission of the author and Alfred A. Knopf, Inc.

[2] Henry Seidel Canby in Saturday Review of Literature.

[3] *A Book About Myself*, by Theodore Dreiser. The Liveright Publishing Corporation.

[4] Current History, Dec., 1932.

[5] *The Emotional Discovery of America*, by Stuart Sherman. Farrar & Rinehart.

[6] *A Hoosier Holiday*, by Theodore Dreiser. The Liveright Publishing Corporation.

[7] *Living Philosophies*. Simon & Schuster, 1931.

[8] *An American Tragedy*, by Theodore Dreiser. The Liveright Publishing Corporation, 1925.

[9] *Newspaper Days*, by Theodore Dreiser. The Liveright Publishing Corporation, 1922.

[10] *Mid-American Chants*, by Sherwood Anderson. Viking Press, 1924.

[11] *Sherwood Anderson's Notebook*. The Liveright Publishing Corporation, 1926.

[12] The Nation, Aug. 31, 1932.

[13] *Main Street*, by Sinclair Lewis, pp. 24–25. Harcourt, Brace & Company.

[14] Ibid., p. 265.

[15] Ibid., p. 269.

[16] Ibid., p. 414.

[17] Ibid., pp. 321–322.

[18] Ibid., pp. 321–324.

[19] Ibid., pp. 185–186.

[20] Ibid., p. 103.

[21] Saturday Review of Literature, Jan. 28, 1933.

[22] *My Antonia*, by Willa Cather. Houghton Mifflin Company, 1916.

[23] *One of Ours*, by Willa Cather. Alfred A. Knopf.

[24] Ibid., pp. 86–87.

[25] Ibid., pp. 86–87.

[26] *Good-bye, Wisconsin*, by Glenway Westcott, pp. 38–39. Harper & Brothers.

CHAPTER FOUR

AMERICAN PICTURE ALBUM

IN his novel, *Grandmothers*, 1927, Glenway Westcott uses an effective technique with which to tie several life stories together into a pattern of unity. His hero, Alwyn Tower, had often turned the pages of an old family album. Storing up in his mind and piecing together the comments and recollections of adults on the various pictures, he had constructed a story to go with each face in the album. The faces in the book were those of members of the family, from the days of the pioneers down to the present. When the boy grew up he put these stories into a book, a chapter to each life, with each face a mirror of a period and location.

It is a method somewhat similar to that of *Spoon River Anthology* and of *Winesburg, Ohio*. More than that, it is a method which has been followed in popular experience. Readers in the United States have for two decades been turning over the pages of an American portrait album. This, of course, is no new experience. It has always been going on. But in the last twenty years or so the pages have been filled with a new type of picture. There has been more pitiless photography and less of an impressionistic and flattering art study. To try to turn the pages, even in the most hurried fashion, of the massive family album which contemporary fiction has presented would be far too large an undertaking for our present study. In this chapter we shall endeavor merely to select a few pictures in realistic fiction, attempting to suggest some moral values in the whole picture album.

Here it may be noted that beyond the contention, already stressed, of the indispensable values to religion and morals of fidelity to fact and truth in the interpretation of life in fiction, is the fact that realistic examination of life, of the effects of existing social condition and environment on personality, in a subtle and inevitable manner raises in the minds of readers the question of the possibility and desirability of change. It orients the mind to change. It disturbs sleep and complacency. On March 15, 1854, Henry Thoreau wrote in his journal: " I am sorry to think that you do not get a man's most effective criticism until you provoke him. Severe truth is expressed with some bitterness." This observation, made almost eighty years ago, is pertinent to much post-war fiction. The observation of life has brought sharp and strong provocation to a group of novelists, and the resulting criticism has been effective, often severe. The novels in turn have been a means of bringing provocation to readers and have helped to induce a critical mood. This result has not come from so-called propaganda novels. The disturbance and provocation come out of the pictures presented. It inheres in the situations themselves, not in any attached harangues or morals. The novels discussed in this chapter are not sociological documents. Fiction which carries the note of rebellion and protest and economic doctrine will be considered in a later chapter. The novels under discussion here as typical examples of realism would all be condemned by the newer school of Marxian fiction writers as hopelessly bourgeois. They have had great significance as a moral and social force simply from their fresh observation of the processes of life with new canons of fidelity and craftsmanship. The result has contributed greatly to the birth of a new critical spirit, the weakening of pious optimisms and sentimentalities, the lifting of questions long suppressed. To religion vitally concerned for the establishment of a more humane and decent order of life, a religion with its faith and hope set on a Kingdom of God on earth, marked by righteousness, justice, and peace, these are major services, the value of which is hard to overestimate.

Toward the close of the last chapter some aspects of the realistic treatment of farm and small town life were considered. Here let us glance at a few novels dealing more specifically with life as affected by an industrial and commercial order.

Robert Herrick, a veteran realistic novelist entitled to be regarded as one of the pioneers of contemporary realism, comes into our period with one novel dealing with industry, *Waste,* 1924. *Waste* is a novel to which the author is entitled to look back with considerable satisfaction, for the ten years which have followed its publication have made quite clear its genuine prophetic quality in its analysis of social and economic aspects of American life. It deals with the social history of the United States from the 1880's to 1920. Herrick's real theme is the lust for possession, the will to power, the profit motive, as they work to blight not only the group of people who make up the characters of the novel but also the whole population. This will to possess wastes the energies of every character in the book, reaching at last the heroine, who held out longest. The contrast between all the rich paraphernalia of living and the spiritual penury which accompanies it is continually drawn. The story tells of the waste of the life of Lewis Thornton, whose spiritual waste began with a mother who felt herself badly used because she was not rich. He gets away from that atmosphere of envy into college, only to have the possible value largely frustrated by the ambition for social prestige and easy money. Herrick's was a voice raised in the wilderness of the upswing of the prosperity boom in 1924, against the dominant mood of the time.

Winston Churchill, after securing a wide audience for his historical fiction in the first years of the century, turned to the problem novel when the muck-raking era set the public interest toward sociological and political questions. In *Coniston,* 1906, and *Mr. Crewe's Career,* 1908, he put New Hampshire politics into fiction. In *The Dwelling Place of Light,* 1917, he turned more to the field of industrial conflict and the effect of the coming of industrialism to New England in the "squeezing" of that class of native New Englanders who did not belong to the Brahmin coupon-clipping class. This novel never won the attention its theme and serious treatment deserved. Perhaps its publication just as the country entered the war was partly responsible. At any rate, it was the author's last novel, up to the present. It deals with a situation very similar to that of the strike in Lawrence, Massachusetts. It draws the economic background with patient detail and makes clear the author's sense of maladjustment and exploitation and his sympathy with the workers. The central figure of the novel is Janet Bumpus, whose father is "a radical failure who worships the Bumpus Genealogy," a gate-keeper in the Chippering

mill. Janet becomes secretary to Claude Ditmer, the manager of the mill, but as the strife progresses and the conflict
grows tense and violent, she joins the I.W.W. who are con-
ducting the strike. Two sharply contrasted types are Rolfe,
the I.W.W. leader, and Brooks Insell, a humanitarian author. The weakness of the novel seems to lie in the fact that
the characters are types chosen to represent the various factors in the strike, and in the fact that no radical solution of
the conflict is offered. Churchill is a liberal and there is
lacking what a later more radical generation of economic
thinkers call a " sense of power politics." Yet the book was
an early projection of the industrial conflict that so marked
the fifteen years that followed. As the work of one of the
most successful of the costumed historical fiction writers,
The Dwelling Place of Light marked a notable right-about-
face in point of view and subject matter. That very change
of theme and method may well serve as a barometer indicating a change of climate in fiction. Worthy to serve also
as an accurate barometer of the coming reaction to many
realistic novels, particularly those dealing with the sacred
idols of business, on the part of conservative traditionalists,
was the comment of the *Catholic World* on Churchill's
novel:

"Frankly we believe the novel merits severe condemnation. Any
man who at this stage of our national life, with a war on our hands
and many internal changes and problems to cope with, will publish
a defense of the propaganda of syndicalism and mob rule deserves
a reprimand." [1]

Louis Bromfield's *The Green Bay Tree*, 1924, and its sequel, *Possession*, 1925, are novels with an industrial background, and observant and detailed drawing of a steel town

in the Middle West. The mills had surrounded the ornate house of John Shane, the owner, making a characteristic setting of an American industrial feudalism, the twentieth century reproduction of the medieval castle on a hill and the clustered huts of retainers and vassals at its foot. John Shane had died ten years before the story opens and his widow lives in the house in the traditions of pride and aristocracy. The social importance of these novels is in their background of economic contrast and conflict. The story itself is one of involved domestic relations.

Edna Ferber's *So Big,* 1924, deserves a high place among the literary achievements of the period, a novel of distinction in its style, in its imaginative creation of character and in its pertinent social criticism. It is a work of real importance for morals and religion, although it does not deal explicitly with formal religion at all. In its heroine, Selina DeJong, a notable character is presented, a schoolteacher in a Dutch community in northern Illinois who marries a farmer and who through the endless drudgery of a farmer's wife never loses a gay unconquerable spirit. She makes a material success when left a widow with an infant son and carries on her truck farm. But her real success is inner and spiritual. She represents the real success of being as opposed to having. She is all the more effective in that the art of the portrayal entirely omits any trace of the didactic. Selina DeJong never bows down to any gold or tin gods of commercialism. But her tragedy is a characteristic one. She cannot transmit her qualities to her son. Dirk, the son, is the common spiritual tragedy of the second generation. In contrast to his mother, " So Big," the son, was a success only in terms of dollars and invitations. One key scene in the novel presents the contrast.

Selina reproaches Dirk for his desertion of beauty, as represented in his profession of architecture, for the accumulation of money in the bond business. Dirk is irritated at his mother's taking his going into the bond business as a betrayal of her hope and faith in him. Her reproach has broken down his assumed self-assurance. When she reverts to the old game she used to play with him when he was a small child and asks, banteringly, "How big is my son," he answers, "So Big" and makes a gesture, not that of outstretched arms, as he used to make when a child, but measures a very small space between thumb and forefinger. Then he realizes that that was the size he actually looked to his mother.

So Big is notable for its effective deflation of the go-getter. It appeared three years later than *Babbitt*. Its method is far more indirect and subtle. It is not vehement in its onslaught; it does not unroll like a comic strip of caricature, as *Babbitt* does to so large an extent. But it effectively pictures the inner emptiness of the tin gods of the temple of big business and the parasitic nature of much of it. In a moment of understanding Dirk sees it with his mother's eyes and confesses, " I'm nothing but a rubber stamp."

A good example of faithful dealing with an industrial situation and its effect on people is Rollo Walter Brown's *Firemakers,* 1931. The scene is the Ohio coal mines, which the author knows by years of close contact. The book carries no load of what the Marxians call " ideology." It does not exhort, it offers no solutions. But it does offer the disturbance of mind which honest pictures of the tension spots of contemporary life bring. The dramatic climax of the book comes toward the end when a group of men are

trapped in a mine. But in a figurative sense, that is the
theme of the whole book — men caught in the mine,
trapped where they cannot get out into life. Luke, the central figure, begins life in the mine at fourteen as a " trap-
boy." He never escapes the trap. He makes a desperate
effort to follow his artistic bent at pottery-making. From
the edge of success he slips back again, but he still cherishes
the hope of success for his son. The informed and sympathetic pictures of the miners of American stock, the strike
and the advent of the militia, the farming life around the
mines, are effective. Similar in its quiet, sincere realism is
Mr. Brown's second novel, *Toward Romance*.

II

To no section of the country has the fiction of the last
twenty years brought such a complete change of approach
as to the South. A fresh and new portrait of the South has
resulted.

One obvious reason for this, of course, has been that the
actual life and conditions of no section had been so heavily
screened by the curtains of a romantic tradition. The South
had been blanketed with a luxuriant growth of honeysuckle and roses. Squalid backgrounds were obscured by
magnolia trees. Just as in the patrician pre-war days the
slave quarters were well out of view from the lawn in front
of the mansion, ugly realities were rather largely out of the
range of vision of the decorous front porch of literature.
Thomas Nelson Page, with his historical stories and romances, well reflected the dominant tradition. The prevalence of the honeysuckle and roses convention in the liter-

ary treatment of Virginia is well illustrated in the fact that when Ellen Glasgow wrote her first novel, *The Descendant,* 1927, she published it anonymously, because, as she explained, she was part of her environment and did not like to be " disloyal " to friends. At that time and, no doubt, to many in the South today, any critical examination of actualities, unrestricted by the " No Trespass " of convention, was treason to the Old Dominion. The change brought about by the advance of the realistic temper and method in fiction and criticism has great significance for the moral, social and political life of the South, for it has resulted in a constant sapping at the base of the intrenchments of traditions and attitudes, a fortified status quo which stood like a row of forts not only against social change but also against the very examination of social problems. It has also a real importance for organized religion, for the church has often been a sacred sanctuary for obscurantism and reaction. It has baptized the existing order and sanctified unholy prejudice and injustice. It has made, in the South as in other sections of the country, " of good report " many things essentially vile. Consequently one of the primary religious services of literary realism has been to break the strangle hold which a conventional and dogmatic type of religion, serving as a rationalization of the prejudices and self-interest of a class, has had on the ethical and religious life. To this result, many writers have made effective contribution.

It would be a great injustice to one of America's foremost novelists, Ellen Glasgow, to think of her as primarily a writer of any one section of the country. She is national and international in significance. Her special contribution to opening the way to a fresh understanding of the life and social problems of the South is indicated in her remark, made in 1925, that "what the South needs now is blood and irony." Her novels have been marked by a continual increase in irony, in an acid sharpness and satire. It would be perhaps unjust to say that there has been a continual increase in realistic treatment of life, for she never has been the victim of sentimentalism. Even in her earliest novels, in the *Battle Ground,* 1902, for instance, dealing with the Civil War, she showed an untraditional treatment of the past of her state. But such a novel as *Barren Ground,* 1924, discloses a much more predominant interest in the conditioning of life by the natural and social forces of its environment.

Barren Ground tells the story of Dorinda Oakley's struggle with the land, of which the " broom-sedge " is the formidable and relentless symbol. Her heroine is a woman fit to stand beside Willa Cather's creations; the story is one of the inner triumph of courage. "We make our living out of barren ground," says Dorinda in words that express both the theme of the novel and the spirit of the heroine. Her father and mother were Virginians who might be identified as the clan of " forgotten men," a little above the poor whites in station and yet much below the landed gentry. The struggle to live is bleak and hard. In addition, Dorinda has to surmount a great personal disappointment in her life, when her intended bridegroom brings home another woman as his bride. With the catastrophe which love meets, she turns to the soil as a fulfilment of life and defeats the broom-sedge after a gallant battle. Her father's barren acres are made to blossom, if not as the rose at least fruitful and green. In the process she gains another and, to the novelist, more important victory; her effort brings the thrill of creation and lifts her life out of the bitterness of threatened defeat and frustration. She can even feel and show compassion to the man who jilted her. She learns how to use adverse circumstances in reaching a goal of fulfilment. The novel is deeply religious in its implications, a moving human documentation to the proposition that " she that loseth her life shall find it."

In her more recent novels, Ellen Glasgow has written in a style much more satirical and much more subversive of established tradition. There is both sympathy for the people who live under an outdated aristocratic social code, an understanding of the values of inherited convention, and at the same time a wit and humor in disclosing the pathetic inadequacies of the tradition and code. Her three latest novels act as a constant erosion on the tradition. This is evident in *The Romantic Comedians,* 1926, in which both satire and cynicism are brought to the " debunking " of conventional sentimentality toward Southern customs. Judge Honeywell, after 36 years of existence as a widower, in the grand manner of loyalty to a departed love, at the age of 65 marries Annabel Upchurch, aged 23. The resulting shattering of illusions furnishes comedy which skirts the edge of tragedy. It must be noted that in the total effect of this humor and irony there is an attitude tending to be subversive not only of Southern tradition but of a much larger area of largely accepted moral authority.

In *The Sheltered Life,* 1932, there is the same ironical spirit, the same shrewd humorous knowledge of human nature, and a devastating criticism of the inadequacy of false sentimentalism. It shows the life of a woman strangled by the attempt to live up to the pretense of a happy marriage, because to admit the ugly reality would be to go against the romantic tradition of her caste. That was the one God above all Gods, a jealous God whose service demanded human sacrifice. Eva Birdsong, a famous Southern beauty, the professional beauty of the roses and moonlight lore of the South, was truly in love with her outwardly attractive but cheap and disloyal husband. To the task of covering up the wretched disaster of her marriage she brings a courage and grace worthy of a much better cause. When the wreckage is made too plain to ignore, through the infatuation of a young girl for her husband, it is the final blow and a tragic shooting puts an end to the futile drama. It is realism blended with imagination and sympathy. There is a revealing bit of symbolism, never emphasized but effective, in the pervasive smell of the gas works which penetrates the old residence district from which all but a few of the former inhabitants have retreated. It is probably no mistake to take that poisonous odor as a symbol of something deadly in the whole false atmosphere of life.

Another invader through the flowered hedge of tradition into the realities of life in the South is Thomas S. Stribling, whose three novels, *Teeftallow,* 1926, *The Forge,* 1930, and *The Store,* 1932, the Pulitzer prize-winning novel for 1933, make up an impressive contribution to a fresh audit of many aspects of Southern life, particularly its ruling moral codes, social practices and economic conditions. Stribling is especially important for our present interest in his many revelations of the defects of a dogmatic orthodoxy, aridly theological and lacking both ethical concern and insight, remote from the life needs of people and communities. To see the vast difference in approach possible to the same social group and background, compare Maristan Chapman's *Happy*

Mountain with Stribling's *Bright Metal*. To the first, life seems to be a bed of roses; to the second, it is a bed of spikes. Yet the same conditions were under observation.

Teeftallow is a bitter dose of realism. Only one who knows well the country described could judge whether or not the contention is justified that it is made up of aspects of the life of the district arbitrarily selected to bear out the author's depressing and pessimistic point of view. The theme is that of humanity caught in the chains of inhuman and petrified religious and moral tradition. The effort to break away from these shackles on the mind and spirit of a community seems hopeless. It is a severe picture, but the whole background of the Scottsboro trials in 1932 and 1933, with their revelation of conditions like many in Stribling's novel, indicate that there is essential truth in the drawing. The novel tells the life history of Abner Teeftallow, born on a poor farm, grandson of a judge and actual heir to a large part of Lane County, Tennessee. The future seems to hold some promise when he falls in love with Nessie Sutton, who has vague but determined ambitions for him. The repressive hand of the ignorant community is laid heavily upon them when it discovers their intimacy. The hill people drive Nessie out of town and attack Abner. The girl finds refuge with a jeweler, a non-conformist to the community bigotry, and Abner escapes to a neighboring town. The book is a vivid commentary on the Scopes trial in Tennessee which occurred the year before its publication. It sets forth the mental environment of bigoted ignorance, the festering of the mind and soul in a secluded pocket of life. The romantic illusions of the hill country are shattered.

The Forge, 1930, aims to throw a searchlight into a day

that is passed, and doubtless has more importance as a social document than as a novel. In it a Southerner looks at his inheritance with an objective attitude and spirit. The novel tells the story of the Alabama Vaidens before, during and after the Civil War. Its description of the Ku Klux Klan and the carpet-bagger is in violent contrast to the shrill hysterics of Thomas Dixon's *The Clansman*.

The award of the Pulitzer prize to Stribling's novel, *The Store*, in 1933 occasioned much dissent in the South and much vigorous protest against it as a warped and false picture. Whatever it lacks as fiction in style and emotional quality, it has impressive sincerity, a wealth of detail of the social and economic background, and a passionate protesting spirit. It is a study in the degeneration of a town, Florence, Alabama, living on an empty memory of past greatness, with a present dominated by exploiting injustice both to blacks and to poor whites and by the tawdry ideals of petty acquisitiveness. Miltiades Vaiden, a Southern gentleman of the old school, seeks to recoup his bankrupt fortunes by blackmail and thieving. The book ends with a melodramatic lynching of Vaiden's mulatto son. The element of greatest value in the story is the description of tension and conflict between the decayed aristocratic class and the most intelligent Negroes and the prejudiced and almost illiterate poor whites. Both white injustice and black resignation are pictured. The exploitation of the Negro is revealed in such an incident as that in which Toussaint, a " white nigger," refused the " nigger pound " which is handed him by an insolent young white clerk:

" ' Ain't it well understood a nigger pound's about twelve ounces? ' asks the irate storekeeper. ' It's a kind of unwritten law — they expect it. An' to have a clerk weighin' out sixteen-ounce pounds would throw everything out of whack, disorganize business!' "

Another " technique " of selling to Negroes is connected with shoes.

" ' What would you do if a nigger woman came in and wanted shoes? ' a clerk was asked.
" ' Do like they do everywhere else,' was the reply. ' Let her look at 'em and buy 'em. If they don't fit 'em when she puts 'em on that's her look out.' "

When Toussaint protests against this exploitation, the end is lynching. Negroes who are defiant against the white man's choice of what is " best " for them, have no place in the society which Stribling depicts. The philosophy is quite simply put by Colonel Miltiades Vaiden.

" ' Colored people,' says Colonel Miltiades, earnestly and sincerely, ' are hurt more than they are helped by education. When a colored person becomes educated there is no place for him.' " [2]

It is fitting that *The Store* should be given the Pulitzer prize in the year of the Scottsboro trial. There is also an impressive irony in the award to this study of a backward social community located a few miles from what has been hailed as a crowning achievement of man's mechanical mastery in the twentieth century, the Muscle Shoals Dam. No better physical symbol of " the social lag " could be selected.

No impression could be farther from the truth than that there has been any unity of point of view or interpretation in the fictional treatment of the South since the war. Indeed it may reasonably be maintained that no section of the country has shown greater divergences. There has been a very prolific group of agrarians, many of whom contributed to the symposium, *I'll Take My Stand,* who rally to the cause of agriculture against an invading industrialism and who at times create the impression that they are giving a modern literary version of Lee's embattled stand in the last defense of Richmond, seventy-five years after Appomattox. Among this group who have written poetry, novels, essays and biography are Allen Tate and John D. Ware.

Farther south there is the lower Mississippi Valley, described by William Faulkner in terms largely of degenerates. Both Faulkner and Erskine Caldwell will be noticed in later chapters under themes to which their works seem particularly related.

Paul Green has dealt in both play and novel with the changing South, with a severe lack of sentimentality, with realism in the dreariest modern tradition substituted for traditional romanticism. In his Pulitzer prize play for 1927, *In Abraham's Bosom,* and other plays he has brought to the dramatic presentation of the Negro an intimate lifelong knowledge which throws fresh streams of light on " the cabin in the cotton." His many treatments of the place and nature of the religion of the Negroes of North and South Carolina show the strange blending of superstition, emotionalism, fear, ecstasy and conscience. Green carries no weight of special pleading; his plays are not problem plays; certainly not economic tracts. They are attempts to picture actuality by one who knows the people and environment. As effective transcriptions of life, however, they are powerful indictments of race exploitation. To use his own words, " Living in the vilest of huts, the prey of his own superstition, suspicions and practices, beaten and forlorn before God

Almighty himself, the Negro has struggled helplessly in the clutch of affliction and pain."

In Abraham's Bosom tells the story of the striving and defeat of Abraham McCranie, a North Carolina Negro, who feels that the very dice of God are loaded against the Negro. " De white man up dere high," Abraham says, " settin' up wid God, up dere in his favor. He git everything, nigger git de scraps, leavings."

In Green's more recent novel, *The Laughing Pioneer*, the real theme is the conflict between the old traditional South, nursing its legends, living in a walled garden of make-believe, and the new South, marked by a trust in the machine and everything labeled Progress. For purposes of contrast doubtless, the representative of the old South, Judge Long, is represented as autocratic, implacable in his hatred of everything but the old aristocracy, bigoted and provincial. The detailed picture of the ruined plantation and the tawdry, shabby life of pretense which Judge Long and his daughter Alice lived on it, is an impressive study of decay, economic, intellectual and moral.

Another Southern writer who has brought understanding and honesty to the representation of the Negro is Du Bose Heyward. His *Porgy* treats the Negro seriously and without patronage. His character Porgy is a notable figure in the American Album. Porgy is a black cripple in Charleston, South Carolina, sitting begging in the sun all day, an occasional gambler but for the most part living silent and remote from his fellows. The coming of love and the loss of his love reveal great strength of character in Porgy, portrayed with sympathy and with an effect of emotional intensity. *South Moon Under,* by Marjorie K. Rawlings, 1933, has attracted much attention, largely from its novelty of background and the sincerity and skill of realistic treatment. It deals with the poor whites of the Florida " scrub," a realm into which fiction had never penetrated. The survivals of the primitive in these people, their almost tribal organization, just a few miles from the parade of plutocracy at Palm Beach and Miami, furnish an ironical element to the story.

III

Edith Wharton, in the forefront of living novelists, has dealt with a restricted setting and, following the tradition of Henry James, has taken the minute depiction of individual character as her chief interest. The word " vivisection " might well describe her process of character drawing. Her field has been the aristocratic class to which she herself belongs and which she knows intimately. But she has brought irony to her analysis of the life of " society." Her most notable novel since the war is undoubtedly *The Age of Innocence,* with the irony of the title strongly reflected in the book. It is a picture of " society " in New York in the 1870's, bringing satire to bear on the Pharisaism which, as she says, was " wholly absorbed in barricading itself against the unpleasant." The cramping conventions, the vulgar concern for respectability, the moral decadence, are all brought under a powerful microscope. The pretensions which have acted as a moral and spiritual plaster cast on a plutocratic society are subjected to a thorough deflation.

At the farthest possible extreme from Mrs. Wharton in almost every particular is Fannie Hurst. In spite of great and obvious limitations of both style and method, limitations from a machine-like pattern for her stories and a constant recurrence of sentimentality, Fannie Hurst has brought fresh realistic treatment to different sections of the populace, " to the Jew first " (to use scriptural language) but also to the Gentile. Her studies of folks " just around the corner " show a knowledge and sympathy for life as it is lived among transplanted Jews, and have helped much to displace mere stock caricature of the Jew by understanding and truthful portrayal. Her most effective novel, *Lummox,* is a strong study of an inarticulate, Bertha, a big powerful servant woman, half Slav and half Swede. Condemned to the hard labor of the exploited, betrayed and wronged, she has elemental strength, denied to those who arrange her destiny, a strength like that of the earth, mysterious, indomitable.

IV

No survey of the influences of realism, no matter how hurried, could leave out of view the so-called " new poetry " which has followed the poetic revival which began in America about 1912. It would be a mistake to consider the most notable poets of the last twenty years as primarily realists. They are primarily poets and their significance is missed if the attempt is made to tag any of them with a hard and fast label. In general, two prominent aspects of the new poetry movement embody elements of realism. These are, first, the inclusion of the common, the familiar, the everyday life over a wide range as proper themes for poetry. A comparison of such poets of the 1890's as Richard Watson Gilder and Thomas Bailey Aldrich, with Edgar Lee Masters and Carl Sandburg, for instance, will make this expansion of the range of poetic theme very clear. The second aspect of the new poetry, realistic in tendency, is the diction. Poetry had become anemic from hackneyed and traditional language; often as remote from life as the dainty shepherdesses of a Watteau picture. The poetic revival in America brought the language of poetry into the realm of the daily speech of actual life and gave it freshness and reality.

The two poets of greatest importance who show this spirit of departure from romantic tradition are Robert Frost and Carl Sandburg. Frost finds his subjects in New England and in many ways is much more traditional in theme and diction than Sandburg. But there is an absence of sentimentality, of the stock *cliché*, in his treatment both of nature and of people, an absence of superficial optimism, a sense of tragedy under commonplace exterior. Frost's work will require mention in the chapter dealing with Disillusionment and Futility; Sandburg's is in the chapter on Rebellion and Social Protest. Here it is sufficient to note the fresh eyesight and insight found in both of them. Much better than a lengthy discussion of Sandburg's realism, is one sample, from a poem called " Onion Days ":

> Mrs. Gabielle Giovannitti comes
>   along Peoria Street every morning at nine
>   o'clock
> With kindling wood piled on top of her head, her eyes
>   looking straight ahead to find the way for her
>   old feet.
> Her daughter-in-law, Mrs. Pietro Giovannitti, whose
>   husband was killed in a tunnel explosion through
>   the negligence of a fellow-servant,
> Works ten hours a day, sometimes twelve, picking
>   onions for Jasper on the Bowmanville road.

She takes a street car at half-past five in the morning,
  Mrs. Pietro Giovannitti does,
And gets back from Jasper's with cash for her day's
  work, between nine and ten o'clock at night.
Last week she got eight cents a box, Mrs. Pietro Giovannitti,
  picking onions for Jasper,
But this week Jasper dropped the pay to six cents a box
  because so many women and girls were answering
    the ads in the Daily News.
Jasper belongs to an Episcopal church in Ravenswood
  and on certain Sundays
He enjoys chanting the Nicene Creed with his daughters
  on each side of him joining their voices with his.
If the preacher repeats old sermons of a Sunday,
  Jasper's mind wanders to his 700-acre farm and
    how he can make it produce more efficiently.[3]

The extent to which the acted drama has shown an increase in realistic spirit and technique may be realized by a
comparison of the work of the most popular and successful
dramatists of twenty years ago with those of the present
time. The drama of conventional pattern, in which the traditions of plot and romantic patterns pressed the play into
familiar molds is clearly evident in the melodramas of
Augustus Thomas, the farces of George H. Broadhurst and
the theatrical romances of David Belasco. The greater
fidelity to actual life situation, the drama of character rather
than plot and stage setting, is illustrated by such plays as
those of Eugene O'Neill, Maxwell Anderson and Laurence
Stallings' *What Price Glory,* Anderson's *Saturday's Children,* Arthur Richman's drama of domestic relations, *Am-
bush,* George Kelly's *Craig's Wife* and *The Show Off,* Elmer
Rice's *Street Scene,* Sidney Howard's *They Knew What They
Wanted, Lucky Sam McCarver,* and his study of possessive

mother love, *The Silver Cord*. Along with such productions, of course, there has gone a flood of machine-made mediocre plays, "crook" and "racketeer" melodramas, slapstick farces and inane romances. But enough first class work has been done not only to make the years since 1915 the most notable in all American history for the realistic interpretation of life in the theater, but also to lift the drama to a new importance as a force in social criticism.

[1] The Catholic World, Feb. 1918.
[2] *The Store,* by Thomas S. Stribling. Doubleday, Doran & Company. Copyright, 1932.
[3] *Chicago Poems,* by Carl Sandburg, p. 6. Henry Holt & Company.

CHAPTER FIVE

REALISM IN ACCOUNT WITH RELIGION

MORE justification than has yet been offered may be felt necessary for the inclusion of even so partial an examination of some of the realistic literature since the war as has been given in the preceding pages. The avowed aim of the present volume is to deal with the bearing of literature on religion. And religion, as such, has occupied but a small part of the attention of the post-war novelists, playwrights and poets discussed.

The justification offered here lies mainly in the fact that, if we are to give any universal weight to the judgment, " Ye shall know the truth and the truth shall make you free," we cannot deny a high spiritual value to the honest reporting of competent observation. Realistic literature can help mightily to set religion free from the blinding bondage of prison walls which shut it in to partial and false views of the world of life of men and women. The proper attitude for organized religion to take to this offering of reporters is that implied in the appeal of Moses to Hobab, who knew the topography and life of the wilderness: " Leave us not, I pray thee, for as much as thou knowest how we are to encamp in the wilderness, and thou mayest be to us instead of eyes " (Numbers 10:31). For here are scores of case studies of enormous importance to religion.

There is lasting value, also, in the definitely religious spirit found in the attitude of wonder prevalent in many of the writers just mentioned. If philosophy begins in wonder, religion is not far away. There is the reflection of Moses' attitude toward the burning bush, " I will now turn aside and see this great sight." There is a standing at attention before human personality caught in various situations, a humility, a sincere effort to understand, a reverence for human life, for the thing that is, which not only has value for religion in its reports rendered, but is itself an essentially religious attitude and experience. With this there has been, much more often than not, an attitude of deep and encompassing pity, of exploring sympathy which is central in a religion whose God is love.

Fiction is particularly important for the unbandaging of eyes and the extension of experience that are necessary if one is to have an adequate view of life, for the reason that no other form of literature gives so nearly the equivalent of actual experience. The personal experience of any one individual, let his immediate contacts with people and situations be as wide and varied as possible, is necessarily limited. Unless there is an extension of trustworthy contact with life through literature, he is condemned to remain more or less a provincial, an easy prey to false generalizations based on too limited data. No other form of literature contributes so directly and fully as does the novel to social awareness and imagination, to a sensitive understanding of another person, another class or race of people, another way of life, a situation never immediately experienced.

A contemporary illustration of the service of truthful delineation of life in fiction in saving readers from misleading delusions is contained in an interesting speculation a literary critic has made concerning Herbert Hoover. He contends that had Mr. Hoover been in any vital touch with the literature of his era, particularly that large section of it expressing criticism and protest, he would not have been betrayed into his relentless adherence to " rugged individualism " as an expression of the temper of the American people. Literature might have been a range-finder, might have provided a means of sympathetic understanding of what was actually stirring in people's minds. Lacking such reports of the people's mind and heart, he " had to fall back on the stereotyped formulas of outdated history books and the grossly inadequate interpretations of such biased political and economic advisers as he took counsel with."

The moral confusion resulting from non-realistic drama is well illustrated in a comment made by Margaret Mayorga on certain popular plays. She selects some very popular pre-war plays and lists the morals taught by each one. The teaching of *Secret Service,* a highly romantic play dealing with the Civil War, was that love triumphs over all obstacles; that of *The Henrietta* was that financial giants operate by some sort of mystical ability; *The Truth* taught that the truth is obvious to perceive and easy to believe; while the moral of *Arizona* was that it is good to sacrifice oneself in order to save another from unpleasant truth. All these morals are, of course, pernicious lies; they are immoral superstitions. While on superficial examination these four plays may seem " wholesome " to the uncritically minded, on any genuinely ethical analysis they are thoroughly " unwholesome." They well illustrate the evil moral and religious effects of conventional sentimentality. Indeed, it is not too much to say that most of the " bad " morals taught by the drama have come from " good " plays.

I

The failure of organized religion to appreciate and profit from this present-day realism has been a calamity of the first order. It has meant a heavy handicap to its efforts to bring spiritual resources to bear on the life of the time. The fact that there are many obvious reasons for this failure makes it none the less tragic. The attitude of most religious people, including ministers, has been too much that of shock at what offended their taste or their morals; they have been too swift in pulling down the shutters of their eyes and minds, at the new, at the depressing, at what they called " unwholesome." The ludicrous, even if pathetic, childishness of the Cincinnati Credit Men's Association's reported action in January, 1933, asking the University of Cincinnati to discontinue a course of lectures on economics because it was " depressing," has a parallel in the attitude of many conventionally religious people toward sincere and competent picturing of the world. It is akin to the quality that has unfitted many ministers to deal helpfully with people in moral difficulty. Their stock response of being " shocked " has prevented them from finding out what the factors in the situation really are and how they might be helpfully dealt with.

Among the reasons for the church's failure to profit as it might from an appreciation of the services of realistic literature, there are six which stand out prominently. The first is the fact that the church has feared any kind of criticism. It has given grudging welcome to any observation and insight which challenged its traditional outlook on life or its official orthodox interpretation of life. There have, of

course, been exceptions to this generalization in the unbroken line of prophets who, from the days of the great
prophets of the eighth century B.C. down to the present,
have refused to mouth the soothsaying of an official optimism complacently blind to fact. This fear of criticism
is, of course, not peculiar to the church; it is one of the liabilities of institutionalism. Its operation in the ranks of
organized religion has resulted in an opposition to realism
in every form of literary art. It has been like the device of
the mind in repressing what is unpleasant or what does not
fit into its ruling and fixed ideas. There has been the additional influence which comes from the fact that the mind
of traditionally religious people has been oriented to sentimentalism by the nature of much of the preaching to which
they have listened. For much preaching has been sentimental in the primary sense that it has been more concerned
with creating the greatest emotional effect on the audience
than with discovering the real truth about the material
dealt with.

A second reason is the historic devotion of both Protes-
tantism and Catholicism, with different emphasis and degree, to Puritanism in individual moral life. This is particularly true in the whole realm of sex. A great deal of
realistic fiction has forsworn allegiance to the taboo on sex;
it has often presented scenes dealing with sex and comment
on sex and marriage relations quite in conflict with the traditional teaching and *mores* of the church. The result has
been that work containing what has been termed " immoral
tendencies " has been either disparaged or put under as much
of a ban as was possible. This, in spite of the fact that often
the very novels and poems condemned were filled with pas-

sionate indictment of monstrous immoralities of another sort, both individual and social.

A third reason for the church's failure to profit from realistic literature is the wide prevalence of a standardized and false view of " spirituality." One of the greatest weaknesses of Christianity as an agency for spiritual and ethical transformation lies in the commonly accepted idea of spirituality. The farther religion has been removed from the concrete situations, choices and issues of life, the more " spiritual " it becomes. It would be both unfair and ridiculous to imagine that this charge is of universal application. Perhaps it does not apply to the majority. But such a vague, abstract, emotional idea of the " spiritual life " does find wide enough acceptance to have made it blur seriously the ethical understanding and spiritual insight of the churches. " Spirituality " has been so predominantly associated with emotional states and personal habits, so tied up with pious devotional practices, so measured by participation in services of worship, that problems and issues of tremendous spiritual significance to millions of people have been shut out from inclusion as spiritual concerns. Membership in the Altar Guild has been often accepted as a mark of spirituality. Work against child labor and tuberculosis, or for a minimum wage, is " secular." That perversion of prophetic religion has played a large part in closing the eyes of people within the ranks of the churches to the fresh resources for understanding the world which much present-day literature has supplied.

Another reason, already suggested, is that traditional religion has been tied up with an unreal outlook on the world, turning a blind eye and a deaf ear to what it considered not uplifting. It has had a viciously unwholesome preoccupation with the wholesome. It has made the tragic mistake of reading too exclusively the contents of its own Sunday school libraries. There is a remark by one of the characters in Norman Douglas's *South Wind,* commonly cited as the apex of cynicism: "There is so much that is wholesome in real life. Let's keep it out of our books." That is cynical. But religious leaders and church people in general would have made ethical and spiritual gain if they had kept more of the " wholesome " out of their reading.

Many different strains of influence have gone into the building up of this blighting tradition of superficial " optimism," some of them noble, some of them base. Undoubtedly the hopeful idealism of the New England of the " Golden Day " contributed much — the optimism of Emerson and Theodore Parker. Through the channel of Unitarianism it pervaded other churches, and became part of widely accepted and influential American " philosophy." The whole Rotarian philosophy of the last twenty years both came from this optimism expressed in the outlook of the churches and in turn augmented it. It is not too much to suggest that the sticky sentimentalities which have dripped from the morning radio in recent years, from the lips of an optimist called " Cheerio," have more than a faint resemblance to the gospel intoned in many sanctuaries. Incidentally, this is a chief reason why the conventional sermonizing and teaching of the churches makes so little appeal to a large part of the younger generation; it represents the very thing against which they are in revolt. If there had been a greater capacity for clear seeing and less addiction to soothing syrup, the churches would have been saved from that falsely optimistic and romantic view of life which has done so much to make religion seem and be unreal. They would have seen more of what Micah saw, what Jesus saw of life. The church has immured herself too much in a Victorian pattern of life, or a rural pattern, and the grim facts of our present industrialism do not fit into either one. It has been said of Henry Adams that his principal difficulty with life was that he had an eighteenth-century education but had to live in the nineteenth century. Change the figures for the centuries and apply it to the church: it has had a nineteenth-century education but has had to live and work in the twentieth century. Dorothy Parker has, quite unintentionally, given an accurate picture of this inadequate grasp of the factors shaping the lives of millions of people in her poem entitled " Interior ":

> She lives in a quiet room,
>   A narrow room, and tall,
> With pretty lamps to quench the gloom
>   And mottoes on the wall.
>
> There all the things are waxen neat
>   And set in decorous lines,
> And there are posies, round and sweet,
>   And little straightened vines.
>
> Her mind lives tidily apart
>   From cold and noise and pain,
> And bolts the door against her heart
>   Out wailing in the rain.[1]

The heart of religion, in its great prophetic hours, has been " out wailing in the rain." Its divine business is not with wall mottoes but with " cold and noise and pain."

There are two other reasons for this lack of appreciation of and learning from realistic literature. One is that it demands the pain of thinking; while the literature of naïve romanticism or rosy optimism can be met with feeling and singing — or, best of all, with sleep. Sir Joshua Reynolds said truthfully: "There is scarcely any expedient to which man will not resort in order to evade and shuffle off real labor — the real labor of thinking." That is not cynicism; it is merely truth. Another reason is that organized religion has had too great a reverence for the business man, in the rôles of both autocrat and wizard. It has been too deeply involved in the established order, has given too many hostages to the status quo, to suffer gladly facts or a point of view which threaten to upset it.

II

All this is particularly tragic when we think of the heritage of the realism which rightly belongs to Christianity. Jesus had a truly terrifying realism. It is a sad irony to think of his name being joined in any manner to the shortsightedness of a chirping optimism, sustained by the blind or cowardly evasion of actual facts. How Jesus hated sentimentalism, emotionalism, blinders and screens! He knew what was in man. His eyes were moral X-rays, never confusing shadow with substance. Recall the occasion when on his entry into Jerusalem his disciples, with the natural curiosity of country men visiting a large city, showed him the imposing buildings, crying out, " Look, Master, what manner of stones." He gave an unexpected answer, " There will not be one stone left upon another." Behind the fair

surface he saw the ethical and spiritual failure. An orthodox member of the Jewish church might well have complained that this prophet from Galilee was not striking a
constructive, optimistic note; that he was pessimistic. Jesus
was profoundly pessimistic about the issue of a way of life not
founded on a rock, about man without God. Selling this
birthright of the penetrating realism of Jesus for a mess of
optimistic pottage is one of the tragedies of Christian history. That high heritage of realism is supremely illustrated
in Jesus' refusal of an opiate or anodyne on the cross, the
putting away of anything that would dull the mind or
blunt the edge of suffering. If the explorations of present-
day writers into the sore and ugly areas of the life of our
times can help us to recover that heritage, they have done
a great religious service.

The insufficiency of realism in literature as an agency of
social and moral progress is clearly seen when we enter the
realm of motive power. Negatively realism has done and is
doing an indispensable critical, destructive service. Realism
has been busy for twenty years pointing out what is wrong;
it seems strangely impotent either to generate the force for
reconstruction or to see and describe a more adequate goal
to be achieved. Hoary stupidities have been exposed; pretense, "bunk," and prejudice have been unmasked; facts
as they are have been faced. But when the inevitable question is reached, "Where do we go from here?" realism in
itself has been at a loss for any impressive or coherent answer. Man cannot live on negations or criticism of existing
structures of thought and action. The smashing of idols
may be, and very often has been, an essential service to
human life and society. But it is obviously a negative serv-

ice which derives its lasting significance from the positive constructive achievement which follows it and which, in some real measure, it makes possible. Two decades of realistic exploration of the existing order of life have sufficed to explode the myth that all that is necessary to secure transformation is to make clear what is wrong. Dr. Henry Seidel Canby has effectively pointed out that there are at present in the United States multitudes who have been shown again and again convincing pictures of what is wrong; and they have shown small inclination and little power to change it. Paraphrasing the words of Edith Cavell, "realism is not enough." Other forces must be brought to bear if men are to build "above the deep intent, the deed, the deed."

In that necessity lies a permanent need for religion.

---

1 *Sunset Gun,* by Dorothy Parker. The Liveright Publishing Corporation.

CHAPTER SIX

DISILLUSIONMENT AND FUTILITY

" Life's a long headache in a noisy street."
                                        JOHN MASEFIELD
" One by one like leaves from a tree
All my faiths have forsaken me."
                                        SARA TEASDALE

DISILLUSIONMENT and Futility are two words widely used in characterizing much American literature since the war. They describe also a larger amount of reading matter which cannot claim the prestige of the word " literature." The words express the moods generated in large numbers of people in Europe and America, not only by the war but by forces active in the preceding decades, disintegrating to many accepted faiths, political, economic and moral as well as religious. It was a sort of spiritual vacuum from which the vitalizing oxygen of faith and idealism had been withdrawn. The wings of the mind and spirit were folded in chill exhaustion.

The history of a progressive distrust both of the inevitability of progress and of the validity of the neat and cozy dogmatisms of traditional religion really starts with the period of the great Enlightenment of a hundred and fifty years ago. Of this glow of trustful optimism which came over the world it could be said truly,

Bliss was it in that dawn to be alive
And to be young were very heaven.

With equal truth can it be said, as much contemporary
fiction and poetry make clear, it was anything but bliss to
be alive when that dawn turned into gray twilight, as it did
so strikingly in the twentieth century. Then, according to
a large and very vocal chorus of young writers, to be young
was very hell. For the Enlightenment furnished a great
height from which to fall. It was a cloud-land of hope, an
almost apocalyptic hope in the natural goodness of man,
in the sure coming of justice, brotherhood and progress.
It was based on the growing conquest of nature by science.
It was a trust in great abstract nouns such as Democracy,
Liberty and Education. When the machine age came in on
wheels, the machine itself became an object of awe and faith,
as in the case of the ancient Philistines who expected salvation from a machine. When the outcome of the French
Revolution brought disillusionment with political Utopias,
faith was transferred to the Industrial Revolution. The
deep descent from that high peak of hope was well started
before the war by the obvious results of industrialism, and
the political code based on it, and by the type of religion which rationalized it. The precipitation given that
descent by the war brought into skeptical contempt many
of the venerated idols, such as the goodness of man, the
possibility of justice, the value as well as the inevitability
of so-called progress and the worth of democracy. As for
man himself, Shakespeare was wrong. We are not " such
stuff as dreams are made of." We are such stuff as glands
are made of and our little life is rounded with a reaction.

In 1922 T. S. Eliot published one of the most discussed and

little read poems of the twentieth century, *The Waste Land*. Stout, indeed, would be the self-confidence of one who undertook to explain the meaning of that dark forest of words. But the main purpose may be grasped even by a wayfaring man. It seems to be an attempt to match in chaotic form the chaos of the generation after the war. *The Waste Land* is a spiritual desert blighted by drought. The action swings from the real world of London to the wilderness of the empty and parched modern soul as represented by the hero. The poem may well stand as a symbol of a " lost generation," to use a phrase descriptive of the spiritual bankruptcy of many of those old enough to go through the war and be affected by it.

I

There were many influences inevitably resulting in this sense of disillusionment and the futility of life which strongly mark so much writing during the 1920's. There was a natural feeling of irritation at the imbecility of civilization, a feeling sometimes mounting to rage, more often simmering as an attitude of cynical disdain for any revered values of such an order. The very uncertainty of life increased the feeling of many that the only sure good was the immediate one of pleasure. The natural effect of horror and hate got on the nerves of many, both of those who participated in the actual slaughter and those who did not. It is not surprising that, after the fatigue and excitement of the war, novelty should appear to be the thing most desirable. The restlessness of fever was much more to be expected than a balanced calm and maturity of judgment. A feeling of instability, like that which follows an earthquake, created an atmosphere in which a feverish urge for self-expression outlawed allegiance to codes or standards, moral and religious. Hence the harsh note so clearly heard in much popular literature, the passing of courtesy, taste and manners, the elevation of noise and speed as chief ends of man. The accompaniment of this change, as it is felt in the realm of religion, is evident in the antagonism to and rejection of any sort of absolutes, whether in art or in morals. In an age of relativity it should occasion no surprise that the great absolute of God should also be rejected. God did not fit in with the spirit of the party. " The idea of God is exacting and exhausting; and the age was tired." In this connection it may be contended with some pertinence that the rejection of the idea of God is not so much a fact about the validity of belief in God as it is a fact about the age.

A typical popular expression of this mood of disillusionment is the song which Noel Coward represents being sung in a London cabaret in 1930 in the last scene of his play, *Cavalcade*. It is banal and trite and crude. But not more so than hundreds of contemporaneous songs. It fairly represents a widely held and shrilly screamed attitude:

> Blues, Twentieth Century Blues, are getting me down.
> Who's escaped those weary Twentieth Century blues?
> Why, if there's a God in the sky, shouldn't he grin?
> High above this dreary Twentieth Century din,
> In this strange illusion
> Chaos and confusion
> People seem to lose their way.
> What is there to strive for,
> Love or keep alive for — say
> Hey, hey, call it a day.
> Blues, nothing to win or lose.[1]

A whole mountain higher in the intellectual scale but not unrelated in feeling is the mood of Edwin Arlington Robinson, in his line:

> I cannot find my way, there is no star.

In quite a different spirit, with a note of sprightly satire on the popular pose of world-weariness, are the verses of Dorothy Parker entitled "Coda," which might serve as a motto for a whole alcove of widely read contemporary fiction:

> There's little in taking or giving,
>   There's little in water or wine;
> This living, this living, this living
>   Was never a project of mine.
> Oh, hard is the struggle, and sparse is
>   The gain of the one at the top,
> For art is a form of catharsis,
>   And love is a permanent flop,
> And work is the province of cattle,
>   And rest's for a clam in a shell,
> So I'm thinking of throwing the battle —
>   Would you kindly direct me to hell? [2]

Attention has already been called to two aspects of the cult of disillusionment which may bear the briefest recalling. The first is that much of the deflation of accepted traditions and reverences is a decided moral and spiritual asset. It has resulted in the needed puncturing of many pretentious lies. This service has been well expressed in Gaius Glenn Atkins' epigram to the effect that "the age of Amen has given way to the age of Oh, Yeah?" The note of jeering skepticism turned on the type of diplomacy which brought on the war, Big Business Geniuses who brought on the depression and the " Stuffed Shirts " of politics, is sweet and holy music to the ears of any one concerned with moral and religious progress. It is an indispensable overture to any genuine ethical advance.

The other fact to be recalled to mind is that the so-called disillusionment and what is often, with doubtful accuracy and lack of sufficient analysis, referred to as the " moral slump " after the war, had part of their origin in the realm of politics. The recoil from idealism in the political sphere had a decided effect in other realms. Those who killed American participation in the League of Nations killed more than a treaty.

II

The Education of Henry Adams is probably the most important as well as massive work of pessimistic disillusionment which the twentieth century has seen. There is a striking fitness of coincidence that it should have been published in the year which marked the end of the war, 1918. The book is not, of course, a reflection of war-time or post-war thinking. It was withheld from publication twelve years after it was written, and its writing was spread over many years before that. It is pre-eminently the expression of the mind and temper of a unique individual, rather than the mood of a group or generation. Yet it served to usher in the post-war period with a reverberation like that of a funeral knell, and its tone of somber cynicism and depression is echoed in many other works. It has been called the autobiography of an American Hamlet. Adams reviews his own life and experiences in many fields — education, diplomacy, politics, literature — and records his successive revolts from each one. It is like a man watching the whole varied pageant of life parade before him and giving the verdict, " Nothing in it." He found no faith, purpose or ideal which might serve as a unifying force in life; perhaps because he found a steadily diminishing faith of any sort in himself.

Perhaps a Freudian interpretation of Adams may be the right one, that his vision of meaningless confusion and purposeless chaos in the world was a projection of an inner lack of unity and purpose within himself. Part of his pessimism has been ascribed to disappointed ambition, his failure to achieve the position of power and influence which he desired. At any rate, it is a profoundly weary and hopeless outlook which he has on the world. Toward the end of his years he is under the grip of a philosophy of determinism, and his favorite thesis of " the degradation of energy," that " the more highly organized an organism the nearer it is to disintegration " — a thesis which in a way was a forerunner of Spengler — only added to the cloud of gloom which settled on his mind. One of his greatest works, *Mont St. Michel and Chartres,* is a glorification of the unity of the thirteenth century, a mystical unity, which he calls " an intensity of conviction never again reached by any passion, whether of religion, of loyalty, of patriotism, of wealth; perhaps never paralleled by any economic effort except in war." There is a strong irony in this man, so completely bankrupt of any sustaining faith, turning to glorify an age completely dominated by faith.

The Education of Henry Adams is one of the great books of the twentieth century. It is full of acute insights, an almost savage criticism of the capitalistic, commercial civiliza-

tion and politics amid which he lived; yet to a large degree
a futile criticism, for he never penetrated to the economic
root causes of the degradation he pilloried. No doubt part
of the large appeal of the book on its appearance was its harmony with the mood of disillusion which was so strong a
mark of the years that followed.

III

It is impossible to do justice to the work of any writer by
trying to include it under any one descriptive adjective or
noun. That warning should be kept in mind in discussing
the authors brought together under the title " disillusionment." Probably the noun applies more accurately to Henry
Adams than to any other author of the period. In considering the work of Edwin Arlington Robinson as " disillusioned " or marked by a sense of futility, it should be con-
stantly remembered that the varied qualities of so great a
poet cannot be expressed by any one label. Yet, with that in
mind, it can truly be said that Robinson has expressed, in the
most poetic and exalted form, the feeling, mood and attitude
of disillusionment. There are evidences of much more positive hopes and adherences in his poetry, as will be illustrated
in the chapter on " The Search for God." In the main,
however, it is a " waste land " in which Robinson lives and
of which he writes, a world of meaningless confusion,
bleakness, hopelessness like the stark, dark, joyless land-
scapes which are the foreground and background of so
much of his poetry. His own phrase, " blind atomic pilgrimage," has kinship to Bertrand Russell's prose poem of
man marching to his pitiless and meaningless doom. The

question he asks, " If there be nothing after now, and we be nothing anyhow, why live? " is one which in various forms is asked throughout his work. It blows through his poetry again and again, like a chill wind.

The feeling that man is an alien or a stray in a universe indifferent to his ethical and spiritual aspiration finds frequent expression, as for instance the classic expression put into the mouth of Shakespeare, in *Ben Jonson Entertains a Man from Stratford,* where Shakespeare affirms that existence is " all nothing," this being a world where emperor and bug " go back to the same dust." It also appears in such a couplet as this from *Cavender's House,* 1929:

> Was ever an insect flying between two flowers
> Told less than we are told of what we are? [3]

This feeling of the futility of existence is found so frequently that it appears to be more personal than merely the delineation of character by speech. Robinson depicts many of his characters in defeat, frustrated by some kink of character or obscure destiny. The well known Richard Cory is an example of this — the individual, fortunate to outward view, who yet " put a bullet through his head."

There is, however, sometimes a note of triumph above defeat, an enduring value to effort to find meaning and light, which no failure quite frustrates. This feeling has resemblances to the "hopeless hope" to be found in Eugene O'Neill. There is also a spiritual aspiration, a search for faith, to be noted later.

Robert Frost has done so much in poetry revealing an appreciation of beauty, a sensuous enjoyment of it, that it may seem quite lacking in understanding to seem to label

him as a poet of disillusion or futility. No single label ever
does justice to a poet; no attempt at label-pasting is here
made. No one can read Frost's poetry of New England,
however, without a strong impression of the bleakness of the
human life depicted. It is a New England gone to seed
that so often appears; human beings gnarled and spiritually
and mentally undernourished, like a scraggly pine on a
Maine headland. The contrast between the optimisms,
spiritual hopes and idealisms of the New England of Emerson and Whittier and the chill human life depicted by
Frost is striking. Many of Frost's poems, despite notable
representation of beauty, give the impression of life like an
abandoned farm. Compare the New England of Whittier's " Snow Bound " with the oppressive picture in Frost's
" Death of the Hired Man," with its grim sense of the hopelessness of the struggle for life on a farm, the niggardliness
of a grudging Nature. Here there is no " light between the
cypress trees." A keynote of much of Frost is his " My
November Guest ":

> My Sorrow, when she's here with me,
>   Thinks these dark days of Autumn rain
> Are beautiful as days can be.
> She loves the bare, the withered tree.
> She walks the sodden pasture lane.[4]

Frost, too, loves " the bare, the withered tree."

IV

Fiction since the war has been much occupied with the
dark capital D's, somber heavy nouns — Disenchantment,
Disillusion, Dismay, Disintegration, Damnation. To these

might be added two other nouns, describing characters making frequent appearance in the rôle of Among Those Present — the Drunks and the Dancers. With the widest differences in detail, in sincerity of purpose and point of view, the fiction which may roughly be called disillusioned is marked by some common characteristics.

For one thing, there is a rather constant preoccupation with the individual. Whatever other objects of worship were cast down from the modern temple, the cult of Narcissus became almost an official religion in fiction dealing with the individual's responses, reactions, mental twistings and moods. It is an interesting bit of irony — this psychology of Narcissism — that in a time when the very existence of the " soul " was so vociferously denied in so many quarters, the soul, or what used to make up the soul, has received more microscopic scrutiny than ever before. In a period when the antique theological word " salvation " has been joyously exposed as a meaningless bogey, the thing itself, the search for salvation in terms of personal fulfilment, has occupied first place on the agenda of the novels here considered.

Very prominent has been the interest, often deserving to be called an obsession, with sex. This feature of the time as expressed in fiction will be considered in the next chapter. Here it is sufficient to note it as a characteristic of so much fiction. The Freudian theories of sex came just in time to fit in perfectly with three contemporary interests or trends: the desire for novelty, the convention of revolt from conventions, moral and religious, and the cult of naturalism displacing the romantic interpretation of love. Love, in the romantic sense, was outlawed by the selfish individualism so much in the literary fashion. Love was removed from the Golden Treasury of the poets and put into an appropriate chapter in the textbook of physiology. The ascendancy of this fashion accounts for much of what Mrs. Rachel Taylor calls the " infantile staccato " of much post-war fiction in England.

A third mark is the prevalence of the note of frustration, often that of futility. In all these features marking so large a portion of post-war fiction there are to be felt the effects of the absence of positive and secure values or any definite vision of the meaning of life.

For purposes of rough classification, fiction and drama are here considered under three divisions. The first may be called the Jazz Party — the picture of those whose watch-word of the new freedom was " Yo, ho, ho and a bottle of rum! " The second may be called the Lost Generation, including more serious portrayals of life carried on when familiar standards and faiths had been forsworn. The third may be called the Pose, including that brigade of writers marching after the parade, writing not so much out of real experience as at the behest of literary fashion and profits. The Great Quest of many writers was not so much " the search for life " as for royalties.

V

Scott Fitzgerald may be considered as opening the Jazz Party with his *This Side of Paradise,* 1920. It was the first widely read offering of what has been baptized as the " cocktail school of fiction." *This Side of Paradise* seems a more sincere study than any of Fitzgerald's other works with the exception of *The Great Gatsby,* and will possess historical value not only as an evidence of what was being written about young people in the heyday of " the younger generation " in the early 1920's but also as a valid expression of the thoughts and outlook of many. It carries a distinct note of futility both in the experience of the hero and the mind of the author. The novel tells the life story, up to the end of his college course, of Amory Blaine, a rich, handsome, pampered young pilgrim of life. He is competently spoiled by a restless, scatter-brained mother and left to fumble eagerly and bunglingly at life. He runs through the usual experiments with love; he finds that college brings no unity or direction or purpose to him; religion is wondered about vaguely, then dismissed as a total loss. In the author's words, he is, at the end, still at sea, less confident, " with no God in his heart, his ideas still in riot, and with the pain of memory." He could not tell whether the struggle was worth while; but the odds seem to be against it. The book was a reflection of the restlessness of the whirlpool below the falls, the whirlpool being in this case the years after the war as they were experienced by a rudderless graduate.

Fitzgerald's second novel, *The Beautiful and the Damned,* reveals more cocktail and less thought. Its characters merit the second adjective at least, whatever doubt there may be about the beauty. It pictures the recklessness of so-called " society people," older than the college generation, a little farther along in the downward rushing whirlpool. It is more hard and tragic; much more consciously " hardboiled " and speciously clever. Anthony Patch's journey to Hell is the theme of the novel. The grandson of a millionaire, sophisticated and wasteful, he meets a match in the flint-like selfishness of Gloria Gilbert, whom he marries. She draws her own picture in the shrill philosophy: " If I wanted anything I'd take it. I can't be bothered resisting things I want." What value the book has lies in its picture of the working out of that characteristic philosophy of freedom from inhibition. Patch fails to inherit his grandfather's millions, with resulting bitterness and bankruptcy, physical and moral as well as financial. Both are dealt an over-melodramatic fate, Gloria left with her beauty waning beyond the power of that port of lost souls, the beauty parlor, to salvage; both damned by their excesses; the husband ripe for a sanitarium for mental wrecks.

Floyd Dell is the historian of the Greenwich Village era and spirit of the 1920's. To say that is unfair to his many books and plays of different types, particularly unfair to his contributions to education. But it is by his pictures of the revolt against conventionality, his sympathetic and understanding tracing of the Odyssey of sensitive youth in a confused world, in the novels, *Moon Calf,* 1920, *The Briary Bush,* 1922, *Janet March,* 1923, that he is best known. The first two novels are marked by a realistic treatment of youth's effort to find itself and to find meaning in life, and also by a sense of tragic bafflement, baffled both by harsh environment and also apparently by something obdurate and evil in life itself. Like much of this type of fiction, *Moon Calf* is biographical, the story of Felix Fay brought to young manhood. This history has been retold in Dell's autobiography, *Homecoming,* 1933. With the handicap of being a dreamer in a misfit family, his father a failure, Felix's life is a long conflict between his dreams and reality. To Felix his dreams are more real than reality. His story is a Pilgrim's

Progress in twentieth century Chicago; much of it, naturally, is through the Slough of Despond, Vanity Fair and the dungeon of Giant Despair; Felix rarely reaches the Delectable Mountains. Youth's excursions into the world are described, the poetic aspirations, an experiment with religion that brings no unity or poise or mastery, rebellion against economic domination, experiments in sex and love. The book is a moving picture of the frustration of sensitive, idealistic youth in conflict with a harsh, materialistic world; it carries an impressive indictment of soul starvation in towns and villages of Illinois. It deserved a much more adequate consideration than the stock reaction which it frequently received — "Keep it out of the libraries." That very reaction is itself an indication of the dominance of traditional romanticism and complacency of the so-called "moral element" of the population.

In the sequel, *The Briary Bush,* 1921, there is a history of Felix's marriage, giving a study of self-centered, individualistic "modern" young people, eager for life but impatient of discipline, tyrannized over by an ideal of freedom which rejects the old because it is old but failing to find any satisfactory basis in the new. While these moderns are pictured as barking their shins against the restraints and responsibilities of marriage, the novel gives also, with the author's evident sympathy, pointed criticism of the cult of revolt, in the judgment that "freedom is playing at life while marriage is taking it seriously."

Ben Hecht and Carl Van Vechten have no assured place in literature, but they occupy prominent seats in the literary jazz orchestra of the 1920's. Hecht no doubt belongs to the group with whom disillusion is more of a pose than a real experience. He is a self-conscious "bold, bad cynic." The hero of his novel, *Eric Dorn,* — a poor excuse for the conventional word " hero " — is a hard-boiled journalist to whom the rapidly shifting scenes of life have no depth or meaning. Melodrama, vulgarity and a specious epigrammatic glitter characterize *Eric Dorn.* Carl Van Vechten in his fiction, *Peter Whiffle,* 1922, *The Blind Bow Boy,* 1923, and several others, has written sophisticated cleverness.

Katharine Brush in her novels *Young Man of Manhattan,* 1930, and *Red Headed Woman,* 1931, is a later example of the novelist who has chosen for her field the hard, more or less glittering, sophisticated " modern " crowd, in American cities and towns, treated with brilliance and satire. She exploits the seamy side of life, a world almost entirely devoid of assured and cherished values, a world where the cruelty of driving self-seeking prevails.

As a footnote to ten years of continual parade in fiction of post-war revels, to the fiction of the jazz age, there is pertinence both as moral evaluation and literary criticism in James Norman Hall's poem, " Youth in These Days ":

> Behold this mighty host that has no might;
> That bears the heat and burden of no day.
> An army?   This disorderly array?
> An army is a noble, heartening sight.
> These have no battered weapons, battle-bright;
> They move, not march, each man in his own way.
> Are any wars afoot?   They cannot say;
> They've heard of none; they keep no watch at night.
> Leaderless, listless, creeps this sorry host.
> Never had soldiers fewer scars to show;
> Never had army lesser cause to boast
> Of hard-fought fields, of given or taken blow.
> Trophies have they neither won nor lost.
> Embattled Youth?   Today?   Who calls it so? [5]

VI

Of far more value as literature, and much more significant for their bearing on religion and morals, are the novels of another group of writers who deal with the disillusionment of the period, a group including Dos Passos, Hemingway, Cabell, Faulkner, and in the drama, O'Neill. Without too much injustice, perhaps, they may be considered under the head of the chroniclers of the "lost generation," for they all give transcripts of life among those who have drifted from any moorings of faith, ideals or purpose.

Dos Passos will perhaps be remembered more as the inventor or at least early practitioner of a technique in fiction than for the lasting significance of his novels. With the technique we are not here particularly concerned, except that it is admirably adapted to convey the impression of the swiftly moving kaleidoscope of modern life. Dos Passos attempts to catch in fiction the inventions of the day, the camera eye, the movie, the newspaper headline. He conveys dates and the background by flashes of contemporary events. The effect on the unity of the novels is confusing, but the representation of confusion is evidently one of the author's chief aims. The "hero" of the novels is the contemporary scene rather than any individual. He attempts to crowd an era, a whole cross-section of a city, or a period of economic development into a novel. It is as a commentator on social movements rather than as an artist dealing with characters that Dos Passos is of most importance. Two of his novels dealing with war, *Three Soldiers* and *1919,* will be discussed in the chapter on war literature.

No American writer has made a more serious attempt to catch the progress of recent American and world history in impressionistic pictures and record the effects and movements on the lives of average Americans as represented by typical individuals. It is a richly detailed though chaotic canvas which Dos Passos spreads, and hardly one to prompt the reader to rise and sing either The Star Spangled Banner or the Long Metre Doxology. He is definitely an historian of a " lost generation " in his *Manhattan Transfer,* 1924, an attempt to picture the life of a city as reflected in people of almost every class, but always people without faith, without discipline or clear purpose beyond that of pleasurable sensation or profit. The inner life of his characters is like their outward environment in New York — confused, noisy, rather terrifying. In formless, episodic manner the fortunes of many groups in post-war New York are presented, people feverishly elbowing their way through crowds, intent on pleasure, or passion, or wealth, within or without the forms of law, or often intent merely on continuing existence without a reason. With no didactic purpose at all, *Manhattan Transfer* is an impressive demonstration in American literature of the petty futility of life which admits no allegiances higher than self-interest, measures itself by no standards other than those of its own group practice, bows at no altars, feels the propulsion of no faith.

In *The Forty Second Parallel,* 1930, Dos Passos has endeavored to catch the movement of a whole economic process extending over two generations, the development of industrial America. The enigmatic title comes from the observation of a meteorologist that in the United States most storms proceed from west to east along the 42nd parallel, the latitude of New York. The novel pictures the flow of population which has reversed the westward expansion of pioneer days, proceeding eastward to New York. The narrative centers on the lives of four pieces of humanity representing different geographical, social and economic backgrounds, all driven like leaves before a storm to New York. The book is even more formless than *Manhattan Transfer*. It conveys the variety and energy, the restlessness and contradictions, of a vast country. It overturns many sacred idols of politics and economics with the blundering ruthlessness of a storm. Dos Passos has acquired a new significance since 1930 as the most accomplished writer of the Marxian political creed. His novels so far are not economic tracts, but they are filled with sharp criticism of the existing order, criticism that has far-reaching ethical and social significance. His work has more value as a stimulant and challenge to religiously inspired social idealism than has all the piously labeled " religious fiction " of a generation.

To Ernest Hemingway has been assigned the rôle of the chief interpreter of the " lost generation." Few American writers of the present time have attained a greater prestige; few have been so widely imitated, at least in manner and style. It is an ideal style for a generation to some extent under the influence of a behavioristic psychology and philosophy. It deals with outward actions rather than inward states. It holds emotion under effective restraints. It is a style stripped of verbiage, almost bullet-like in its short declarative sentences. It proved popular; it was easy to imitate; hence the market was flooded with minor Hemingways. As the style is stripped of surplus words, so the characters are stripped of soul; we are told the exterior facts about them; any inner strivings of spirit are beyond the restricted gaze of the author. It is indeed a spiritual " waste land " which is pictured. The land is peopled by the tribe of the hard-boiled bull-fighters, prize-fighters, gunmen, prostitutes, professional soldiers, dope fiends — " the simple annals of the callous," as Lee Wilson Dodd described his volume of short stories, *Men Without Women*. His first great success, *The Sun Also Rises,* depicts a group of human derelicts in Paris, on whom the sun has set, enveloped with a cloud of post-war pessimism and aimlessness, in which alcohol inebriates but does not cheer. The success which that book attained is due partly, at least, to the manner in which it expressed the popular aversion to romanticism and sentimentality. It portrayed a paralyzing disillusion so strongly that in the words of Clifton Fadiman, " he takes a spiritual *malaise* and translates it into something vivid, vital, even splendid, giving to bitterness an exuberance that joy itself cannot match." It is hard to find much exuberance in Hemingway, outside of his spirited zest in extolling brute force and cruelty, and aside from the love story in *Farewell to Arms,* which owes its strength not so much to callous realism as to deeply sentimental romance. Mr. Fadiman's comment, however, does probably indicate a real source of attractiveness in Hemingway, that he has most powerfully expressed the disappointed idealism, cruelly shattered by the war and its aftermath. His strongest novel, *Farewell to Arms,* brings to bear on the war a clarity of objective observation which makes its incidental criticism of war all the stronger.

No more penetrating comment on the moral world of Hemingway's characters has been made than that of Joseph Wood Krutch in his discussion of Hemingway and Aldous

Huxley. He writes of the characters described by Huxley and Hemingway:

" In a generally devaluated world they are eagerly endeavoring to get what they can in the pursuit of satisfactions which are sufficiently instinctive to retain inevitably a modicum of animal pleasure, but they cannot transmute that single animal pleasure into anything else. They themselves frequently share the contempt with which their creator regards them, and nothing could be less seductive, because nothing could be less glamorous, than the description of the debaucheries born of nothing except a sense of the emptiness of life." [6]

James Branch Cabell is an acquired taste, probably to a greater degree than any other contemporary American writer. Indeed, the sense of being one of the sophisticated few who understand him and appreciate him has undoubtedly contributed to such vogue as he has had. Cabell undoubtedly bulks far greater in criticism and discussion of his work than in number of actual readers. For that reason his influence is easily overrated. He has become the prophet of a highly sifted group of the world-weary and disillusioned. It became a rigorous convention for the sophisticated to burn incense at his shrine.

But it was Mr. Cabell's enormous good fortune to have *Jurgen* run foul of the censor and thus acquire the prestige of the forbidden. Without the aid and comfort of the censor, his fame would be far less than it is. Cabell has combined realism and romanticism. He is realistic in his expression of complete disillusionment with life, the conviction, as expressed in *The Cream of the Jest,* that life is a bad dream with even its illusions empty and unsatisfactory; he is romantic in his style and the world of illusion which he has invented and mapped, a mythical medieval French country named Poictesme, and in which he gives the history of Dom Manuel and his descendants. Cabell explains his retreat to a world of fancy as a necessary refuge from ugly and futile reality. As he explains in *Beyond Life,* which is a sort of literary apologia, he " perceives this race to be beyond all wording petty and ineffectual," and accordingly he follows the "instinct of any hurt animal to seek revenge" — in the field of imagination. His hero, ever reappearing under various names, pursues the dream, trying to escape from the ignoble and degrading reality, and in the end the dream is shattered. It is a philosophy of stark negation of values put into esoteric fable. Cabell expressed the mood of many contemporaries in his sharp expression of the contrast between the charm and beauty of the dreams of youth and the ugliness which reality proves to be. This is the theme of *Jurgen.* Outside of his dreams, Jurgen is an unimpressive pawnbroker in the middle ages, married to an ill-tempered wife. The bulk of the book consists of his amatory adventures, in a land of illusions, as he packs " the follies of a quarter of a century into a year." Thus the author combines the triple attractions of cynicism, a beautifully wrought style, and veiled pornography. In the end, as always, Jurgen finds only the emptiness of frustration, as expressed in his own words: " Oh, nothing can help me, for I know not what thing it is that I desire. . . . For I am Jurgen, who seeks he knows not what. . . . I have gone romancing throughout the world, . . . nowhere have I found what I desire. . . . I am compact of weariness and apprehension, for I no longer discern what thing is I, nor what is my desire, and I fear that I am already dead." [7] Jurgen confesses in one passage in the story that he is

" forced to jeer out of season." Cabell is the master of cynical mockery, the artist of the jeer and the leer.

VII

To consider Eugene O'Neill in a chapter devoted to the expression of disillusionment and the sense of futility in current literature is to do no justice at all to the many-sidedness of his significance. His services to the drama, his large share in making it a vehicle for thought as well as entertainment, his dramatic innovation and technique, as well as his poetic and literary quality, lie well beyond the scope of the present volume. O'Neill is the towering figure of twentieth century American drama moving across the stage much like a Colossus. In addition to that, his work has the aspects of a dark forest, quite too intricate and obscure to be mapped by any neat set of charts designed to " explain " his meaning. The one aspect of his plays singled out for emphasis here is that of the repeated appearance of the sense of frustration, lives enmeshed by a strange dark web of destiny, sometimes apparently a web of chance, sometimes more definitely that of a malignant fate, sometimes a web woven by the destiny of human character. There is a preoccupation with defeat and death; yet often surging up a mystic sense of spiritual triumph even in death, which makes the total picture by no means that of stark determinism or unrelieved gloom. Some aspects of his plays which bear definitely on religion as concerned with cosmic reality, those which relate, to use his own words, to " the death of the old God " and the search for a new faith to put in his place, are to be considered in the chapter on " The Search for God."

O'Neill's Pulitzer prize play, *Beyond the Horizon,* 1920, well illustrates the aspects of the author mentioned in the preceding paragraph. It is a treatment of a theme common in the literature of the decade of the 1920's, the conflict of illusion with the harsh edges of reality and the ironical frustration of the dreamer. Two sharply contrasted brothers are the central characters, one a sensitive poetic person who feels that beauty may be found just "beyond the horizon." His older brother is a hard-headed practical New England farmer. Both fall in love with the same girl, who responds to the romance of the dreamer rather than to the greater security promised by the realist. It is the practical one, however, who gets beyond the horizon in travel to seek his fortune. Robert, the younger brother, is condemned to stay at home and wage an unequal, futile battle with the soil. Characteristic O'Neill tragedy overwhelms him, laid on thickly enough to suggest a stubborn malignancy of fate. The farm fails, his baby dies, he is stricken with tuberculosis. When the brother comes back home wealthy, Robert's wife transfers her affections to the successful one, away from the defeated failure. Withal a sort of exalted mystical triumph comes at the end. Robert, dying, crawls to the top of a little hill looking out over the sea to watch a sunrise, and his finding of the beauty "beyond the horizon" voices a note of hope surviving even complete defeat. He cries:

"You mustn't feel sorry for me. Don't you see I'm happy at last — free — free — freed from the farm — free to wander on and on — eternally! Look! Isn't it beautiful beyond the hills? I can hear the old voices coming to me — (exultantly) and this time I'm going! It isn't the end. It's a free beginning — the start of my voyage I've won to my trip — the right of release — beyond the horizon!" [8]

The note of struggle and defeat appears in play after play; in *The Emperor Jones,* a powerful dramatization of fear; in *The Hairy Ape,* the awakening of Yank, the stoker on a transatlantic ship, the personification of the brute force at the bottom of society, his baffled endeavor to " belong " in the scheme of life, ending in his making his way to the zoo, the only place left for him, apparently, and being there crushed to death by a gorilla. Frustration is strongly apparent in that mixture of sordid gloom, *Desire Under the Elms,* where warped and repressed individuals are shown caught in the toils of dark forces too great for them and are drawn on to tragedy. *All God's Chillen Got Wings,* 1923, a drama of racial intermarriage, is a sample of what often seems to be O'Neill's deliberate search for repellent themes. Jim Harris, the Negro, is a typical O'Neill character striving for the unattainable and doomed to defeat.

The closing words of one of his early short plays, *The Straw,* give a clue to an idea of O'Neill's which recurs frequently. The nurse in the tuberculosis sanitarium answers the question why she has given a " hopeless hope " to a patient. She replies:

" Isn't everything we know just that, when you think of it? (Her face lighting up with revelation.) But there must be something back of it — some promise of fulfilment, somehow — somewhere — in the spirit of hope itself." [9]

Life a hopeless hope — and yet some promise of fulfilment in the very existence of hope itself! That is not a misleading key to some of O'Neill's philosophy. In the midst of much else in that modern parallel to the great Greek tragedy, *Mourning Becomes Electra,* there is the play of marionettes in the hands of fate, moved by hatred and lust, marked by almost entire absence of pity. It seems to convey an overtone of a sort of theological doctrine of defeat, of frustration and hopelessness. There was real pertinence in the remark of a Boston woman, after witnessing the five-hour production: " Can't we find a nice pleasant morgue in which to spend the rest of the evening? " Certainly the dominant conception of *Mourning Becomes Electra* stands in sharp contradiction to Hebrew and Christian ideas, which stress both man's power to choose between right and wrong and the power of love and compassion.

Far exceeding O'Neill in selective choice of repellent subjects and gloom of treatment is William Faulkner, whose novels and short stories, including *Sanctuary, Light in August, The Sound and the Fury* and *These Thirteen,* present a gallery of individuals unmatched outside the wards of a psychopathic hospital, and scarcely to be equaled there. Faulkner devotes a brilliant talent to the analysis of human derelicts of Mississippi and the " deep South." No phase of life is to be denied to the novelist, and Faulkner's narratives combine impressive power of realistic treatment and implied acute criticism of society which produces such misfits and monstrosities. He is in many respects a literary sadist specializing in horror, brutality, mental derangement. Perhaps the preoccupation with lust, rape, murder, idiocy, sheep-like stupidity of both blacks and whites, is due to Faulkner's leaning over backward to avoid the charge of romanticism. Perhaps in a realistic revolt against the predominance of honeysuckle and magnolia in the Southern vegetation he planted his own garden with thistles and skunk cabbage. The very themes of his novels give an idea of the morbid pictures of life he gives. *The Sound and the Fury,* 1929, chronicles the decay of a Southern family, told in part by an idiot son. *As I Lay Dying,* 1930, deals with a sorry funeral journey made by a dazed and crazed father and children carrying the body of their mother, in a homemade coffin, across a wide swamp to her old home. *Sanctuary,* 1931, gives the tragic and terrifying experiences of an eighteen-year-old college girl who goes into a Tennessee moonshiner's cabin in search of liquor. Faulkner has drawn attention to vicious social maladjustments in the South and their results in mangled personalities and lives. His confining his attention to the wrecks and depraved gives his work an effect of extreme morbidity and pessimism.

Others whose work falls partly, at least, into this classification of the literature of disillusion are Edgar Lee Masters in his poetical narrative *Domesday Book,* 1920, in which a coroner's inquest is taken as a means of examining a wide spread of life in America; Evelyn Scott in *A Calendar of Sin;* David Burnham, in *This Our Exile;* and Morley Callaghan.

VIII

No glimpse of the annals of a generation of which loss of faith and ideals is a marked symptom could be complete without recognition of a large amount of fiction and journalism in which disillusion is more a pose than a genuine experience. Such a group includes the mass of writing devoted to shocking revelations of " wild young people." Novels of this type have already become museum pieces, useful largely for showing some interests and ideas of the post-war decade. Yet such novels of third and fourth rate importance have added their evidence of a large company of people who put away all religious faith, all idealisms of any sort, all convictions of absolute moral values and were thrown back upon themselves in a spiritual isolation which brought nothing but despair. "Life," says one typical author, Thomas Burke, "is an unreconstructed blur of pain and joy and despair."

The opening words of Ernest Hemingway's first novel, *In Our Time,* were these: "Everybody was drunk." That might stand for a popular school of fiction. Scott Fitzgerald set the fashion of being more or less happy over youth's disillusionment. The philosophy ran thus: "God died yesterday leaving His whole estate in bankruptcy. Let's eat, drink and be merry." That was the program. The first two items on the agenda were always well carried out. The third usually slipped, somehow. To mention only one of the recent works of this sophomore class in literature, *New England Holiday,* by C. A. Smart, is a degenerate "Tales of a Wayside Inn." Each guest tells his story, with the revelations described thus by one unimpressed reviewer: "These young people — and in a way not intended by the author — seem as shallow and empty as they think themselves to be profound, tortured, introspective, emotionally alert and what not. They remain overgrown children." [10] This crowd, and the dramatis personae of a hundred other novels, are well described by a newly invented but long needed word, "Sophomoron." Yet the type of mentality and attitude described is one frequently met, a real factor in the life of the time, though now greatly in decline. The churches, moreover, had better not draw aside their gaze with too unconcerned an aversion. It is a question whether the unreal optimistic gospel of the pre-war era so prominent in the Protestant churches is not partially, at least, responsible for the depth of the drop from idealism in the succeeding years.

The extreme of disillusionment, the sense of the futility of life and the world, has given a name to a group of novelists, " the futilitarians." Mr. Chesterton satirized these novelists engaged in passionately declaiming the worthlessness of life in his remark made while on a visit to this country ten or more years ago, that the chief difference between *Spoon River Anthology* and *Main Street* seemed to him to be that in the former book the people all had taken prussic acid, while in the latter they were only thinking about taking it. There has been a good deal of prussic acid in the diet. There have been a good many fictional rehearsals of the belief that

> The world rolls on forever like a mill.
> It grinds out death and life and good and ill,
> It has no purpose, heart or mind or will.

Sometimes it is an oppressive strain of pessimism, made blacker by selective attention to the black. A typical volume of the more serious sort is Glenway Westcott's *The Grandmothers*. It pictures the long burdensome struggle with the soil and the small gain from it. Frustration runs through it like a threnody. The novel begins with the one who relates it seated on a balcony at night in a mountain resort in Europe. Before his imagination the sad procession of his blighted ancestors passes. Each one is a futile being. They all die of their own unvoiced despair. Love and hate alike end in soul starvation, heart sickness, despair. He sees the new generation as very probably preparing to go around the same meaningless circle: " Too soon the holiness was going out of the land. There were modern inventions for warming the heart, and certain fires with too bitter smoke had been allowed to go out — except upon old-fashioned, unattractive hearths. And perhaps those hearths, reared in, embittered and half intoxicated by the smoke, would have to do the work. . . . Stronger than their fathers, because, lacking a God of resignation and forgiveness, failure would be even more intolerable. The future of America, if it was to be worth troubling about, depended on them." [11]

The lack of anything to catch hold of, the angry and bitter feeling that the accepted orthodoxies of the teachers, the solons of business, the preachers and the laurel-crowned writers had deceived them, was a dominant feeling with many people. It resulted in a wholesale throwing overboard of faiths, precepts and codes, done either with sadness or adolescent glee. Cynicism became the style, like shorter skirts. The bright green covers of the American Mercury were a badge of sophistication. The Peck's Bad Boy of criticism, H. L. Mencken, sat enthroned on the seat of the scornful. While the season lasted, Mencken's word was law and gospel to an army of liegemen. A characteristic feat of the era was the progressive treating by John Erskine of such stories as Homer's tale of Troy, Galahad, Tristram, and Adam and Eve. It was a clever piece of literary dexterity, and he worked the vein till it ran completely out. Erskine's stories have received severe criticism. Many who were shocked at his " vandalism," however, failed to appreciate his frequent acute moral insights imbedded in his humorous comment on stock notions.

IX

As was inevitable in such a mental climate, smartness, ranging from genuine wit down through jauntiness and callousness to mere impudent exhibitionism, found voluminous expression. This vogue of smartness flowered in scores of biographies, till all the figures in history were staked off by prospective biographers, like claims in a gold country. Many a lusty battle was waged by competing squatters for the right to be the first to "debunk" their hero. This "biography of assassination" has been well satirized by Charlotte Perkins Gilman:

> Lives of great men all remind us
> We can make our lives unclean
> And, departing, leave behind us
> Data for more "Lives" obscene.

> Let us then be up and doing,
> With a heart for any shame,
> Still achieving, still pursuing,
> Learn to live for long ill fame.

The recognition of the genuine ethical and spiritual values in contemporary realism must not blind us to the wide practice of that particular sort which is well called "dead cat realism." It is built on the theory that there is valuable truth to be achieved merely by dragging into the parlor all the dead cats one can find in the street and saying, "Here, look here, this is America." William Lyon Phelps is authority for the statement that Schiller used to do his writing in a room fragrant with decaying apples. That same invig-

orating odor steals through an appallingly large number of
third and fourth rate novels, widely read — fiction which had
little but the odor to recommend it. George Meredith more
than a generation ago pointed out in *Diana of the Crossways*
the superficial fallacy of this " dead cat realism." He writes
of Diana: " She mused on their soundings and probings
of poor humanity, which the world accepts for the very bottom truth if their dredge brings up sheer refuse of the
abominable. The world imagines those to be at our nature's
depths who are impudent enough to expose its muddy
shallows."

Laura E. Richards has done no injustice to these spe-
cialists in muddy shallows in her biting " Prayer of a Natu-
ralist ":

> Let me be dreary, O god of the garbage-can!
>   Let me be dreary, and largely obscene!
> All that is bright, may I see it obfusculate,
>   All that is gold, may I see it as green!
> Green, not of grass that the donkey may nibble at,
>   Green, not of leaves that may pleasure the fool.
> Nay! but of mould that the sexton may dibble at;
>   Nay! but of slime that o'er-mantles the pool!
> Give me for beauty the contents of sinks;
> Give me for fragrance no attars Victorian
>   Nay! but a compound of manifold stinks.
> Let me be dreary, O god of the garbage-can.
>   Let me be dreary, and largely obscene.
> Grant me obscurity; grant me impurity.
> But for the sake of an anguished futurity
>   Make it not easy to see what I mean.[12]

Given a generation marked by the throwing off of restraints, by the weakening of ethical and spiritual traditions,

by the inevitable moral upheaval which has always followed war, and it is not a matter for surprise that the period was one in which sex was a constant theme. Innumerable Columbuses discovered sex and reported their voyages *seriatim* and *in extenso*. As one said in the early 1920's, " It is sex o'clock."

There were many to " greet the obscene with a cheer." In the frantic revolt to get away from the drawing room, many have bolted clear out to the pig pen. In a reaction against reticence, the facts of life have been shouted through a megaphone with strident and tiresome repetition. The aim has been not so much the delineation of character as the excitement of nerves. The sex interest was exploited by commercialism. Mammon soon realized that there was " gold in them thar hills " and took over Aphrodite as general manager and promoter. Reference has already been made to a " barbarian invasion." In the field of sex there has been an invasion of the barbarian, as defined by Santayana: " A barbarian is one who regards his passions as their own excuse for being, who cannot discipline them either by controlling them or conceiving them for their ideal good."

There are obvious reasons for this invasion of the barbarian. In an age of revolt it was natural that much of the revolt should be directed against the orthodox code of sex relations. In a time when the swing was so largely away from faiths, attention was focused on sensations. When God fades out of life, the first substitute which often has been found, historically, is physical sensation. The temple of Aphrodite is always erected beside the abandoned ruins of the altar of Jehovah or Christ. A third reason lies in the reputed " discovery " of the unconscious. When the unconscious swam into the ken of the public, and particularly of the novelist, it was readily, and in view of Freud's theory, naturally, seized upon as a great down-in-the-cellar preoccupation with sex. Sex was opposed to love, in the despised romantic sense. It was something to be indulged, as a physical need. Love, on the other hand, was an upsetting nuisance. Pushed to the extreme, this rôle of sex made infidelity almost a matter of solemn doctrine. Constancy acquired the status of a naïve heresy.

This parade of sex license has been with many writers like a Fourth of July celebration over a new Declaration of Independence. It is not a moralistic preacher, but one of the leading contemporary poets of England, Humbert Wolfe, who sums up the invasion of the sex-obsessed writers, following the wake of D. H. Lawrence, James Joyce and Aldous Huxley:

" Their slogan is: ' Conventions are dead. Live the Conventions.' The Victorians denied the existence of sex; they deny the existence of anything else. The Victorians were guilty of a sickly sentimentalism; they are guilty of a sickly anti-sentimentalism. The Victorians pretended to a virtue they did not possess: they claim vices of which they are incapable. In a word, the wheel has come full circle. The dull stupidities of non-sex have yielded to the stupidities no less dull of universal sex. Indeed, one may say bitterly, of the two extremities it is sex of one and sex of the other. ' Nothing too much,' cried the Greeks. The Victorians read that as ' too much of nothing,' but our contemporaries yodel ' Nothing can be too much.' And both are equally wrong." [13]

Accompanying this license of expression, has been a solemn philosophy, an acrobatic scheme of morals, which achieves originality by simply inverting values. It resembles the devotions of the juggler who stood on his head. These acrobatic moralists represent a higher hooliganism in ethics. The latest thing in sexual morals turns out to be nothing but recollections of forgotten memories of very primitive ancestors. The charter of freedom may be found in many of the words of H. L. Mencken.

Self-indulgence has rationalized itself as a " freedom from miserly Puritanism." The call of the hour was " instincts to the quarter-deck." " The fear of the Lord " which was mistakenly supposed to be the beginning of wisdom has given way to the terrible Freudian fear of the consequence of disobedience to one's instincts. " Have I the right to disobey this instinct? " asks the hesitant soul. Echo answers, " No! " And so another soul is saved from the perdition of repression.

That vogue has happily to a large extent passed into history. Other views of man, besides that of a muddleheaded animal " with a sex urge and delusions about himself," are at present in the ascendant in fiction, as in life. But that vogue has left an ugly smear.

Back of all these notes of contemporary literature noted in this chapter lies the major fact of the gray twilight of religious faith. The extent to which this diminished place of religion in literature is an accurate gauge of its place and influence in the life of the country is a matter for dispute. That it strongly marks the writing of the time is indisputable. In many the attitude to this loss is that of having made a happy disposal of a heavy incumbrance. Santayana's classic sonnet, written many years before the war, expressed this feeling and fairly represents a large number of writers:

Farewell my burden! No more will I bear
The foolish load of my fond faith's despair,
But trip the idle race with careless feet.
The crown of olive let another wear;
It is my crown to mock the runners' heat,
With gentle wonder and with laughter sweet.[14]

At the opposite extreme is the attitude feelingly described by W. P. Montague: "If God is not, then the existence of all that is beautiful and in any sense good, is but the accidental and ineffectual by-product of blindly swirling atoms, or of the equally unpurposeful, though more conceptually complicated, mechanisms of present-day physics. A man may believe that this dreadful thing is true. But only the fool will say in his heart that he is glad that it is true. For to wish there should be no God is to wish that the things which we love and strive to realize and make permanent should be only temporary and doomed to frustration and destruction. . . . Atheism leads not to badness but only to an incurable sadness and loneliness." [15]

Whatever the attitude toward the eclipse of faith, the fact interprets wide areas of literature and the life from which it came. To use the language of Amos, " the sun went down at noon." The descending shadow sits like an Arctic darkness over the life and thought of many of the most widely heard voices of the time. The effects of this religious twilight are evidence of unassailable authenticity and importance of the relation which religion bears to literature. That evidence will be more closely examined in the next chapter.

[1] *Cavalcade,* by Noel Coward.   Doubleday, Doran & Company.   Copyright, 1931, 1932.

[2] *Sunset Gun,* by Dorothy Parker.   The Liveright Publishing Corporation.

[3] The Macmillan Company.

[4] *Collected Poems,* by Robert Frost.   Henry Holt & Company.

[5] Harper's Magazine, Oct. 1931.

[6] *The Modern Temper,* by Joseph Wood Krutch.   Doubleday, Doran & Company.

[7] *Jurgen,* by James Branch Cabell.   McBride & Company, 1919.

[8] *Complete Plays,* by Eugene O'Neill, Vol. 1.   Random House.

[9] Ibid.

[10] New York Herald Tribune.

[11] *The Grandmothers,* by Glenway Westcott, pp. 374–375.   Harper & Brothers.

[12] Saturday Review of Literature, July 30, 1932.

[13] Ibid., May 7, 1932.

[14] *Poems,* by George Santayana.   Charles Scribner's Sons, 1923.

[15] *Belief Unbound,* by W. P. Montague.   Yale University Press.

Chapter Seven

SOUNDINGS

ANY attempt to assess, even tentatively, some principal implications of the literature discussed in the
preceding three chapters, for religion of the Christian and Hebrew tradition and for the ideals of conduct historically associated with those traditions, meets inescapably
the fallacy of generalizing about a mass of material widely
different in character. The impossibility of doing that in
any just manner limits the value of any conclusions reached.
The observations here to be made are intended to apply particularly to that large field of fiction, so characteristic of the
post-war period, part of which belongs to the so-called
" naturalistic " school, much of which delineates the cult of
freedom and self-expression, so prominent and vociferous,
and much of which may not unjustly be called the literature
of disillusion.

I

One criticism of the bulk of this fiction immediately suggests itself. Along with the fullest recognition of its values
for the understanding of the life of our time must go a recognition of its narrow selective range of attention — its one-
sidedness. What we have in so much contemporary fiction
is an inverted romanticism. Its motto is, " Whatever is, is

wrong." It is not so much a case of inaccurate reporting as of too narrow a focus. Too small a segment of life has been held under the magnifying glass. A distortion of impression is secured when this highly selective group of experiences is taken for a complete picture. Multiply this effect by the imitative repetitions which follow in the train of every original work, repetitions dealing with the same segment of life, and an unbalanced out-of-drawing picture is the result. There are more things in Main Street than are dreamt of in Lewis's philosophy; more people in Winesburg, Ohio, than got into Sherwood Anderson's census of psychic cripples. This judgment is well expressed by Henry Seidel Canby:

" Half the attention lavished on the abnormalities and perversions of human nature is born of a vision too restricted to see man's passions and weaknesses in the perspective of the whole complex, pitiful, magnificent drama of human existence, just as half of the strained, fantastic, banal manner of expression which has passed as writing has arisen from lack of all standards that can serve as a touch-stone to style." [1]

Parallel to this is the comment expressed by another author, who cannot be accused of any moralistic or religious bias, James Norman Hall, in his sonnet, " In a Library ":

Sometimes when I have read a sordid tale
Of our own times, some story writ to show
How vile is humankind, how lecherous, low,
How worse than any vermin — past the pale
Of help or hope — all this in bleak detail,
Page after page, I close the book and go
In thought over the names of men I know:
All kinds of men, both in and out of jail.

No vermin, these, not one of them. Instead,
Struggling creatures like myself I find.
Some are maimed, it may be; some are weak;
Some dwarfed and twisted by the bitter wind
Of adverse fate; but those of whom I've read
I never find, no matter where I seek.[2]

Even if he could find them his rebuttal would still have
pertinence.

In January, 1927, Dr. Henry S. Canby picked out at random nine current novels and showed the following motley
collection of heroes and heroines (God spare the mark!):

" (1) a predatory sharper willing to sacrifice anything to his vanity;
(2) a congenital alcoholic prostitute whose social position kept her
out of jail; (3) a monstrous egoist who could not decide between two
women, and so ruined both; (4) a mean-spirited woman who spent
twenty-odd years in nagging, or being nagged by, two old women
whom she was paid to care for; (5) a man who deserted his wife
because she loved him too much; (6) a woman who preferred bossing
men to loving them, or indeed to life itself; (7) a noisy drunkard who
uses the power of great wealth with about the spiritual insight of a
ten-year-old boy; (8) a young girl who marries an old man for his
money, gives him dyspepsia, and runs away from him to live on his
money with someone else; (9) an artist so brutally selfish and so
irrational outside of his art that he mars every life he touches, including his own." [3]

No doubt the census of every town in America would
show parallels of these figures. In the proportions, however,
in the total view which an unsophisticated reader would get
from these nine novels, and from ninety and nine others,
the picture is out of focus. Much of the dominant realism
has just the bias pointed out by the classic comment on
Gorki: " He looks at life from a basement into which no

sunbeams can penetrate and from which he sees only feet of men passing by rubbish pails that stand near his windows." There is genuine literary criticism as well as pointed burlesque in the following bit of newspaper verse, satirically entitled, " The Seeing Eye, the Daring Pen ":

> My father's vest is stained with bits of egg;
> My mother, drunk, sits sobbing in her tea;
> Young Michael's kicking sister in the leg,
> While mad desire stirs restlessly in me.

> A frightful noise assails my vibrant ear;
> I look to see the author of the call.
> My uncle stands there yelling for his beer,
> As grandma scuffs her slippers down the hall.

> I ask myself why I should longer stay
> Within these walls of turbulence and rack;
> A thousand times I've tried to run away,
> But lack of opium always brings me back.

> " Here's Truth indeed," the younger critics cry.
> " This man sees life, and seeing, dares to write."
> But as I read their words I faintly sigh
> And wish that God had given him better sight.[4]

That is a perfect theme for a Faulkner novel!

One obvious result of this myopic selectiveness has been the steady driving in of the idea that life is a much more gray or black and sordid thing than normal human experience finds it. This idea is for the most part unconsciously absorbed, and is the more influential for the very reason that its subtle insertion into the mind does not arouse defenses or conflict or definite rejection. The result is a tendency to hold life cheaply; to dismiss nobility as an exposed illusion.

II

A second fact that stands out with inescapable clearness is the dulness of a great body of post-war fiction — a dulness that has a large part of its explanation in a lack of moral issues. The words of Oliver Wendell Holmes may have a hopelessly pious ring in the ears of many today: " It is faith in something and enthusiasm about something which make a life worth looking at." But it is also that which makes a life worth reading about. One could put one's hand on scores of recent novels which are convincing evidence of that truth. A sense of the reality of moral alternatives is indispensable to fiction of lasting significance.

> When the fight begins within himself,
> A man's worth something.

Yes, and a book's worth something too. Rebecca West has put this truth with her usual keenness when she says, " The corpse on the library floor is a poor show compared to the three-ring circus of Charles Dickens." The creation of real character set in the midst of real moral issues gives zest and enduring life to fiction. The story of intrigue, of comedy, or of the merely puzzle-picture sort, is a poor substitute for ethical issues. The demonstration of that truth which contemporary literature gives is significant first-hand evidence regarding the place of moral questions in life.

Take, for instance, the following advertisement of a typical specimen of the cocktail school of fiction, *Weep no More,* by Ward Greene. It begins with a speech of one of the women in the novel:

" ' We're all kind of crazy . . . I reckon I ought not to think at all, I ought not to do anything at all. About things. Let 'em rip. Just let 'em rip.' Sister Craycraft *had* let 'em rip.. It seemed the thing to do. Cocktail parties — road houses — other men's wives and other women's husbands — that was the aristocratic South as she knew it. Just drink — and ' play ' — and some fine day, perhaps, put a bullet through your head. . . ."

" Let 'em rip," be the " ripping " fast and hard as it may, gets to be a very thin recipe for fiction!

Another form of the same truth is this: Art needs moral categories. There is a profound psychological and literary insight in the prayer of the Psalms: " If I forget thee, O Jerusalem, let my right hand forget its cunning and my tongue cleave to the roof of my mouth." That is exactly what always happens. Let Jerusalem, using that city as a symbol of the moral and religious element in life, sink out of sight, and the writer's hand loses its highest skill and the singer's voice flats. The thinness of a hundred tales of the jazz age comes from the fact that there is a dimension lacking. Lest this be taken as the kind of comment made entirely from the point of view of an interest in morals, catch its expression in the judgment of a journeyman book reviewer, written from no other standpoint than that of literary criticism. It occurs in an unsigned review of a novel typical of a whole litter of the late 1920's, Vina Delmar's *Kept Woman:*

" This novel has all the faults of the short stories; it is full of ' facts ' — such as frying bacon, lipstick, automobiles, Greta Garbo and John Gilbert, radio announcing, gin and the 1929 round of wise-cracks. But of drama there is a mere paltry indication; and of the exploration of that complex of feelings, thoughts and wonder that go to make up what must be termed the soul there is virtually none at all. For all the psychological insight that one gets from *Kept Woman* one might as well spend the time reading a jacket blurb version of the story. The ' facts ' do not speak for themselves, whether they are presented synoptically or in Vina Delmar's extension of them." [5]

Whitman's old complaint that the American literature of his day did not furnish to the people any heroic models, which lack resulted in a derelict drifting for need of charts and direction, is very pertinent in our day. Mere negation and the spectacular blowing up of inhibitions makes a lively and noisy party while it is going on, but leaves no significant or enduring direction or momentum. It is just this need of moral categories, even moral absolutes, which is stressed in the assertion of W. B. Yeats: " Every writer, even every small writer, who has belonged to the great tradition has had his dream of an impossibly noble life and the greater he is the more does it seem to plunge him into some beautiful or bitter reverie."

III

One other observation is just as fully and convincingly documented. It is that indignation, to be convincingly portrayed in literature, needs a religious background. In much of the examination of the social and economic scene, in the delineation of life, there is little of what may be called, in the classical phrase, noble indignation. There is satire. Lewis and Mencken, Ring Lardner, Elmer Rice, Hoffenstein, Kaufman and Connelly, to name but a few, are full of it. There is anger. Dos Passos and Upton Sinclair blaze with it. There is burlesque. There is pity and sympathy, as in Willa Cather, Dreiser, Ellen Glasgow, O'Neill. But there is little of high and moving indignation. Part of the reason, in the case of some leading writers, is the absence of a religious outlook on life. Indignation depends for its fullest and highest expression on a tremendous sense of the value of people who are being maimed and blighted by evil forces. That sense of the value of personality has historic roots in the religious interpretation of reality, in the religious conception of the sacredness of personality. One does not have the same consuming indignation, for instance, in saying to an exploiter of people, " Stop, you are doing wrong to these accidental collocations of atoms," that Moses had when he thundered to Pharaoh, " The Eternal has said, Let my people go! " Compare, for instance, the indignation of Vachel Lindsay and Carl Sandburg with its absence in Lewis and Mencken. Joseph Wood Krutch in *The Modern Temper* has argued in great detail that an age which has lost religious faith cannot produce great tragedy. Certainly when religious faith is absent or flickering, the power of indignation is shriveled.

IV

One impression deepened by the reading of a large number of novels is the poverty of the love affairs. That also has a direct and close relation to a conception of life which has religious roots. It is not in quantity that love affairs are poor; it is in quality. It is in their lack of depth. They are in large part endless splashes in a wading-pool six inches deep. They are a succession of adventures without vital meaning. In O'Neill's play, *Strange Interlude,* one of the lovers of the heroine says to her, " I loved you horribly at that time, Nina — horribly." That's exactly it. As has often been pointed out, many of these lovers in current fiction do love — horribly. As Mr. Krutch remarks with sharp insight concerning Ernest Hemingway and Aldous Huxley: "To them love is at times only a sort of obscene joke. . . . But the joke is one which turns quickly bitter on the tongue, for a great and gratifying illusion has passed away, leaving the need for it still there. . . . If you start with the belief that love is the pleasure of a moment, is it really surprising that it yields only a momentary pleasure?" [6]

A flood of light is thrown on this poverty by Lovelace's familiar couplet:

> I could not love thee dear, so much
> Loved I not honor more.

There is more than meter and grace in those lines. There is an ultimate truth about human relations. There can be no deep love without a high sense of personal significance and values. A classic passage in this connection is that of Joseph Wood Krutch:

"If love has come to be less often a sin, it has come also to be less often a supreme privilege. If one turns to the smarter of those novelists who describe the doings of the more advanced set of those who are experimenting with life — to, for example, Mr. Aldous Huxley or Mr. Ernest Hemingway — one will discover in their tragic farces the picture of a society which is at bottom in despair because, though it is more completely absorbed in the pursuit of love than in anything else, it has lost the sense of any ultimate importance inherent in the experience which preoccupies it; and if one turns to the graver of the intellectual writers — to, for example, Mr. D. H. Lawrence, Mr. T. S. Eliot, or Mr. James Joyce — one will find both explicitly and implicitly a similar sense that the transcendental value of love has become somehow attenuated, and that, to take a perfectly concrete example, a conclusion which does no more than bring a man and woman into complete possession of one another is a mere bathos which does nothing except legitimately provoke the comment, ' Well, what of it? ' " [6]

That " what of it? " is the terrific anti-climax which occurs when life has no background of ultimate values. It is very interesting to note the number of writers who can bring veracity, with narrative skill, to the description of flirtation, seduction, domestic shipwreck, divorce, and yet have nothing with which to plumb the experience of love. Dreiser's portrayals of love, for instance, are like lectures on China by one who has never been there. So far as any penetrating understanding of the deep places of the soul stirred by love is concerned, many books proclaimed by the blurbs on their bright jackets to be " starkly realistic," " stripped of rosy mists," " daringly unconventional," are simply themes by the awkward squad of the Freshman class.

V

In its relation to religion, the most important data brought by post-war realism are in what it did not at all set out to report. There is an emphatic report of an entire failure to realize either a sense of completion or happiness. Lest this seem to be a partisan and biased judgment, it is well to read into the record the testimony of Walter Lippmann:

" There is now a generation in the world which is approaching middle age. They have exerted the privileges which were won by iconoclasts who attacked what was usually called the Puritan or Victorian tradition. They have exerted the privileges without external restraint and without inhibition. Their conclusions are reported in the latest works of fiction. Do they report that they have found happiness in their freedom? Well, hardly. Instead of the gladness which they were promised, they seem . . . to have found the wasteland." [7]

It is not madness but the words of truth and soberness which declare that among the most persuasive of the " hot-gospelers " of religion in our time have been a group of real-istic novelists. They have depicted, as Thackeray once wrote to his mother before writing *Vanity Fair* that he intended to portray, " a set of people living without God and without hope in the world, only that is a cant phrase." If a Pulitzer Prize for Christian Evangelism were to be awarded, strong claims could be made for its bestowal upon Dorothy Parker's *Laments for the Living,* Hemingway's *The Sun Also Rises,* or Dos Passos' *Manhattan Transfer.* They show blank deserts utterly without happiness, without peace, without anything of meaningful significance.

Mrs. Parker's volume of short stories, *Laments for the Living,* is well named. Between its covers move for the most part a company of people who live on a diet of " wisecracks," whose one reaction to life is to " laugh it off." " Faced by sit-uations too tragic to be ' laughed off,' their lack of inner re-sources is complete." Her 1933 volume of short stories, *After Such Pleasures,* furnishes more of the same effective evidence. Hemingway's *The Sun Also Rises* is the classic picture of " the lost generation," set in a barroom that stretches across France from the English Channel to the Pyrenees. The utter absence of any religion or idealism is accurately matched by the absolute absence of happiness or a remote reflection of it. The following satirical comment on it, writ-ten by Marion Sanders, has deep truth under its style of banter:

" It is the great moral tract of the age. It will drive all the ama-teur reprobates in the English speaking world to cold showers and bran muffins. Mr. Hemingway has painted the most unalluring picture of vice yet achieved, to my knowledge, by mortal pen. It is the same old orgy from start to finish. A pathetic round of drinking, cussing and immorality. Good enough for the week-ends, but a man has to have a vacation some time. No one can stand a continuous grind of monotonous gaiety forever. It's just an endless cycle of dreary dissipation. After hearing Mr. Hemingway's characters classify each other for the ninth time as good or bad drunks (practically the sole diversion of these poor drudges), you feel that they really have a nice hectic game of croquet coming to them, just to put a little color in their drab lives. They may be bad eggs, but surely God never meant the least of his creatures to be so bored." [8]

Negative, unintended testimony to the necessity of a spiritual content to life is just as persuasive as positive assertion, and has this additional worth in that its force carries in many quarters where the more positive form of assertion would be dismissed as moralistic preaching.

There is both value and opportunity for religion in the inescapable demonstration which novels of this general type have made that mere freedom in itself is an empty gain.

Freedom has been a popular war cry. It might, if one wished to lapse into burlesque, be called the watchword of the Children's Crusade of the 1920's. As a rebellious youngster in Walpole's *Wintersmoon* phrased it, " My aim is, above all, to help rid the world of the past, the rotting, clogging, hampering past." It is a false estimate, of course, to call this frenzy for freedom a Children's Crusade. Scott Fitzgerald says very truly that what began as a children's party was taken over by the elders. But for young or old, freedom, merely in the sense of throwing overboard all the ballast of the ship, fails, as it always does, to bring the prizes so naïvely counted on. It has been an insight of the wisdom of the ages, brought freshly to mind in our generation, that it is just when we are free to do exactly what we like that our real troubles begin. The burglar-parson in Shaw's play, *Too True to be Good,* expresses this forcibly. In verbose monologues he expounds the breakdown of negative philosophies of life. All the old faiths and affirmations are gone. Unlimited freedom has brought only the exclamation, "I am healthy, I am free, I am happy — and I am miserable!" Freedom as the mere absence of restraint ends in merely a moral vacuum. And in that vacuum the spirit dies for air. This is another emphasis of historic Christianity for which impressive evidence is to be found in our generation's literature.

VI

"The blight of contemporaneousness" is a charge which may fairly be brought against a dominant spirit in the writing since the war. It is inevitable, when a wholesale discarding of traditional values and codes takes place, a discarding often without any critical discrimination, that a high appraisal should be put on whatever supplants it, and that anything which did not originate with the present generation is "dated." This frenzy to be "in date" has been perfectly satirized by Mrs. Charlotte Perkins Gilman in her quatrain:

> The little front wave ran up on the sand
> And frothed there, highly elated;
> "I am the Tide," said the little front wave,
> "The waves before me are dated."

The only really unforgivable sin is to be out of date. This obsession for this year's models in thought and practice runs through much of the literature of the time like the college yell of a Sophomore class. That insistence on being feverishly up to date is the reason why so much of the literature of the short period of fifteen years is already " dated." In this we see not the type of arrogance pilloried in the book of Job which says: " Wisdom shall die with us," but the far more subtle arrogance which says, " Wisdom began with us." Consider the following words which occur in a review of Fritz Wittels' book on Freud. They are written by one of the distinguished psychiatrists of the United States, Dr. Frankwood E. Williams. He says: " We shall not long concern ourselves with pre-Freud ideas of psychology, sociology, religion, philosophy, ethics, morals, law, economics." [9] Rather a clean sweep, that! It seems that the world began last Saturday night! Eight of the major fields of human achievement through five thousand years sunk without a trace! Indeed, the only areas of thought and creation in which anything seems to be left at all are art, literature, and music. We may be grateful that by a surprising generosity (or was it an oversight, since the sentence was already heavily loaded?) a little of Phidias, a few lines of Shakespeare, a few chords of Beethoven, are given a chance to escape oblivion. Yes, and the multiplication tables. Thank God, they apparently stand unchanged, visible, towering like Mount Ararat above the flood! But Plato, Socrates, St. Paul, Justinian, Spinoza, Kant, Coke, John Locke, Jesus — all, all are gone, the old familiar faces!

This obsession for the contemporaneous, and the disdain for the timeless, has not been a mental trait which religion would find congenial. But it is a type of thinking from which religion, resting on the timeless and permanent intuitions of the mind and heart, has nothing to fear and to which it has much to give.

We may bring this series of general observations to a close by mentioning two growing realizations which emerge clearly at the end of our period, within the last few years. One is the undoubted revolt from cynicism, either genuine or posed. It has often been pointed out, by Lippmann among others, that our time has witnessed a rather new spectacle, that of a generation disillusioned from its own cynicism, tired of its own revolt. Partly this is due, of course, to the fact that the mind of a nation, or even of a considerable group, cannot strike an attitude and hold it forever, like a figure on a Grecian urn. Partly, however, it is due to the fruits of experience, that cynicism is thin diet and one cannot permanently feast on the east wind. The depression at least gave a hearty push to that convention as it limped off the stage.

The other realization has been that realism is not enough to furnish any ground for a better order of life. For twenty years we have had piling up an impressive total of remarkably able pictures of life, of the inner life of individuals, of the social scene as a whole. This has had, as we have tried to indicate, values which are ethical and religious assets. But what has been the result of this painting and snapshotting of facts? There has been an illusion that if the facts in a given situation were only faithfully reported, they in themselves would furnish a motive power sufficient to generate the will to change undesirable conditions. That illusion has not paid twenty cents on the dollar. In fact, it has suspended payments altogether. Too often the response has been a morally indifferent " What of it? " We have learned again, what has been taught often before, that knowledge is not virtue. There has been growing up a new skepticism of the idea that a literature of reporting, merely in itself, had some magic capacity to create energy for social change.

What then does the sum of these appraisals mean for religion? One thing stands out clearly. That under all costuming of modern clothes and moods, all the changing stage scenery of environment, there are problems of the human spirit that will not down. One of the most specious delusions of the mind is that when man changes his clothes and his tools somehow his essential nature and needs undergo a similar change. But when we look beneath the surface, when literature shows us both that which it sets out to tell and that which it unconsciously and unintentionally reveals, we learn anew that the heart knows the same desires, bitterness and needs under the smokestacks of Pittsburgh and Detroit as under the pyramids of Egypt. Man cannot live by bread alone. From the distracted life of our day, and from the literature which comes out of it and makes it vocal, there comes a challenge to religion to meet three general types of need: the need in personal life, felt in the strain which modern life makes; the need arising from economic distress, agonizing and acute and shrieking to a heaven all too brazen; and the need coming from intellectual difficulty and perplexity. There is an empty place in the heart of modern man, in spite of a clutter of assorted merchandise amid which man's heart is unsatisfied. A religion honest enough, robust enough, to meet these needs, can take that place and fill it.

1 Saturday Review of Literature.

2 Harper's Magazine, Oct. 1932.

3 Saturday Review of Literature.

4 The Conning Tower, New York World, 1927.

5 New York Herald Tribune.

6 *The Modern Temper,* by Joseph Wood Krutch.   Harcourt, Brace & Company.

7 *Preface to Morals,* by Walter Lippmann, pp. 202–203.   The Macmillan Company.

8 New York World, 1927.

9 New York Herald Tribune.

CHAPTER EIGHT

WAR LITERATURE

The contemplation of human grandeur and imbecility in a concentrated and paranoic form. . .

THOMAS BEER

ATTITUDES toward war developed within the fields of creative literature and organized religion show a striking parallel since 1918. The World War is marked off from any other ever fought in history in a large number of respects. Not least significant among these is the fact that the World War was followed by a critical revulsion from and attack upon war as an institution, far surpassing in volume and intensity anything ever before witnessed in history. Some of those who are still able to retain any flickering social hope in the 1930's, when any reasonable hope has been at a high premium, feel that this critical aftermath of the war, finding vigorous expression both in religious thought and activity and also in literature, may appear in future years to be the one fact of greatest importance about the whole war and its results. However that may be, the critical attitude toward war has been the occasion of a new and important relationship between literature and religion.

Of course the question may be asked, Granting all this fresh criticism of war, what has it to do with religion? War is a matter of politics, diplomacy, economics, social psychology. Religion is primarily the worship of God. Why call the opposition to war a manifestation of religion?

There is much reasonable basis for such a question. It becomes all the stronger when it is recalled that historically religion has been a chief support of war, " a bulwark never failing." When General Crozier of the British Army wrote in his *A Brass Hat in No Man's Land* that " the church has been the greatest creator of blood-lust that we have," he was only giving extreme expression to a commonplace of history. More than that, at the present time some of the most vociferous exponents of a rampant, chauvinistic patriotism and nationalism are to be found among the ranks of the members of the churches.

This fact emphasizes the importance of the spiritual and ethical insight displayed at the present time by the keenest minds and most sensitive consciences of those within the churches into the profoundly anti-religious aspect of war. It has amounted to a growing recognition that war and religion — or, as that question comes to those of the western world, war and a theistic, ethical religion, as represented by Judaism and Christianity — are completely incompatible. It is the recognition of war as the ultimate atheism. As it has been put, " Christianity must either destroy war or war will destroy Christianity." Or, in another form, " War means everything which Jesus did not mean, and nothing that he did mean." A part of this spiritual insight is expressed in the recognition by a growing number of people of nationalism as the supreme rival and enemy of Christianity. In an emphatic way the present unusual harmony of thought between many prophets of religion and writers is seen in the fact that the fifteen years since the war, years marked by an unprecedented attack on war from the ranks of religion, have also witnessed the most thoroughgoing exposure of the futility of war and deflation of the prestige of war which has ever come from literature.

Of course, much of this realistic picture of war in contemporary literature is entirely lacking in conscious religious motivation, in the conventional sense. That fact does not affect the results and significance for religion which come from a large amount of the literature dealing with the war. As someone has pointedly said concerning the literary treatment of war in novel, play and poetry, " The present temper of mind with regard to war is prompted by nausea rather than idealism; our only consolation lies in the fact that a pain in the stomach may sometimes serve an ultimate purpose quite as well as an idea in the head." That is a fair picture of realistic war fiction and the poetry of derision and satire, as a close ally of religion in the extermination of war — " a pain in the stomach and an idea in the head," both serving an ultimate spiritual purpose.

It has always been true that the critical thinking about a war — to the extent that in the past there has ever been much — does not come until a number of years after it is over. This is natural. The glamour of the war mood, built up by the conflict and by all the forces of propaganda, does not wear out in a few months. Mental and spiritual demobilization is a long process. The ablest minds do not turn to the war as a theme until years after the conflict, when it can be treated historically or artistically without the disturbance of heated emotion or the distortion of the near view. Like muddy water, the war mind takes time to clear. It is unquestionably too early, fifteen years after the war, to judge with any accuracy the permanent literary reflection of the war or the effect of the war on popular thinking and literature. But a large body of literature has been produced giving evidence of a spirit and attitude towards the war which not only indicates a startling change from the mood of 1917, but which is unmatched in the literature following any previous war in history.

As late as 1920 in America, in fact up until the publication of Dos Passos' *Three Soldiers* in 1921, there was little indication that any radical change in literary treatment of war was in store. This was partly true in Great Britain also, although there, owing to the far greater involvement in the war, and the vastly greater list of casualties and the more serious economic situation, the voices of disillusionment and cynicism about the war and its outcome, and of grim skepticism concerning patriotic myths and legends, politicians and the military hierarchy, made themselves heard sooner. The public was tired of war in 1919 and for several years afterward. The idealisms generated during the struggle, both sincere and specious, were exhausted. " Back to normalcy and forget it," was the general mood. Incidentally, it was " normalcy " turning bitter in the mouth which had much to do with the fresh exploration of war from the standpoint of hard realism. Within five years after 1918 was evident a strong trend toward the revaluation of war, not so much as " emotion remembered in tranquillity " as remembered in a fresh clarity of vision.

I

In America there had been very little realistic thinking about war in either literature or popular attitude. Stephen Crane is almost the only prominent literary figure who comes to mind in that connection. One early exception should be made for Lowell's treatment of the Mexican War in his *Biglow Papers*. Crane in his story, *The Red Badge of Courage,* brought honesty and psychological insight to bear on the stereotype of war. His satirical poem, "War is Kind," is powerful in its quiet restraint — the sort of thing which has been common in recent years — but is almost a solitary voice in American literature up to 1920:

> Do not weep, maiden, for war is kind.
> Because your lover threw wild hands toward the sky
> And the affrighted steed ran on alone,
> Do not weep.
> War is kind.
>
> Hoarse, booming drums of the regiment,
> Little souls who thirst for fight,
> These men were born to drill and die.
> The unexplained glory flies above them,
> Great is the battle-god, and his kingdom —
> A field where a thousand corpses lie.
>
> .   .   .   .
>
> Mother, whose heart hung humble as a button
>   On the bright, splendid shroud of your son,
>   Do not weep.
>   War is kind.[1]

It took thirty years to recover any such penetration and redeeming cynicism. The Civil War was too long past to have any effect on the 1900's. The war with Spain was too much a military and naval holiday to break up the conventional pattern of thought. It went to the head of the nation like a drink of whiskey; it even set back critical thinking in the economic and political realm for years.

At the entrance of America into the World War there was little expressed antagonism to war as such. There was much question as to the wisdom of going in, but that was largely argued on the basis of expediency. When the United States finally entered the war, it became, as one orator boasted, "one single swinging sword." A moratorium was put on minority opinion. There was no voice like that of Romain Rolland in France, a voice above the battle, sounding against waste and murder. There was in the United States no work at all comparable to that of Barbusse, in France, whose *Under Fire,* published in the very midst of the war, went through 200 editions in France alone and was translated into almost every language and received the *Prix Goncourt* in 1917. It had an impressive mixture of stark realistic description of what mechanized war means, and intense passion. Latzo's *Men in War,* 1918, was another European book, published during the conflict, of a type not produced in America during the war or the years immediately following. Latzo was an Austrian army officer and his realistic sketches of war, cast in fictional form, portray a revolt against war, a hatred not of the enemy but of war itself. The book is particularly significant for its lack of the distortion of conventional patriotism and its picture of soldiers thoroughly sick of war, an innovation in 1918 but thoroughly familiar by 1930.

Of course there was in the United States a protesting minority, some of which found expression in literature. An outstanding voice was that of Randolph Bourne, too early dead at the threshold of his work. His book, *Untimely Papers,* written during the first year of the war and published in 1919, stands as a monument of far-seeing social thinking. He predicted with tragic accuracy what war would do to social progress. Edna St. Vincent Millay is thus glimpsed in war-time by Floyd Dell: " She hated war, and walked up and down courtroom corridors with her socialist and pacifist friends, saying her most beautiful poems to them for comfort while they were waiting for the jury to decide whether they would have to spend the next twenty years in prison." But for the most part there was no minority report to make discord with the strains of " Over There." The sentimental war fiction of Coningsby Dawson, the crude and lying heroics of Arthur Guy Empey, the correct patriotic verse of the thousand newspapers, were the popular fare. This lasted for two years after the war, unchanged for the most part. It is significant to note that the section on war in Marguerite Wilkinson's discriminating book of interpretation and anthology of poetry, entitled *New Voices,* published in 1921, does not contain a single line by an American, amid all the war poems noted, which challenges the official view of the war or questions war in general.

The new mind on the matter was bound to come. It was helped by the prevailing temper and technique of realism, which was inevitably applied to war. It was accelerated, no doubt, by the disillusionment brought by the ruthlessness of the Versailles Treaty, which gave a cynical victor's sneer to all the idealistic propaganda about a " war to end war."

Unquestionably this bitter reaction was made all the more severe by the boomerang which the government prepared in the thoroughness with which it did an educational propaganda task in explaining the high aims of the war to soldiers and civilians alike. Never had any government gone into such painstaking detail inculcating a highly moral and spiritual interpretation of a war. When events belied that version, the reaction was all the more strong. One great force making for a revision of attitude toward war was undoubtedly the recovery of the church from the moral and spiritual asphyxiation into which it fell when the bands began to play in April, 1917.

II

In 1921, *Three Soldiers,* absent without leave from headquarters, walked across the stage of literature, and marked the advent of a new spirit in the treatment of the war. This book by Dos Passos was not a pretty book and was not meant to be. It was not encumbered with such a lofty purpose as that of an attack of war. It was one man's record of what war did to men, to three ordinary doughboys picked from a cross-section of American life. The three soldiers were from different social backgrounds and were of different temperaments. One is of Italian parentage, Dan Fuselli, a conformist anxious both to rise in rank and to avoid all clashes with "the brass hats." The second, Chrisfield, is an Indiana farmer boy addicted to severe homesickness. John Andrews, musician, college graduate, is the third, hating army life and unfitted for it. The book shows all three broken in different ways by their experiences in the war, a conclusion documented in specific and revolting detail. Andrews is left at the end to face the firing squad for desertion — desperate, yet calm and defiant. The book was recognized as painfully real by multitudes of men who knew war at closer range than through the pages of a government statement of the aims of war, or a four-minute man's speech selling liberty bonds. It tore the veil from romantic pictures of modern war; it revealed the ugliness of the moral degeneration which war fostered. Worst of all, from the military point of view, it showed the muddle-headedness of the "brass hats." *Three Soldiers* is an honest, courageous, savage book — "the harmonious expression of a well-chewed rage."

In the library of fiction dealing with the war, Dos Passos' *1919,* published in 1932, is unique. It deals with the effect of the war on the civilian rather than the soldier, on the whole country rather than on a group of individuals. The form, or rather formlessness, follows the technique of the author's *Forty-Second Parallel.* The narrative is interspersed with headlines, news stories, the "camera eye," every device available to flash on the mind an impression of the contemporary scene. The result is a book which seems to have more relationship to such histories as Allen's *Only Yesterday* than to the novel in general. Dos Passos gets nearly every phase of life in the United States in the chaotic year 1919 before the eye of his literary motion-picture camera. The central threads, picked up from time to time, deal with the story of four varied characters: Evaline Hutchins, a clergyman's daughter from Chicago; Dick Savage, a Harvard graduate; Ben Compton, a radical; Joe Williams, a sailor battered about the world on a tramp ship. Not only is the casual aimlessness and lack of meaning in these particular lives conveyed, but also the ramifying social effects of war are portrayed, the cynical diplomacy, political hypocrisy, profiteering, the conditioning of individual lives by social forces.

An early novel dealing with a change of attitude to war, unmatched for sheer intensity of feeling by any American war novel, is *Plumes* by Laurence Stallings, a novel worthy of far more attention than it received. Perhaps it was too bitter, too full of pain, too complete in its deflation of flag-waving patriotism, to appeal to a large number. Stallings got a great deal of the same savage mood which dominates *Plumes* into the cripple who finally returns home in his motion picture, *The Big Parade. Plumes* tells of a romantic patriotism gone sour. The Plumes were a North Carolina family who had been patriotic fighters since the romantic days of the Revolution. When the United States entered the war Richard Plume followed the tradition of the family, resigned a teaching position in a Southern college, left his wife and sailed for France. He comes back a battered wreck to spend months of agony in hospitals. He finally gets around with the aid of a torturing iron brace. The theme of the novel is his suffering and disillusion while trying to make a living in Washington after the war — an experience which led him to renounce the romantic military creed of his family as a creed for soft-headed fools. The hatred of the hero is directed against the selfishness and stupidity which cause and tolerate war. Of all American fiction dealing with the war, *Plumes* is the most thoughtful.

William Faulkner's *Soldier's Pay*, 1926, is a bitterly realistic book, cynical in tone. It deals with the homecoming to a Southern town of a soldier horribly mutilated in the face

and suffering from lost memory. Two chance acquaint-
ances on the train, wondering with pity what his homecoming will be, decide to see him home. The sorry story
of his tragic return drives home the fact that there was
little use for, and scant understanding of, the disabled soldier. Nothing of the glamour of war is left.

Hemingway's *Farewell to Arms* is not so directly critical
of war as any of the three foregoing novels. Its wide success was probably due more to the author's style, to the grip
of the narrative, its love story, and its generous supply of sex
episodes. Yet by its very restraint, its entire absence of patriotic heroics, it brings strong criticism of the official version
of war. The aversion of the common soldier to the language
of glory dear to the heart of the orator and employed in military citation and monument inscriptions is well illustrated
in the words of the hero, Lieutenant Henry, an American
who enlisted with the Italian army on the Italian-Austrian
frontier, when a friend tells him, grandiloquently, " What
has been done this summer cannot have been done in vain."

" I was always embarrassed by the words sacred, glorious, and sacrifice, and the expression in vain. We had heard them, sometimes
standing in the rain almost out of earshot, so that only the shouted
words came through, and had read them on proclamations that were
slapped up by bill-posters over other proclamations, now for a long
time, and I had seen nothing sacred, and the things that were glorious
had no glory and the sacrifices were like the stockyards at Chicago
if nothing was done with the meat except to bury it. . . .

". . . Abstract words such as glory, honor, courage, or hallow
were obscene beside the concrete names of villages, the number of
roads, the names of rivers, the numbers of regiments and the dates." [2]

" The things that were glorious had no glory and the
sacrifices were like the stockyards at Chicago " — these clear

words of Hemingway's convey the honest report of an open
eye and interpret a whole library of war fiction and poetry.
They are also an index of a significant social force and an
asset to any thoroughgoing religious view of the world.

Among other books which helped to make up an impressive total were such works as Emery Pottle's *Stretchers,* 1930.
There is no touch of propaganda for definite opinion in it,
yet the cumulative force of its objective facts builds up a
strong impression of the futility of war. It records the experiences of a hospital unit during the war. The five-months
outlook on active fighting from the point of view of a hospital surgical room gives a sharp feeling of the cost and pain
of war. A rough history, impressive in its very unpleasant-
ness, is Liam O'Flaherty's *The Return of the Brute,* 1930,
telling the story of nine men who were victims of the war,
members of the same bombing squad. Through hunger,
pain, filth, drunkenness, fear, the novelist marches each to his
separate death. W. T. Scanlon's *God Have Mercy on Us* is
much more representative of the official military view of
the army. Yet its unadorned direct statement, even though
incorporating a good deal of patriotic legend, conveys the
feeling of both waste and horror.

Fourteen years after the armistice came one of the strongest of all the American novels dealing with the war, *Company K* by William March. It follows a familiar model,
that of assembling the personal histories of members of one
company. In form it is a sort of prose *Spoon River Anthology;* each of the gallery of soldiers " speaks his piece " and
helps to build up a total effect. The author's burning hatred
is felt in nearly every flash of the picture; also his despair-
ing hopelessness. Chapters of this book could well be sub-

stituted for the opening prayer at American Legion conventions!

A rather continuous note in this fiction, whether intended or not, is the sense of frustration, the spiritual deflation, revealing, in the words of J. E. McAfee, "the minds of men as a scarred acre on which grass never grows again." [3]

This appraisal of war by a squad of writers with military experience was something new. Literature had been, up to this time, almost universally on the side of the battalions, the drill-masters, the brigadiers. But here were soldiers reporting in infinite and often revolting detail that war is a chaotic, obscene spectacle. One ironical feature of this was the manner in which the selective draft gathered into its net so many writers, and thus prepared for the war system and the whole gold-braided military interpretation of civilization a thundering rebuttal that exploded with a detonation like that of a big Bertha. For many of these soldiers were not "mute inglorious Miltons"; they were "platoons of Homers." Squads made up of such doughboys as Dos Passos, Hemingway and Stallings were not born to blush unseen or to die with all their grating music in them.

III

Perhaps even more effective in fixing a critical attitude and a protest mixed with cynicism and ridicule was the first war play of this spirit, *What Price Glory,* 1925, by Maxwell Anderson and Laurence Stallings. No wonder the military authorities writhed over it and longed for its suppression. Here was the soldier in undress uniform. More, here was war itself, caught outside of story books to be recommended to schools by the D. A. R. In the midst of its profanity and its sex episodes was strong moral realism which acted as a powerful agent applied to the blustering arrogance of war and military prestige. Take two speeches from it, not parlor speeches, but full of ethical and religious insight. The first is made by one of the leading characters, Captain Flagg: " Damn Headquarters! It's some more of that world-safe-for-democracy slush. Every time they come around here I've got to ask myself is this an army or is it a stinking theosophical society for ethical culture and the Bible-backing uplift! I don't want that band of Gideons from headquarters. . . . In ten minutes we're going to have another of these round-headed gentlemen of the old school here giving us a prepared lecture on what we're fighting the war for and how we're to do it." [4] That man is not befuddled; he is a realist. He knows what war is and has too much integrity of character to try to disguise it by pious camouflage.

The second speech is from the non-commissioned officer, Kiper: " The chaplain said my folks was all praying for me to come through, and for God to spare me after hearing their prayers. God, I ain't that dirty a coward! That's a case of saying, Oh God, don't kill our child. Kill every kid in the neighborhood, but bring the one marked Kiper safe back home. . . . No, I don't want none of that for mine. And you can take all your New Testaments with the khaki backs and throw them in the incinerator so far as I want anything out of 'em. I'd rather have a book of cigarette papers any time." [4] There is more downright understanding of a genuinely Christian theology in that speech than in hundreds of prayers uttered in Christian pulpits for " the success of our armies," or " the protection of our boys."

Gilbert Emery's *The Hero* was another play making much the same effect. A musical comedy, *Strike Up the Band,* 1930, in its humorous setting forth of the progress of " The Henry J. Fletcher Memorial War to End Wars " added the telling force of ridicule to the trend. By some strange miracle, Hollywood for the moment stepped out of its usual glorification of war and offered itself to the fine talent of Laurence Stallings and produced *The Big Parade.* Undoubtedly an influential force tending to produce a new attitude in the popular mind was Channing Pollock's play, *The Enemy.* It made a great popular success, against the adverse judgment of many dramatic critics. The thesis of the drama was that the real enemy of mankind is not any other nation but suspicion, fear and selfish diplomacy.

IV

The expression of this clear-eyed criticism in poetry would fill many volumes. A very few examples of this type of poetry must suffice. The first is from the fiery lines of Carl Sandburg's " Killers," with its true, deep feeling of horror:

I am singing to you
Soft as a man with a dead child speaks;
Hard as a man in handcuffs,
Held where he can not move.

Under the sun
Are sixteen million men,
Chosen for shining teeth,
Sharp eyes, hard legs,
And a running of young warm blood in their wrists.

And a red juice runs on the green grass;
And a red juice soaks the dark soil.
And the sixteen million are killing . . . and killing and killing.
I never forget them day or night;
They beat on my head for memory of them;
They pound on my heart and I cry back to them,
To their homes and women, dreams and games.
I wake in the night and smell the trenches,
And hear the low stir of sleepers in lines —
Sixteen million sleepers and pickets in the dark:
Some of them long sleepers for always,
Some of them tumbling to sleep tomorrow for always,
Fixed in the drag of the world's heartbreak,
Eating and drinking, toiling . . . on a long job of killing.

Sixteen million men.[5]

Illustrative of the satirical type of treatment is Sandburg's poem, "And So Today," where, amid the solemn description of the burial of the Unknown Soldier, he stops to listen to the "honorable orators":

" The honorable orators, always the honorable orators,
Buttoning the buttons on their prince alberts
Pronouncing the syllables — sacrifice,
Juggling those bitter salt-soaked syllables,
Do they ever gag with hot ashes in their mouths? " [6]

The religious note is found in many of Lindsay's poems dealing with the war, as in the poem *The Unpardonable Sin* in which he calls speaking " of bloody power as right divine " the sin against the Holy Ghost.

The difficulty of squaring war with the teaching of Jesus is thus put sharply by Charles Badger Clark in describing the difference between himself, a soldier in the World War, and his father who fought in the Civil War:

And now what about
Me in my own day of battle?
Could I put my prayers behind a slim Springfield bullet?
Hardly, except to mutter: " Jesus, we part here.
My country calls for my body, and takes my soul also.
Do you see those humans herded and driven against me?
Turn away, Jesus, for I've got to kill them.
Why?   Oh, well, it's the way of my fathers,
And such evils bring some vast, vague good to my country.
I don't know why, but today my business is killing,
And my gods must be luck and the devil till this thing is over.
Leave me now, Lord. Your eyes make me slack in my duty."
My father could mix his prayers and his shooting,
And he was a rare, true man in his generation.
Now, I'm fairly decent in mine, I reckon;
Yet, if I should pray like him, I'd spoil it by laughing.

What is the matter? [7]

The note of rebellion which comes from prophetic religion is found in elevated expression in William Ellery
Leonard's " The Prophet ":

> Into a world of Blood and Flame
> The Prophet with his Voices came.
>
> And the Battle stopped and the People said:
> " For ourselves, our children, and our dead! "
>
> And he journeyed by sea in times of awe
> To write in a Temple the Book of the Law.
>
> But (housed with Greed, and Feud, and Wit)
> New worlds of Blood and Flame he writ. . . .
>
> With the Prophet's Voices the People in wrath
> Scourged the Prophet from their Path.

With the Prophet's Voices themselves they wrought
The Book of the Law whereof he taught.

For out of the People, blind and dumb,
The Prophet's Voices, unknown, had come.[8]

A typical expression of an idea appearing often in the poetry on war, the contrast between the martial frenzy of the incitement of war fever and the inevitable aftermath, is Lola Ridge's " Song ":

That day, in the slipping of torsos and straining flanks
On the bloodied ooze of fields plowed by the iron,
And the smoke, bluish near earth and bronze in the sunshine,
Floating like cotton-down;
And the harsh and terrible screaming,
And that strange vibration at the roots of us . . .
Desire, fierce like a song . . .
And we heard — do you remember? —
All the Red Cross bands on Fifth Avenue,
And bugles in little home towns,
And children's harmonicas bleating
AMERICA.

And after . . .
(Do you remember?)
The drollery of the wind on our faces,
And horizons reeling,
And the terror of the plain,
Heaving like a gaunt pelvis to the sun
Under us — threshing and twanging
Torn-up roots of the song? [9]

Two valuable anthologies containing poems dealing with war from many points of view are *Red Harvest,* edited by Vincent G. Burns, and *Poems of Justice,* edited by Thomas Curtis Clark.

American and British treatments of the war show many contrasts. For one thing, the revulsion from war came earlier in England, doubtless owing to the far greater numbers engaged and the severity of the losses. American poetry has not matched that of England in the exalted expression of the high emotion which the war generated in its early period — such poetry as Rupert Brooke's sonnets — nor did American poets often express the extremely bitter and savage cynicism of such poets as Siegfried Sassoon and Wilfred Owen. Again, there is lacking the art and satire of such a writer as C. E. Montague in *Disenchantment, Fiery Particles* and *Right off the Map.* The latter is perhaps the most delicate yet devastating satire on war which has ever been written. Not least among its achievements is the ironical portrayal of the part played by the organizations of religion in whooping up the martial spirit. Thus Montague etches a pompous bishop blessing the carnage: " I thank God from my heart," says the bishop, " for using us to show to mankind how much a just war can do for a nation, how it molds and disciplines man's character, how it sifts and purifies and steels them for all noble purposes, I thank God . . . thank God for all that He and He alone has done today! "

Outside the field of fiction, drama and poetry is the large contribution to the molding of opinion made by a growing number of works such as the treatment of war-guilt by Professor Sidney B. Fay, serious explorations of the whole question of war such as Kirby Page's *National Defense,* Charles Clayton Morrison's *The Outlawry of War,* and such recent exposures of the pension and veterans' rackets as *Peace Veterans,* 1933, by Roger Burlingame and the sorry history of graft unrolled by Talcott Powell in his *Tattered Banners,* 1933. The totaling of the cost of paying the piper after the dance of war is ended, as revealed in these two last named books, ought to be made required declamations on Memorial Day programs.

One alluring delusion needs to be rigidly guarded against. No multiplication of the horrors of war will ever suffice to outlaw it. Telling the plain, ugly, filthy truth about war will do much to debunk the romantic glamour which has given it so much of its stranglehold on humanity, but the task of putting war into an historical museum demands more than realistic fact. It calls for a more positive dynamic conception of peace and a more adequate and enduring motivation than either fear or horror.

---

[1] Collected Works of Stephen Crane. 12 vols. Alfred A. Knopf.

[2] *Farewell to Arms,* by Ernest Hemingway. Charles Scribner's Sons.

[3] Atlantic Monthly, Vol. 123, p. 234.

[4] *What Price Glory,* by Laurence Stallings and Maxwell Anderson. Harcourt, Brace & Company.

[5] *Chicago Poems,* by Carl Sandburg. Henry Holt & Company.

[6] Ibid.

[7] By permission of the author.

[8] *The Lynching Bee and Other Poems,* by William Ellery Leonard. Vanguard Press.

[9] *The Ghetto and Other Poems,* by Lola Ridge. Viking Press.

CHAPTER NINE

SOCIAL DISCONTENT AND PROTEST

ON October 30, 1929, the day after the great crash in the stock market, one of the New York newspapers published a cartoon showing a man buried under a mountain of ticker tape. Beneath the drawing was the title, " The End of the Day."

It proved to be the end of a day in a far more decisive sense than anyone in 1929 could dream. Not for a good many years will it appear in how far-reaching a sense it may have been an end of a day. There are some who think that that date, marked as an earthquake at the beginning of the economic collapse, may be taken in the future as a point of time marking a water-shed of history. One thing, at least, has already become clear. The date marks the turning of a page in American literature; the impact of new influences; the end of the dominance of certain moods. It is a convenient point at which to mark the end of the jazz age. Literary saxophones are still moaning and dancing is still going on. But the overturn of the economic world has brought a sobering not unlike a " morning after." It is forcing a fresh attention to an outward social world as opposed to a decade's emphasis on inward personal reactions. It has brought a reassertion of interest in social change, in reconstruction, in economics. It is giving to literature, in a real degree, an orientation to the future. To some extent the situation, as the 1920's gave way to the 1930's, may be pictured in the familiar words of Byron's lines on Waterloo:

> There was a sound of revelry by night,
>
> . . . .
>
> The lamps shone over fair women and brave men,
> A thousand hearts beat happily;
>
> . . . .
>
> But hark! a deep sound strikes like a rising knell!

The deep sound was that of stocks hitting the bottom for an " all-time low." The party, some features of which have been noted above, was rather definitely broken up. That judgment should not be taken to mean that the note of American literature has become overnight predominantly that of social criticism; nor that the so-called literature of the depression represents a major or a lasting school or tendency. But such a far-reaching condition and experience in the life of a whole nation and world has had inevitable effects on the expression of that life in literature. No area of life and thought has failed or could fail to reflect it. Perhaps the safest generalization to be made is that both in literature and in religious thought and life we are witnessing the re-emergence of concern with social reform, with transformation, with the future in economics and politics, which had such a marked smothering by the war.

Joseph Warren Beach has summed up the chief central interests of periods of both American and British fiction in the last half century thus: in the Victorian era, individual morality; in the Edwardian era, individual psychology; in the Georgian era, the general social situation.[1] This judgment must be taken with the remembrance that in no period was any one type of interest predominant, and that in recent years there has been a continuance of interest in individual psychology. In this connection it is interesting to note that the very years of the depression, when there has been such an increase in interest in economic and social questions, have also brought a revival of interest in themes far removed from the present preoccupation, as represented by the work of Elizabeth Maddox Roberts, by such historical novels as *Anthony Adverse* by Hervey Allen, and by such a popular novel as *As the Earth Turns,* 1933, by Gladys Carroll.

There is a parallel to this in the eclectic period of architecture following the late 1880's, when Gothic and Romanesque, Greek and Georgian buildings were erected in confusing variety side by side.

With that obvious caution, however, Mr. Beach's generalization expresses the chief trend of movement in fictional interest, growing during the last ten years. A comparison of the 1920's, marked by the "revolt from the village" typified by the best seller of the year, *Main Street,* and the loudly advertised "revolt of youth," with the interests of the present day, will make clear the advent of a new type of social interest and criticism.

The relation of this tendency to religion is close and clear. It is a movement in a realm which historically has been a primary concern of prophetic religion. This mood of social discontent in literature, of rebellion, of criticism of the social order, may seem to have little in common with religion in its cosmic aspects. Religion is more than social criticism or social reform. But much of this spirit of criticism and revolt has roots deeply intertwined with religious attitudes, roots which cannot be separated into secular and religious. This spirit of protest in literature may be nearer to that of Amos than to Saint Paul, but it carries an overtone of a moral order which cannot be outraged without penalty, a passionate concern for justice, a sympathy for men, a sense of sin in the feeling of participation in social wrong, and belief in human values, which are at the heart of a theistic and Christian outlook on life. These are the very warp and woof of a religious attitude to life. To the Christian, and to the Hebrew faith, they are grounded in the ultimate reality of God.

I

In many respects much of the literature of today, in both fiction and poetry, presents strong contrasts to that of the early 1920's. As we have seen, a chief theme of those years was personal reactions to the American environment. It was a cultural concern, rather than economic and social in the broad sense, including the political. Dr. Canby characterizes it as " slapping at nuisances." The symposium edited by Harold Stearns entitled *Civilization in the United States,* 1922, is typical of the loud protests which went up to the effect that the American scene was an impossible one for the life of an artist. Between the covers of that volume was the familiar indictment of the " land of the Pilgrim's pride " that it was dull, provincial, narrow, materialistic, repressive, frustrating. Mencken struck his mighty tuning fork and sounded the pitch for a great Anvil Chorus, in his words: " The American people, taking them by and large, are the most timorous, sniveling, ignominious mob of serfs and goose-steppers ever gathered under one flag in Christendom since the fall of the Eastern Empire." [2] This preoccupation was pushed from the center of the stage when the outward scenery changed to winding breadlines and the shaking of the leaning towers of capitalism.

During most of the 1920's there was strongly felt the definite quietus which the war put on liberalism and the interest in social reform. That snuffing out was decidedly marked in literary expression. Indeed the end of the reform interest was foreshadowed even before the war in the collapse of the Progressive movement. The crowds which paraded through the streets of Chicago in 1912 to the strains of "Onward, Christian Soldiers," marching to Armageddon to battle for the Lord, were not, as they thought, opening a new era, but were, as the following twenty years made clear, singing the swan song of one coming to an end. Many of the crusaders of 1912 lived to fill the ranks of the tired radicals of the 'twenties.

The rattle of the stock-ticker, the song of the salesman, the clink of currency, during the seven fat years of the 1920's, also helped to drown out, as a predominant note, the voice of social discontent and protest. That voice kept on speaking, as we shall see, in many writers whose perceptions, unbefuddled by the loot of a specious prosperity, grasped the bankruptcy of the official economic and social orthodoxy long before the crash revealed the extent of that bankruptcy. But their voices sounded too much like that of Cassandra either to dominate or to win wide acclaim.

Many causes of a change in mood in a significant minority operated before the depression forced open the eyes and ears of the multitude. The reaction from the orgy of repression, marked by Attorney General Palmer's red raids, by the frenzy of professional patriots and the Ku Klux Klan, was sharp and strong. The D. A. R. and the National Security Leagues did far more than the Socialist party to stimulate radical thinking. The vast movie of communized Russia unrolled before the eyes of the world had far-reaching effects in getting fresh questions before the national mind, even though successive administrations refused to admit that there was such a country as Russia. The whole trend of realistic fiction inevitably led many readers into the habit of looking underneath surfaces and refusing bedtime stories.

As we look back over the past fifteen years from our present knoll of observation, 1933, one trait comes out clearly regarding nearly all the most prominent literary figures of the era, particularly the novelists. That is the extremely superficial quality of their boasted " realism " in dealing with economic forces. Dreiser, Anderson, Lewis, Mencken, all wrote from an essentially undisturbed middle-class point of view. They did not grasp the underlying causes of the havoc, the effects of which engaged their attention. They had no challenge to the underlying assumption of an economically sanctified individualism, no penetration of the root causes of the chaos they saw. In that respect, their social criticism was about as penetrating as that of a troop of Boy Scouts. Both Dreiser and Sherwood Anderson, since 1931, have published books which seem to be indications of a belated perception of that weakness. Dreiser's *Tragic America* is a long, rambling, amateurish excursion into communism; Anderson's *Beyond Desire,* unquestionably his poorest novel, deals with a labor strike in North Carolina led by communists. Both are marked more by a foggy sentimentalism than by economic understanding.

Steadily through the years there has been a spirit in fiction and poetry that was more than a dissatisfaction with American culture and the American environment. It was a deeper discontent with the causes and the workings of intrenched privilege, with an economic order which issued in sharply seen human effects. In this body of literature there is need to distinguish tin from steel. There has been much fiction dealing with the seamy side of life, with human wreckage, with squalor and waste, which has not been based on a reasoned analysis or a deep desire for fundamental change. It has been rather a fashionable cult of ugliness and pain. A great many so-called " strong " novels have had a very simple formula for their manufacture: a good sprinkling of profanity, the shock of unaccustomed subjects and language dragged into print, and a general atmosphere of gloom and squalor.

An emergent note of this fiction of protest is to be found in the dictum of Karl Marx: " Up to now the philosophers have only been interpreting the world; now it is a question of changing it." What we have in many of the writers now coming into prominence is more than the familiar portrayal of confusion and hopelessness bordering on despair. There is a more positive interest which runs beyond the mere realistic portrayal of the scene they look upon. There is a desire to change it and to bring order out of confusion. It is more than a lamentation over the waste of life; it is a questioning of the whole tradition which has produced such insane waste, and sometimes this questioning rises to a demand for a new cooperative order of society.

This, of course, does not date from 1930. In 1927, during the days preceding the execution of Sacco and Vanzetti, Dorothy Parker was arrested and fined five dollars for "loitering and sauntering" around the Charlestown State Prison. That minor police court item has considerable value as a symbol, for all during the years since the war there has been an increasing tendency to "loiter and saunter" about the sore spots and tension points of American civilization. Jack London died in 1916, so that his propaganda socialistic fiction does not come within the post-war period. The other figure associated with the fiction of rebellion, Upton Sinclair, continued writing and did some of his best work in *Oil!* and *Boston*. Sinclair achieved real historical importance with his *Jungle,* 1916, the first novel of radical social criticism to become a best seller and to generate social and political force. Yet it is a commentary on the imperviousness of the popular mind to radical criticism of industrialism that the public interest centered on the revelation of the contamination of meat, rather than on what was Sinclair's chief interest, the exploitation of labor. Sinclair himself complained that he "shot at the public's head and hit its stomach."

II

Sinclair's easily caricatured defects as a propagandist have resulted in an undue disparagement of him as a novelist. His fads, his conceit, his tendency to exaggerate, his shrill denunciation, his bias which readily transmutes every criticism of him into a plot of capitalism — these are obvious points of attack and have minimized his influence both as critic and as novelist. After all these are duly recognized, however, there remains a validity of critical content and literary art far more considerable than is generally admitted. Three of his novels written since the war began justify his place as a leader in the treatment of broad social themes in fiction.

King Coal, published in 1917, had to compete with the war in public interest and failed to win wide attention. It pictures faithfully the unorganized coal-mining camps of Colorado, with full documentation based on sworn testimony taken under government supervision. The whole case of the unprotected miner against the powerful corporation is presented with detail and, for Sinclair, impressive restraint. As a result of arguments in college regarding conditions in the mines, a rich boy works as a mule-tender and later as a miner's helper in a summer vacation. He discovers how the company has got into its grip all the forces affecting the life of the miner, suppresses personal rights, thumbs its nose at social welfare, and even stoops to petty larceny at the weighing machines. Every one of the issues raised by Sinclair has been a constant source of conflict. Indeed, the whole harrowing tragedy of the miners in feudal West Virginia and Kentucky during the last five years makes an impressive confirmation of the point and accuracy of *King Coal.*

Oil!, 1927, puts the oil scandals of the Harding administration into fiction. But in the process it does more than that. It spreads out the confused welter of life in Southern California, centering in Los Angeles, the "angel city" which Sinclair calls the "Devil's Playground." The book pictures the moral degeneration brought by the lure of "easy money," the bribery, class-warfare and international competition inherent in big business as largely practised in America.

Boston, 1928, is an attempt to construct a picture of Boston through the lens of the Sacco-Vanzetti trial as a symbol of the immovable mind of a static society, dominated by the creed of property and class. It tells the whole history of the seven years' trials and the execution as seen through the eyes of the principal character, an aristocratic rebel. There is too much sincerity and careful detail in the novel for it to be lightly dismissed as the biased caricature of a fanatical radical. Sinclair's main positions have been borne out by the conclusions of such investigators as John Dewey and Felix Frankfurter. Its interpretation of that trial as an index of the degradation of Massachusetts justice is similar to that which has found extensive expression in poetry in the year following the execution. In 1922 Sinclair attempted social criticism more definitely from the standpoint of an interpretation of the teachings and personality of Jesus in his novel, *They Call Me Carpenter,* using the familiar device of a return of Jesus to modern life and the description of the treatment which would be accorded him. The conclusion he reached, that Jesus would be no more welcomed by the America of today than by the Jerusalem of 30 A.D., is one hard to controvert.

In addition to fiction, Sinclair has poured forth a stream of " exposure " of modern society in indictment of the churches, the press, the colleges and schools and the writing profession, as purchased supporters of Mammon. His uncritical extravagance and his habit of unduly simplifying complicated forces have vitiated much of his criticism. Yet, after all necessary deductions are made, there is an impressive residue in his indictment of religion, the press and education for their failure to act as free and courageous critics of the injustices of American life. These are found in *The Profits of Religion*, 1918, *The Brass Check*, 1919, dealing with the press, and *The Goose Step*, dealing with the colleges. A sample of the vigorous style in his attack on the subservience of the church to wealth is found in the following parody of the denunciation of the Pharisees by Jesus:

"Woe unto you, doctors of divinity and Catholics, hypocrites! for you shut up the kingdom of Heaven against men; you don't go in yourself and you don't let others go in. Woe unto you, doctors of divinity and Presbyterians, hypocrites! for you foreclose mortgages on widows' houses, and for a pretense you make long prayers. For this you will receive the greater damnation! Woe unto you, doctors of divinity and Methodists, hypocrites! for you send missionaries to Africa to make one convert, and when you have made him, he is twice as much a child of hell as yourselves. (Applause) Woe unto you, blind guides, with your subtleties of doctrine, your transubstantiation and consubstantiation and all the rest of it; you fools and blind! Woe unto you, doctors of divinity and Episcopalians, hypocrites! for you drop your checks into the collection-plate and you pay no heed to the really important things in the Bible, which are justice and mercy and faith in goodness. You blind guides, who strain at a gnat and swallow a camel! (Laughter) Woe unto you, doctors of divinity and Anglicans, hypocrites! for you bathe yourselves and dress in immaculate clothing but within you are full of extortion and excess. You blind high churchmen, clean first your hearts, so that the clothes you wear may represent you. Woe unto you, doctors of divinity and Baptists, hypocrites! for you are like marble tombs which appear beautiful on the outside, but inside are full of dead men's bones and all uncleanness. Even so you appear righteous to men, but inside you are full of hypocrisy and iniquity. (Applause) Woe unto you, doctors of divinity and Unitarians, hypocrites! because you erect statues to dead reformers, and put wreaths upon the tombs of old-time martyrs. You say, if we had been alive in those days, we would not have helped to kill those good men. That ought to show you how to treat us at present. (Laughter) But you are the children of those who killed the good men; so go ahead and kill us too! You serpents, you generation of vipers, how can you escape the damnation of hell? " [3]

Samuel Hopkins Adams's *Revelry,* 1926, treated in fiction the corruption of the Harding administration. It failed of its possible effect by its mixing of fiction and fact in a way that made it impossible for the reader to separate the two. It is a vigorous journalistic piece of work, however, the main contentions of which were abundantly borne out by later court decisions. The burlesque quality as well as the cynical point of view is seen in the names the author gives to the posts in the Harding cabinet: " Secretary of Deals, Secretary of Pardons, Bootlegger General, Secretary of Office Sales, Receiver General of Graft, Secretary of Purchasable Contracts."

An influence making for this type of critical protest in fiction reaches back into the pre-war era, in the increased attention given to the unromantic people on the lower flights of the social and economic stairway. O. Henry, in his snapshots of *The Four Million,* had social influences which he little intended. His work was not realistic at all, for in his detailed settings of Bagdad-on-the-subway he told romantic stories which outdo the Arabian Nights. But by his choice of characters he stimulated interest in people.

A picture often is a criticism and an interpretation, even when it has no didactic purpose whatever. America was given a large picture book to look at in the generation 1900-1930, and the study of that album, prepared by poet and novelist, by dramatist and critic, added enormously to the force and range of the literature of protest. Eugene O'Neill's *Hairy Ape,* 1922, opened up the hatches so that the lower order of humanity might be seen, and more — heard! They were heard increasingly. It is no exaggeration to say that the voice from the Yank, the Hairy Ape in the stokehole, echoed increasingly down the years that immediately followed and is destined to echo farther:

" 'Hell in de stokehole? Sure! It takes a man to work in hell. Hell, sure, dat's my fav'rite climate. I eat it up! I git fat on it! It's me makes it hot! It's me makes it roar! It's me makes it move! Sure, on'y for me everything stops. It all goes dead, get me? . . . I'm at de bottom, get me? Dere ain't nothin' foither. I'm de end! I'm de start! I start! I start somep'n and de woild moves! It — dat's me! — de new dat's moiderin' de old! I'm de ting in coal dat makes it boin; I'm steam and oil for de engines; I'm de ting in noise dat makes yuh hear it; I'm smoke and express trains and steamers and factory whistles; I'm de ting in gold dat makes it money! And I'm what makes iron into steel! I'm steel — steel — steel! Slaves. We run de whole woiks. All de rich guys dat tink dey's somep'n dey ain't nothin'! Dey don't belong. But us guys, we're in de move, we're at de bottom, de whole ting is us!' " [4]

Not a lovely voice — that. Out of key, raucous, grating, unmusical. But a human voice, and one that will be listened to.

III

This approach to criticism by way of sympathy, of recognition of the under dog, giving the emotional momentum necessary for the intellectual attack to be formulated later, finds large expression in poetry. The great poetic revival in America dates roughly from 1912. Its sources of renewal lay in the new themes to which poets gave their attention, and the new diction of poetry, suited to real people with real emotions, as opposed to stock poetic *clichés* of theme and language. This social criticism set to music, this blending of eyesight and compassion, is a strong mark of much poetry. Two strains in this poetry can be illustrated in two contrasting poems. The first is just a portrait, not a beautiful one but having the quality of Dutch painting — honesty. It is Agnes Lee's " Mrs. Malooly ":

> Mrs. Malooly has gone to her rest,
> Who scrubbed Manhattan's marble aisles.
> She has forgotten, forgotten, forgotten
> The mop and broom
> And the patterned tiles.
>
> Mrs. Malooly has gone to her rest
> In the smooth-dug loam, to a rest so deep
> She has forgotten, forgotten, forgotten
> The unmade bed
> And the whiskey sleep.[5]

A text for theme and mood of this protest in poetry might well be found in Carl Sandburg's restrained and moving picture, " The Masses ":

Among the mountains I wandered and saw blue haze and red crag and was amazed;

On the beach where the long push under the endless tide maneuvers, I stood silent;

Under the stars on the prairie watching the Dipper slant over the horizon's grass, I was full of thoughts.

Great men, pageants of war and labor, soldiers and workers, mothers lifting their children — these all I touched, and felt the solemn thrill of them.

And then one day I got a true look at the Poor, millions of the Poor,
  patient and toiling; more patient than crags, tides, and stars;
  innumerable, patient as the darkness of night — and all broken
  humble ruins of nations.[6]

This fresh feeling and theme of poetry led one conservative critic, William C. Brownell, to complain gently that
"poets who are not adorning the golden calf are incensing
the under dog." It is interesting to observe that he used the
metaphor of worship in describing the new spirit. There
is far more in the figure of speech than his sarcasm grasps.
It was not so much the incensing of the under dog in what
he observed, as it was an outraged sense of human values, an
attitude religious in nature. Poetry of this sort has done
great service to religion in dramatizing the tension between
religion and the world in which it is set. That dramatization in many poets came before that tension was acutely
realized by many within the churches. Indeed, it is not
acutely realized by the majority even today, in spite of the
fact that it has become one of the most important features
of the religious situation in our generation.

The literary critic may say, and in fact has already said
emphatically, that this class of poetry is too choked up with
emotion, carries a too heavy load of impediment in the form
of propaganda, to be poetry of the first order. The work we
are considering here, however, is not propaganda; it is not
loaded with any particular economic or political ideology or
dogmatism. Some may not be in the highest rank in American poetry, but it is characteristic poetry, authentic music,
and convincing evidence of a deep and new spirit. The poet
is a voice for inarticulate thousands who speak through him.
Those of the Christian tradition can but recognize it as a

divine as well as a human inspiration; divine because it wells up from human experience.

The deepest thing in Vachel Lindsay is not new forms of verse, not jazz singing on Olympus; it is his ethical outlook, his moral idealism, his sensitiveness to the possibilities of life which are being thwarted. This finds expression, again and again, in connection with widely different themes. Sometimes the theme is political, as he pictures his own Middle Westerners in the poem on " Bryan," a theme strangely timely in the present years of agricultural collapse. Lindsay pictures the Middle Western farmers as caught in a gigantic spider web spun in the East.

The sense of the tragic cost of a sky filled with the smoke of mills, the red blood of men mixed with the black smoke, is a recurring one with Carl Sandburg.

A bar of steel — it is only
Smoke at the heart of it, smoke and the blood of a man.
A runner of fire ran in it, ran out, ran somewhere else,
And left smoke and the blood of a man
And the finished steel, chilled and blue. . . .
In the blood of men and the ink of chimneys
The smoke nights write their oaths:
Smoke into steel and blood into steel;
Homestead, Braddock, Birmingham, they make their steel with men.
Smoke and blood is the mix of steel.[7]

A vehement protest, more direct and sharp, marks many of the poems of one as far removed from Carl Sandburg as a poet of the same generation could well be, Edna St. Vincent Millay. Her poem written after the final decision in the Sacco-Vanzetti case is a powerful expression of restrained emotion and challenge. After a moving description of a New England homestead she concludes:

What from the splendid dead
We have inherited —
Furrows sweet to the grain, and the weed subdued —
See now the slug and the mildew plunder.
Evil does overwhelm
The larkspur and the corn;
We have seen them go under.

Let us sit here, sit still,
Here in the sitting-room until we die;
At the step of Death on the walk, rise and go;
Leaving to our children's children this beautiful doorway,
And a blighted earth to till
With a broken hoe.

Miss Kathleen Millay has combined in an unusual manner a sensitive appreciation of beauty with both social sympathy and rebellious protest. A typical note in her verses is this:

> The anguish of the world is on my tongue,
> My bowl is filled to the brim with it; there
> is more than I can eat.[8]

Another evidence both of the repercussion in poetry of the Sacco-Vanzetti execution and of the note of social protest in contemporary poetry is Arthur Davison Ficke's noble sonnet, " Prayer in Massachusetts ":

> Upon this soil may no tree ever grow.
>   In this land may no lips ever again
> Speak the word justice, now that all men know
>   Those lips have long boasted and in vain.
> May never young men hither come to learn
>   What cruel elders have no power to teach.
> May no lights burn here save witch fires that burn
>   Along some desolate and abandoned beach.

May this dour land go back now whence it came —
   To early granite, to implacable sea.
May there descend on it the cleansing flame
   Of some supreme remote catastrophe
Divorcing it forever with its shame
   From men who would be generous, wise and free.[9]

It is not often that a single poem can be found which may be taken as the keynote of a significant part of the succeeding poetry of a generation, as is true of Edwin Markham's " The Man with a Hoe," published in 1900. There were many elements of prophecy in that poem. Its description of the rise of the inarticulate and defrauded remains the best poetic description of the Russian Revolution, written seventeen years before the event. Markham's poem did much to affect the social thinking of the Rooseveltian era. It also marked the beginning of a fresh interest of poets in social questions, economics and politics. It is interesting, consequently, to note Markham's treatment of the same theme a generation later in one of the poems of his " Eighty Songs at Eighty," published in 1932:

Behold, O world, the Toiling Man,
Bearing earth's burden and her ban.
Because of his all-giving grace,
Kaisers and Kings have held their place —
Because he gave ungrudging toil,
The Lords have had the world for spoil —
Because he gave them all his dower,
Great ladies glittered out their hour.
He clothed the paupers, gave them bed,
Put into their mouths their daily bread
And his reward, a crust to taste,
An unknown grave upon the waste.

Outcast and cursed, befooled and flayed,
With earth's brute burdens on him laid,
He only reacht out humble hands,
Reacht out his mercies on all lands.
How silent down the world he trod —
How patient he has been with God! [10]

That last line recalls another line, which might well be read
with apprehension by those who are greeting these days of
economic judgment with nothing but a sleepy mental snore:
" The long, long patience of the plundered poor." Much of
the work of a score of poets should be recognized in any estimate of this emphasis in contemporary poetry. Sarah N.
Cleghorn, Dana Burnet, Herman Hagedorn, Louis Unter-
meyer, James Oppenheim, Arthur Davison Ficke, Zona Gale,
Ralph Cheyney, James Rorty, William Ellery Leonard, are
only a few among many who might be named. Thomas
Curtis Clark, himself a poet, has rendered a large service in
the taste and skill which he has brought to the editing of
several anthologies of poetry dealing with religion and human sympathy — *Poems of Justice, The Master of Men* and
Quotable Poems. It has been a contribution to poetry dealing with religious themes comparable to that rendered to
poetry in general by Harriet Monroe during the last twenty
years.

Merely from the standpoint of literary appraisal, a dis-
tinctive feature of much of this poetry of criticism, of sympathy, of the cry for justice, is its religious spirit and often
its religious content, particularly its employment of the figure of Jesus. When we examine this poetry from the viewpoint of its relationship to religion, the theme of Jesus becomes all the more significant. The emergence of Jesus as

a theme and motive is apparent not only in so-called religious poetry but in poetry unqualified by any adjective. Since 1910 there has been a new resurrection of Jesus from the tomb of convention and tradition. It has been another chapter in the long history of the rediscovery of Jesus. This cannot be regarded as a resurgence of interest in creedal Christianity; it is rather interest in Jesus as a personality, a source of inspiration, a refuge to which the poet turns under the shock of the present scene or situation. Richard Watson Gilder in the 1890's drew the contrast which describes the religious spirit of this poetic trend:

> Not the Christ of our subtle creeds:
> But the brother of want and blame,
>   The lover of women and men,
> With a love that puts to shame
>   All passions of mortal ken.

The same feeling finds expression in the verses of Elizabeth Waddell in her poem "Crusaders":

> They have taken the tomb of our Comrade Christ,
>   Infidel hordes that believe not in man.
> Stable and stall for his birth sufficed
>   But his tomb is built on a kingly plan.
>
> They have hanged him round with pomp and parade,
>   They have buried him deep under steel and stone,
> But we come leading the great crusade
>   To give our Comrade back to his own.[11]

Let it be freely granted that some of the use made of Jesus in verse dealing with social questions has been that of a convenient stereotype. Many references to Jesus have evidently been made not as tributes to one looked up to in devotion, but as convenient sticks with which to beat the employer or the exploiter. The prestige of Jesus, literary and religious, has been claimed by many to whom the religious faith of Jesus, his discipline, his demand for self-sacrifice, would be abhorrent. Yet while recognizing that, the sincerity and extent of this interest in Jesus, as source of vision, of moral energy and as court of appeal, cannot be overlooked or doubted. It is found in the most unexpected sources. Edwin Arlington Robinson's sonnet " Calvary " is not only a powerful poem but also a significant evidence of the attraction of Jesus for one outside the ranks of creedal subscription:

> Friendless and faint, with martyred steps and slow,
> Faint for the flesh, but for the spirit free,
> Stung by the mob that came to see the show,
> The Master toiled along to Calvary;
> We gibed him, as he went, with houndish glee,
> Till his dimmed eyes for us did overflow;
> We cursed his vengeless hands thrice wretchedly —
> And this was nineteen hundred years ago.
> But after nineteen hundred years the shame
> Still clings, and we have not made good the loss
> That outraged faith has entered in his name.
> Ah, when shall come love's courage to be strong!
> Tell me, O Lord — tell me, O Lord, how long
> Are we to keep Christ writhing on the cross! [12]

A frequent theme in the poetry of protest is the appeal to Jesus in pointing the contrast which he makes to attitudes taken, complacence revealed, evils tolerated by individuals and organizations which bear his name. Illustrative of this is Edna St. Vincent Millay's sonnet " To Jesus on His Birthday ":

For this Your mother sweated in the cold,
  For this You bled upon the bitter tree;
A yard of tinsel ribbon bought and sold;
  A paper wreath; a day at home for me.

The merry bells ring out, the people kneel;
  Up goes the man of God before the crowd;
With voice of honey and with eyes of steel
  He drones Your humble gospel to the proud.

Nobody listens. Less than the wind that blows
  Are all Your words, to us You died to save.
O Prince of Peace! O Sharon's Dewy Rose!
  How mute You lie within Your vaulted grave!
The stone the angel rolled away with tears
Is back upon Your mouth these thousand years.[13]

An example of still another type of the poetic use of
the figure of Jesus in social conflict is Sarah N. Cleghorn's
" Comrade Jesus " (quoted in part):

Thanks to Saint Matthew, who had been
At mass-meetings in Palestine,
We know whose side was spoken for
When Comrade Jesus had the floor.

" Where sore they toiled and hard they lie,
Among the great unwashed dwell I —
The tramp, the convict, I am he;
Cold-shoulder him, cold-shoulder me."

By Dives' door, with thoughtful eye,
He did tomorrow prophesy:
" The kingdom's gate is low and small;
The rich can scarce wedge through at all."

Ah, let no local him refuse!
Comrade Jesus hath paid his dues.
Whatever other be debarred,
Comrade Jesus hath his red card.[14]

Naturally much of the current poetry is finding first appearance in magazines and newspapers. Typical of a considerable volume of verse making use of the figure of Jesus, both in criticism of the church and in the appeal for justice, is Verne Bright's " Comrade Christ ":

> Give us Jesus Christ, the Carpenter.
> What to us is your white-liveried God?
> O men of the anvil, of the loom, the sod,
> They have hid our God in a golden sepulcher;
> They have made our Christ a sniveling pampered priest,
> A paltry giver of fine bread and wine —
> Our Christ is a God of Men, as men divine,
> Holding in brotherhood the lost and the least.
>
> He toils in the desert place by our side;
> He delves with us beneath the granite hill;
> He weeps above our brothers who have died;
> He dreams with us in the darkness hot and still;
> No surpliced shriver of the sins of men —
> Christ, the Carpenter, has come again.[15]

Two final samples from a large volume of poetry similar in nature must suffice. One is the Christmas poem of James Rorty, a poet quite outside the ranks of conventional religion, a poem in which " the high cross " of Jesus is appealed to as a symbol of justice and revolution:

In the dark days, the early evenings of December,
With summer gone, and autumn, and the pale towers of the sky-
    scrapers withered in the high cold, or blind in rain,
And the people stumbling home, sick with small fears, the little lies
    of trade, the multiple loneliness of crowds,
Then the Christmas bell-ringers come forth, the mute whiskered false-
    faces, each with his iron kettle and his bell.

Ting-ling-ling, ting-ling-ling — how hesitant, how humble these priests; is something really born, are they sure?

Long ago the desert villagers heard this bell; then the tired Greeks, the Romans, even the reindeer people of the north — all fed the myth and the myth sustained them.

By this faith the pale towers rise, the myriad lights burn, the shoaled motors race and stop, overhead a great ship drills a lighted wake through the new ocean of the night air.

One small scrap of ancient holiness — out of this we have built a world unholy, terrible and fierce; but we are neither fierce nor terrible.

The blood of the lamb grows thin; next year or next century will the bell-ringers come again to the street corners?

Not for long shall we dream this dream; when fierceness wakes again in our blood we shall want not bells, but trumpets, and again the high cross.[16]

The challenge which the figure of Jesus brings to indifference and complacency has been the theme of many poems. It is feelingly expressed in Thomas Curtis Clark's sonnet "Questions," written at the time of the Eucharistic Congress in Chicago:

> Is this a tribute to the Nazarene,
> Beloved of children, brother of the poor,
> The peasant teacher turned from door to door;
> Without a home save on God's friendly green?
> This mitred pomp, these gilded lords of pride,
> These surging peoples awed by thronging priests,
> By old tradition, storied fasts and feasts —
> Is this for Him who on a rude cross died?
> How great His gain, who now commands such zeal,
> Such loyalty, beyond His fairest thought!
> In His high name what wonders have been wrought!
> How proud His kingdom — this we see today!
> If He were here — who walked a pilgrim way —
> If He were here. . . .[17]

IV

The novels of the past four years reflecting the inevitable turning of interest to economic and social conditions, a concern with the oppressed, the victims of economic stupidity and injustice, are already many. Some lack art, some are too heavy with propaganda to sail gracefully, but in general they show an immense vitality which gives large promise for fiction dealing with social conditions. The mood of the time, which has resulted in this vital interest, is perfectly expressed in Gilbert Maxwell's poem " This Year of our Lord," published in January, 1933. It is rarely that a single poem so catches the literary mood of a time and expresses it so forcibly:

> I am sick in my soul of the poets who sing
> Of the star in the sky and the bird on the wing,
> While Life lies down in a filthy shroud
> And cannot be spoken about aloud.
>
> I am weary of women with perilous eyes
> Who cover their lust with a fat disguise
> And prate from a bounteous fireside
> Of a vision lost and a dream denied,
>
> While chaos is thundering under the earth
> And laborers beggared of right and of worth,
> Standing in line for a meager crust,
> Humbly entreat the mercy of dust.
>
> A canker is gnawing the roots of my heart
> That such as these can shiver and smart
> Under the thorn of mock despair
> While children suffer for light and air. . . .

Better oblivion breaking the mind
And the blood run dry and the soul gone blind
Than this — to sob and snivel above
The little anguished body of Love! [18]

Three novels and one play may be selected as typical of the most significant works of this character.

The first is Michael Gold's *Jews without Money*, 1931. It is a powerful novel, richly detailed from the varied life experiences of its author. Gold has described what might be called the education of a novelist: " All in all, I have worked in about 36 jobs entailing manual labor, and on 12 newspapers as reporter and copy-reader. I have been chased by the cops in about 40 street demonstrations and have helped in about 20 strikes." The novel pictures the fortunes of a Jewish family on the East Side of New York, a boy's education on the streets and his progress as a result of that education to communism as the solution of chaos and tragedy. It is a novel that ought not to be neglected. It is not an economic tract; it is a moving human picture, instinct with tenderness and pity as well as rebellion. The author sees, as do many of today's novelists, society as the villain. He has an understanding of the individual villain and hatred of the group villain. He writes: " One hates gangsters, as one must hate all mercenaries. Yet some are unfortunate boys, bad eggs, hatched by the bad world hen." Of Louis, the One Eye, he writes:

" He would have been handsome but for his one eye, and the hard sneer fixed upon his mouth. They disfigured him like wounds. They were the fatal wounds given him by Society. . . . The State had turned a moody, unhappy boy into this evil rattlesnake that struck a deathblow at the slightest touch of man." [19]

The emotional quality of his social radicalism comes out in many passages. One typifies it: "Mother! Momma! I am still bound to you by the cords of birth. I must remain faithful to the poor because I cannot be faithless to you. I believe in the poor because I have known you. The world must be made gracious for the poor! Momma, you taught me that." [20]

Again, at the end of the novel, at the end of the recital of the futile struggle to escape out of poverty:

"A man on an East Side soap-box, one night, proclaimed that out of the despair, melancholy and helpless rage of millions, a world movement had been born to abolish poverty.

"I listened to him.

"O workers' Revolution, you brought hope to me, a lonely, suicidal boy. You are the true Messiah. You will destroy the East Side when you come, and build there a garden for the human spirit.

"O Revolution, that forced me to think, to struggle and to live.

"O great Beginning!" [21]

One sentence gives a determining conviction — "Kindness is a form of suicide in a world based on the law of competition."

Two years later, in 1932, appeared one of the most stinging pieces of depression literature, *Nobody Starves,* by Catherine Brody. Miss Brody is not the literary artist that Gold is but she is an accomplished reporter, and against a veracious background she tells a story that hurts from page one to the end. It is a chapter in the short and simple annals of the poor in Detroit in 1931. It is one of what have come to be called "proletarian novels," although it is written by an intellectual of the middle class. The book takes a young American boy and girl through several jobs and factories, dealing with the insecurity of life even before unemployment came. The couple marry and drift to Detroit, where the man becomes another cog in an automobile factory, understanding neither the industrial process nor its economic background. The wife goes to work to help the attempted climb up into the middle class, largely by means of instalment payments on furniture. The man loses work, the home is lost, she has to return to her people. A sorry drama which has played out in just the same terms in Detroit by thousands in the last two years. In a nervous collapse, the husband shoots the wife, kills her, fails to accomplish suicide and is left in jail as the book ends. The bitter satirical note is expressed in the fact that " nobody starves." One emphasis is the lack on the part of the people in the book of any grasp on the underlying economic causes of their distress. Except for occasional outbursts of cursing, they are dumb. They do not fight, they do not understand.

A novel of 1931, *Call Home the Heart,* by Olive Tilford Dargan, writing under the pseudonym of Fielding Burke, far greater in literary skill and emotional power than the preceding, is one of quite a number of recent novels dealing with the industrialism of the South. The novel does not carry a large load of propaganda and it is all the more effective for being, for the most part, a deeply human story. It contrasts the two contemporary backgrounds, that of the mountains and that of the towns down in the valleys and plains. The only choice which the mountaineer has seems to be that of starving in the hills or going down to starve in the towns. The strike at Gastonia comes into the story, with its beatings and its legalized murder; but it is the full-canvas picture of the people which makes the real theme. The sen-

sitively appreciated beauty of the mountain home of the
heroine, before she leaves her husband to fly to the mill
town, stands in glaring contrast to the supernatural ugliness
of the town. The whole human bearing of the " stretch-out
system," the use of people as cheap raw material, their heart-
rending helplessness, all have detailed presentation. It is a
human situation which gives the communist organizer a
great opportunity.

Elmer Rice's drama, *We the People,* produced in January,
1933, was an ambitious effort to put the " depression " on the
stage. It was not an outstanding success on the stage, yet it
ran for several months. No doubt too steadily insistent on
its " moral " to make an artistic drama, it is a significant
achievement in the dramatic presentation of ideas. It is a
stinging challenge to " rugged individualism," both in its
passionate declamation and in its satire of the college president and senator who do the bidding of the industrial mag-
nate. The dramatist takes a family apparently secure in the
days when Mr. Hoover was promising the abolition of poverty. The father of the family had worked for twenty years
as a foreman in a factory. The daughter was a teacher, the
son a student in a university. Then the illusion of prosperity
broke; the father loses his job, is wounded in a massacre of
workers, evidently patterned after the shooting of unemployed men at Dearborn, Michigan, by Mr. Ford's con-
stables; the son is falsely accused of shooting a policeman
during a radical meeting and condemned to be electrocuted.
The foreclosure of mortgages, bank failures, the woman
who spends a fortune for a painting while her husband lays
off hundreds of workers, hunger and hopelessness, all get
into the play. The purpose of the play is brought out in the

concluding speech, delivered at a meeting of protest over the sentencing to death of the son of the family. It is delivered by a liberal professor at the University, who was dismissed from his position for protesting against the murder of unemployed men:

"'It is of such lives — Allan's and Mary's and Helen's and a dozen others I might name — that a strong and free people could be built. But what do we do with them . . . . we waste them, squander them, throw them on the scrap heap. The right to live, that is what Mary asks. That is all that any of them asks. And no social system that denies them that right has a claim to a continuance of its existence. In the name of humanity, ladies and gentlemen, in the name of common sense. We are the people — ladies and gentlemen, we — you and I and every one of us. It is our house: this America. Let us cleanse it and put it in order and make it a place for decent people to live in.'" [22]

Mary Heaton Vorse's *Strike,* 1931, deals with the Southern industrial problem. It is more directly propagandist, for the author went to North Carolina to aid the strikers. Grace Lumpkin's *To Make My Bread* is a striking instance of the trend which has been described as " Southern novelists forsaking the magnolia tradition for a scrutinizing of their social institutions." The three novels of Mrs. Dargan, Mrs. Vorse and Miss Lumpkin agree completely as to their details. People from the mountain fastness are followed as they are drawn down to the textile mills where steam is more valuable than people. The authors indeed reveal the conclusion that the people might have starved at home much more conveniently. Other novels which have drawn indictments of the social order, not in lawyers' briefs but in pictures of life, are Henry Harrison Kidd's *Three Brothers and Seven Dad-*

dies and John Herman's *Summer is Ended*. Erskine Caldwell's *Tobacco Road* might well take a Pulitzer prize, if one were offered for sheer depressing theme and detail. The hero is one of the most unattractive characters who have dragged their way across the pages of American fiction. He is a human derelict thrown up by the economic collapse of agriculture. It is not a pleasant story to read, but the human tragedy behind falling prices in agriculture is not a pleasant one to take part in. One can hardly read Caldwell without getting an impression, which he never put into words, of an appalling social stupidity which breeds such results. John L. Spivak in *Georgia Nigger*, 1932, tells the story of the chain-gang penology of Georgia, accurate in its facts, strong in its pity. Another novel, not marked by the outraged sense of justice shown by Spivak, is Wellborn Kelley's *Inchin' Along,* which pictures as part of its theme the difficulties of " share croppin'." One of the most notable works of sheer reporting of the " depression " background is Jack Conroy's *The Disinherited,* 1933.

In a class by themselves are the two books of Edward Dahlberg, reminiscent of Gorki's *The Lower Depths* or Arthur Morrison's *Tales of Mean Streets*. This is not propaganda literature, but its searing portraits constitute social criticism of the most powerful type. His novel *From Flushing to Calvary* digs down far beneath the middle class and reports life among the real under dogs, people who are forced down to the cheap, coarse, vulgar level which industrialism has provided as a human sub-cellar. The author's style is fitted to the environment and the whole effect is sordid — as it is rightly designed to be. Dahlberg's first novel, *Bottom Dogs,* was even more drearily realistic in detail, dealing also with

the slum center and fringe which every American city pos-
sesses.

Factual pictures movingly interpreted mark Clinch Cal-
kins' memorable book on the lives and deaths of the unemployed, *Some Folks Won't Work*. Another book of remarkable reporting was Edmund Wilson's *American Jitters,*
perhaps the strongest recording of the United States in the
second year of the depression, 1931. The whole panorama
is there — breadlines, the lines of applicants for work at the
Ford plants in Detroit, soup kitchens, communist meetings,
farmers' " holidays " and labor strikes. It is a highly selective picture book, of course. Wilson is one of the authors
who make up the intellectual wing of the communist party,
a group which includes, either as party members or sym-
pathizers, Sidney Howard, the playwright, Dreiser, Lincoln
Steffens, Waldo Frank and Dos Passos.

V

The spectacle of hunger and homeless woe as the end product of an opulent civilization has furnished a theme for
many poems. Three typical poems here quoted are indicative of the character of a large volume of present-day poetry.
A sample is Ogden Nash's parody of William Blake, entitled " The Beggar ":

> Beggar, beggar, burning low
> In the city's trodden snow.
> What immortal hand or eye
> Could frame thy dread asymmetry?
>
> In what distant deep of lies
> Died the fire of thine eyes?

What the mind that planned the shame?
What the hand dare quench the flame?

And what shoulder and what art
Could rend the sinews of thy heart?
And when thy heart began to fail,
What soft excuse, what easy tale?

What the hammer? What the chain?
What the furnace dulled thy brain?
What the anvil? What the blow
Dared to forge this deadly woe?

When the business cycle ends,
In flaming extra dividends,
Will He smile his work to see?
Did He who made the Ford make thee? [23]

The second example is also on the beggar as the abysmal
anti-climax of " civilization," by Anderson M. Scruggs:

This is the depth, the end of all despair:
That man for whom the planets toil and sing —
Inheritor of earth and sea and air —
Should come to be this starved, forsaken thing
Whose soft, obsequious words and pleading eye
Invoke the heedless masses of the street,
Hoping that in the crowds that pass him by,
Some fat-faced god may deign to let him eat.
Here is the deepest wrong, the darkest deed
That man must answer in some distant dawn:
That in this fecund earth there should be need
For such as these — the beggars that pass on
Down dim-lit streets and byways of the night,
Asking of man what should be man's by right. [24]

A third is from a poem by Nels Francis Nordstrom entitled *Cinder Snappers,* the slang term for young steel workers employed as helpers. It gives two pictures of the steel mills of South Chicago, one in the boom year 1928, the other in 1933. The lines here given are from the picture of 1933:

Man triumphant — rides through the mountains —
  Over the desert.
Man triumphant — builds a new heaven
  Fifty stories high.
Man triumphant — laughs at the Gods
  Who hid the ore, the coal, and the intricate processes that make the
    steel.
Man triumphant — stands silent — alone,
  His hands idle, beside the stopped machine.

" At the gate " — we are all alike — " Spicks," " Dagoes,"
  " Polacks," " Wops."
Ours is the same answer — the same waiting.

I am Youth! Number 1533 — Unemployed.
  I walk the pavements, counting the cement blocks to the Yard Office.
No Work Today! This must I do — that Number 1533 may live.

I know the ways of Man — the toil of idleness!
I know the pain of time — the quietness of the shutdown machine.
I have travelled the streets from shop to shop —
Stood outside the gates — walked along the red fence,
Barbed wire at the top. No Work Today! Yet the months toil on.
The stacks stand in silent rows. Not a cloud of smoke.
I can see the rust. The fires are out.
There are men everywhere. Strange — different.
Their faces are clean, pale, lost.
We sit on the street curb and talk —
But Hell! we can't — it's the same old " line."

The tomorrows are like the todays and yesterdays. " No Work To-
day."
Even with the gang I am lost, alone.
Only I can face my tomorrow.
 I can see the rust. The fires are out.
 I can see no further. The gates are closed.[25]

VI

Another field of interest is that of the entirely new note
which is heard in Negro literature in America since the war.
It is no longer " the white man's Negro " who speaks most
compellingly. It is no longer the characteristic religious
plaintive note of the spirituals which is the predominant one.
It is no longer the smooth cadences of a Paul Laurence Dun-
bar. It is the Negro awakened to economic and social exploitation, to injustice, to violation of right, to racial hypocrisy and white complacency. Some of the most impassioned
poetry of social discontent produced since the war is that
which expressed the Negro's protest against injustice. Negro
literature is escaping the domination of the traditional figures, Uncle Tom and Uncle Remus. Two poems, separated
by several years in their composition, when taken together
reveal clearly this new spirit and mood. The first is a series
of questions asked by James Weldon Johnson in his poem
" To America ":

> How would you have us? As we are
> Or sinking 'neath the load we bear,
> Our eyes fixed forward on a star,
> Or gazing empty at despair?
>
> Rising or falling? Men or things?
> With dragging pace or footsteps fleet?
> Strong, willing sinews in your wings,
> Or tightening chains about your feet? [26]

The other may fairly be considered an answer to that question; an answer on the basis that America has decided that she prefers the Negro "falling." It is by Langston Hughes, also as Johnson, a Negro. It is entitled "I, Too":

> I, too, sing America.
>
> I am the darker brother.
> They send me in the kitchen
> When company comes.
> But I laugh,
> And eat well,
> And grow strong.
>
> Tomorrow
> I'll sit at the table
> When company comes,
> Nobody'll dare
> Say to me,
> "Eat in the kitchen"
> Then.
>
> Besides, they'll see how beautiful I am
> And be ashamed, —
>
> I, too, am America.[27]

The heart of the mood is to be found in two lines of Countee Cullen, one of the ablest Negro poets:

> Yet do I marvel at this curious thing,
> To make a poet black and bid him sing.

The last twenty years have been marked by the opening of eyes of educated Negroes to the economic and social realities of their world. These years have been marked by disillusionment over the fruits of the attitude of cooperation represented by Booker T. Washington and a prevalence of the more radical, race-conscious insistence on rights, represented by W. E. B. Du Bois. Dr. Du Bois has very recently, in an address at Washington, May 18, 1933, given voice to the spirit of the radical Negro group. He declared:

" That all previous efforts on the part of Negroes had in fact failed to win for them recognition as an integral part of American civilization or of modern culture, and urged re-direction of their efforts in the future to prepare themselves for the new world order which, he said, was surely coming.

" I propose as the next step which the American Negro can give to the world a new and unique gift. We have tried song and laughter and rare good humor, and the world has received it; we have given the world work, hard, backbreaking labor, and the world let John Henry die breaking his heart to beat the machinery.

It is now our business to give the world an example of intelligent cooperation so that when the new industrial commonwealth comes we can go into it as experienced people and not again be left on the outside as mere beggars. Twelve million people in the United States can work for themselves and feed themselves; can pay themselves and organize their own industry; unless they are incurably stupid."

The most vigorous expression of this rebellion is perhaps that of Claude McKay's poem " If We Must Die ":

If we must die — let it not be like hogs
Hunted and penned in an inglorious spot,
While round us bark the mad and hungry dogs,
Making their mock at our accursed lot.
If we must die — oh, let us nobly die,
So that our precious blood may not be shed
In vain; then even the monsters we defy
Shall be constrained to honor us though dead!

Oh, kinsmen! We must meet the common foe;
Though far outnumbered, let us still be brave,
And for their thousand blows deal one death-blow!
What though before us lies the open grave!

Like men we'll face the murderous, cowardly pack,
Pressed to the wall, dying, but — fighting back! [28]

In this whole literature of protest and rebellion, there is
an impressively large amount which has kinship with the
ethical insight of religion in its highest prophetic eras. In
all of it there is an inescapable challenge to religion to make
its resources available for the crying needs of life.

[1] *The Twentieth Century Novel,* by J. W. Beach. The Century Company.
[2] The Nation, New York, 1923.
[3] *The Profits of Religion,* by Upton Sinclair, pp. 291–292. Vanguard Press.
[4] *Nine Plays,* by Eugene O'Neill, p. 48. Random House.
[5] By permission of Ralph Fletcher Seymour, Chicago.
[6] *Chicago Poems,* by Carl Sandburg, p. 6. Henry Holt & Company.
[7] *Smoke and Steel,* by Carl Sandburg. Harcourt, Brace & Company.
[8] By permission of the author.
[9] By permission of the author.
[10] *Eighty Songs at Eighty,* by Edwin Markham. Doubleday, Doran & Company.
[11] Used by permission of the author.
[12] *Children of the Night,* by Edwin Arlington Robinson. Charles Scribner's Sons.
[13] *The Buck in the Snow,* by Edna St. Vincent Millay. Harper & Brothers.
[14] *Portraits and Protests,* by Sarah N. Cleghorn. Henry Holt & Company.
[15] The Christian Century, May 6, 1931.
[16] The New Freeman. By permission of the author.
[17] The Christian Century.
[18] "This Year of Our Lord," from *Look to the Lightning.* Dodd, Mead & Company.
[19] *Jews without Money,* by Michael Gold. Liveright Publishing Corporation.
[20] Ibid.
[21] Ibid.
[22] *We the People,* by Elmer Rice. Coward-McCann Company.
[23] The New Outlook, Nov. 1932.
[24] Harper's Magazine, June 1933.
[25] The Survey Graphic, July 1933.
[26] By permission of the author.
[27] *Fine Clothes to the Jew.* Alfred A. Knopf, Inc.
[28] *Harlem Shadows,* by Claude McKay. Harcourt, Brace & Company.

CHAPTER TEN

TRENDS IN CRITICISM

AT the close of the Spanish-American War, in the exaltation of the first flush of the adventure of the United States in imperialism, Richard Hovey addressed these lines to " Unmanifest Destiny ":

> There is a Hand that bends our deeds
>   To mightier issues than we planned;
> Each son that triumphs, each that bleeds,
>   My country, serves Its dark commands.

> I do not know beneath what sky
>   Nor on what seas shall be thy fate;
> I only know it shall be high,
>   I only know it shall be great.[1]

Sixteen years later, in 1914, another poet, a much greater one, Edwin Arlington Robinson, addressed his country in a very different tone and speech, in a poem bearing the ominous title *Cassandra*. In that poem Robinson records Cassandra's accusation that America's only word was the dollar, and that the dollar's wrath was its only fear.

The contrast between these two poems may be fairly taken as an indication of the changed temper which criticism in American literature has undergone since the early years of the twentieth century. Indeed, there is more than a change to be recorded. The years from 1910 to 1930 have been marked by what is virtually a new type of criticism, only very faintly evidenced in the years preceding. It is a realistic evaluation of American life in the light of freshly applied social, political and moral standards. It has escaped from the fog of a mystical trust that, whatever America does, its fate will be " high and great." In fact, in most part it is quite confident that, unless radical changes are made, its confident voyage will end on the rocks.

That contrast is made clear, in this year of the vaunted Century of Progress Exposition in Chicago, by recalling the lyric romanticism of Harriet Monroe's " Columbian Ode," 1893:

> Columbia! Men behold thee rise
>   A goddess from the misty sea.
> Lady of joy, sent from the skies,
>   The nations worshiped thee.
> Thy brows were flushed with dawn's first light,
> By foamy ways the stars bedight
>   Thy blue robe floated free.[2]

Contrast this worship of Columbia, " Lady of joy, sent from the skies," with the chorus of derision which has greeted the irony of a " Century of Progress " in 1933, where the uncatalogued exhibit of a city looted, bankrupt, with unpaid school teachers, with a fifth of its population in need of public relief, is more striking than the advertised show. " Columbia, the gem of the ocean " is no longer the sacred anthem of American criticism.

No department of literature has shown greater growth or change in twenty years than that generally included under the classification of " criticism." From Randolph Bourne's

Youth and Life, 1911, and John Macy's *The Spirit of American Literature,* 1913, down to Calverton's *The Liberation of American Literature,* 1932, there has been the ferment of new ideas, the clash of battle between the iconoclasts and defenders of tradition. The largest part of this literature lies beyond the scope of the concern of the present volume. It can be dealt with in only a very limited manner. No exploration, however, no matter how superficial, of the relation between literature and religion in the present day, could overlook certain features and consequences of trends in criticism. Aspects of that relationship may be considered under four general lines of influence.

Literary criticism of the present day is much more concerned with life than that of earlier generations. It is not restricted to the examination of books. Thus it has emerged into the wider area of the life of which the books are a product, thereby entering the field with which religion is also primarily concerned.

A vigorous, independent, realistic evaluation of tradition and the status quo has developed, a revolt from the conventions of genteel literature and from the codes and traditions which have created and upheld the economic order. These latter, of course, have been so deeply intertwined with the religious orthodoxy that the effect of much of this movement in criticism has been an undermining not only of traditional religion but often of all religious belief. On the other hand, the skeptical spirit directed against the intrenchments of privilege, against the hypocrisies inherent in the standing order, against the social results of chaotic profit seeking, have contributed enormously to clear the way for the ethical reconstruction of society which must be a primary concern for any religion which aspires to be a molding force in the life of its time.

Much of the criticism which includes life as well as literature for its field has brought to bear on the examination of life far more thorough-going ethical standards and criteria than have ever before been applied in history. This judgment may fairly be applied to the work of writers so widely different in their field of work and point of view as Van Wyck Brooks, James Truslow Adams, Henry Seidel Canby, Stuart Chase, Stuart P. Sherman, Charles A. Beard, to name but a few from a large number. This has made a contribution of large importance to the spiritual assets of American life.

On the other hand, there is not to be overlooked the pervasive effect of a widely ranging re-examination of tradition. That effect has been suggested above — the effect on many readers subversive of all definite religious belief and faith.

I

Van Wyck Brooks' *America Comes of Age,* 1917, played a large part in giving a new quality and direction to literary criticism and establishing that type of criticism which dealt with life as well as its literary interpretation. It was a torpedo directed at the school of the genteel tradition which had so long dominated criticism as well as fiction and poetry. His main attack was on the ethical dualism which ran through so much of life, particularly on the way in which this dualism was perpetuated by an education which proclaimed ideals and did not provide for their being expressed in acts and institutions. Brooks found in the average baccalaureate sermon the symbol for the ethical and social chaos of American life.   It dealt, he said, with lofty idealisms which had no connection with prevailing practice.   The popular literature, Brooks maintained, was made for the American whose sole educational bill of fare was " a sort of orgy of lofty examples, moralized poems, national anthems and baccalaureate sermons."   This, by the way, was the same criticism made by Mr. Mencken's description of the culture of the politicians: " What they know of sound literature is what they got out of McGuffey's Fifth Reader."   Brooks' forceful criticism of the ethics of a profit-dominated society is felt all through *America Comes of Age* and his recent *Sketches in Criticism,* 1932.   In the former volume, a key-note is to be found in his description of the typical American. He says: " He has been encouraged to assume that the world was a stamping-ground for every greedy and aggressive impulse in him; that, in short, society is fair play for what he can get out of it."   In *Sketches in Criticism,* writing of some latter day historians, doubtless with James Ford Rhodes in mind, he thus pictures the futility of a criticism which is remote in experience and understanding from the economic and social realities of the time:

" Latter day historians (Parkman and Prescott are in quite a different category) grew up in a world in which dollars and cents, and the infantile romanticism that issues from the same mint, were the sole desideratum.   They consumed the newspapers, interviewed the great financiers that they met at their clubs, visited the political conventions, and now and then, to get a breath of the bustling activity, to prove to themselves that they were not mere Scribes and that ' manifest destiny ' was really coming off, they took a trip through the Great Lakes or down the Mississippi.   They prate for the business men . . . and the business men occasionally snatched a moment to enjoy the casual pleasure of perceiving that history approved of them and their children." [3]

That is a modern parallel to the Hebrew prophet's cry — "My people are destroyed for lack of knowledge." Brooks did much to supply that lack.

This weighing of American life on new balances was a desperately needed service, if freedom from the hypocrisies and self-deceptions which enveloped the land was to be obtained and any real understanding of ethical realities was to be won. This pointed criticism found expression in various authors such as Lewis Mumford in *The Golden Day,* 1926, and *Sticks and Stones,* 1924; Waldo Frank, *Our America,* 1919, and *The Rediscovery of America,* 1929; James Truslow Adams in *Our Business Civilization,* 1929; and in the work of such very different men as Stuart Chase, Elmer Davis, Vernon L. Parrington, George Soule, Lincoln Steffens. To such a company belongs much of the credit for breaking up what Matthew Arnold justly called " the American rhapsody of self-praise." The timeliness of such a body of critical work and its possible service, are thus put by Mr. Brooks:

" The recent damming up of our social energies through the closing of the frontier at the West and the slackening of immigration at the East enables us really for the first time to submit to a candid scrutiny our prepossessions in regard to property and every other fundamental issue, to desire a great and beautiful corporate life." [4]

II

Of a very different sort, and yet with interesting relationship, has been the work of the most widely read critic of the twentieth century in the United States, H. L. Mencken. His production has been enormous, his twenty published volumes being only a small part of his writing. His vogue, though passing or passed, has been great, his influence extensive. Mencken's savage gusto in attacking what he did not like, his contempt, his joyous onslaught on religion, have made it impossible for a large number of people to see him in any other rôle than as the Devil's vicar general. It is hard to tell whether assigning to Mr. Mencken any place on the side of the angels would irritate his antagonists more than it would him. Yet any audit of his services to his time must include achievements of far-reaching social and spiritual value. No one could possibly whirl as wicked a slingshot on the public thoroughfare for twenty-five years as Mencken has done without hitting some things and people whose laying low must be counted as meritorious service in the army of the Lord. Consider what public enemies he has charged with a vicious onslaught: the oracular hokum of "big business"; the hypocrisy of the laudation of "service"; the prostitution of religion as variously practiced by religious organizations; the sheep-like gullibility of so many Americans; the viciousness of hundred per cent Americanism. That in the puncturing of so many shams he attacked many genuine idealisms does not minimize the value of his blows to such a collection of bogus respectabilities. As the typical exponent of the post-war reaction away from idealism, as the most daring bold, bad gunman of a consciously bold, bad generation, Mencken attained a wide following. Van Wyck Brooks has pointed out that his criticism seems so exceptionally savage because Americans had been in the habit of always having their fur stroked the right way.

His waning influence is due to many factors, including

the change of intellectual climate; but, most of all, to the fact that he had only one act and that act went stale. There is no trace of any growth in his ideas; he took very little trouble even to rearrange them. Mencken is the American Punch and Judy show. The fury of his lambasting is diverting sport, whether he has in hand the clergyman, the professor or the Rotarian. But after the audience has seen the performance two or three thousand times it begins to get a rough idea, at least in its broad aspects, of how the thing works. " Boob-thumping" had its obvious limitations.

The value of his criticism has suffered greatly from its entirely negative character. It has been pointed out that he continually leans against the thing he attacks; withdraw it and he has nothing positive of his own to stand on. Another fatal weakness in a decade turning increasingly to analysis of the economic basis of society, his almost naïve lack of any thoroughgoing knowledge of economic realities, caused a great deflation in his prestige as a prophet. His ambitious treatment of religion, *Treatise on the Gods,* carried him far out of his depth, his analysis of religion as the product of fear and the chicanery of priestcraft being much more clearly the indulgence of a grudge than any serious contribution to the subject.

Probably the most exciting literary prize-fight of the last twenty years was the long battle between Mencken and Stuart Sherman, for many years professor in the University of Illinois and for the last two years of his life editor of " Books," the literary supplement of the New York Tribune. Sherman gained his fame as the opponent of " naturalism " in fiction, the defender of standards in literature, and a vigorous champion of Puritanism. His interpretation of

Puritanism, as opposed to the stock caricature, was that of the Puritan as the historic liberal non-conformist in many realms. The Puritan, according to Sherman, was marked by " dissatisfaction with the past, the courage to break with it, readiness to accept discipline in order to attain a nobler life, and a serious desire to make the better life prevail." Sherman's appreciation of the best in tradition, of the place of discipline in life, of the relation of happiness to discipline, was a notable contribution to the thinking of his generation.

III

A movement in criticism in recent years which has a close relation to religion is that known as literary " humanism." The two chief leaders in the movement, Professors Irving Babbitt of Harvard and Paul Elmer More of Princeton, had been writing and teaching for a generation, exerting a strong influence on a limited circle of those who accepted their general positions. In 1929 they attracted a much wider attention from the general reading public by the emergence of a definite movement for humanism, which created quite a stir, sharp if temporary, in literary circles. The chief record of this controversy is to be found in two volumes giving the opposing sides in the controversy, *Humanism and America,* edited by Norman Foerster, 1930, made up of contributions by a dozen humanists, including Babbitt and More; and *The Critique of Humanism,* a collection of essays by antagonists to the school of literary humanism, edited by C. Hartley Grattan and including Lewis Mumford and Burton Rascoe.

Humanism has undoubtedly suffered greatly from the lack of a clear and accepted definition. All through the discussion there has been on the part of the humanist a struggle for a definition. This is due in part to the fact that humanism is an attitude to life and literature rather than a formulated creed. In general, humanism has pleaded the cause of " the centuries against the hours "; it has contended for standards and control of appetites against the chaos and license of naturalism; it sets up as a standard the enduring values of the two great traditions of the Western world, the Greek and the Christian. Professor Babbitt emphasizes poise and proportion in his attempt at definition in *Humanism and America:* " Humanism has two main meanings — an historical meaning in its application to the scholars who turned away from the Middle Ages to the Greeks and Romans; and a psychological meaning, as one may say, that derives directly from the historical one: humanists in this latter sense are those who, in any age, aim at proportionateness through a cultivation of the law of measure." [5] Perhaps as satisfactory an untechnical description as any of the central attitude of humanism is to be found in the words of one of its ablest and most appreciative interpreters, Professor Percy H. Boynton of the University of Chicago: " Humanism stands for controls, balances, standards of life. It would have man cultivate his humanity, those traits that make him different from the other animals. It would have him cultivate poise by moderate and decorous living. It would have him normal, if the word can be defined. The humanists want a harmonious development of body, mind and, in the case of the religious humanists, soul." [6]

In this whole attitude and point of view there is much that is central in theistic religion and in the standards of conduct inherent in Hebrew and Christian religious tradition. Literary humanists have been contending for many of the values associated with religion, whether they have labeled themselves religious humanists or not. Mr. More has taken definitely to the position that religion is necessary as a support for humanism in its contention against naturalism. Mr. Babbitt in recent years, in more guarded terms, has inclined to the same view. "Humanism," he says, "may work in harmony with traditional religion. In that case there must be a careful determination of boundaries. Though humanism and religion both lie on the same ascending path from the naturalistic flux, one must insist that each has its separate domain. It is an error to hold that humanism can take the place of religion. Religion indeed may more readily dispense with humanism than humanism with religion. Humanism gains greatly by having a religious background in the sense that I have indicated; whereas religion, for the man who has actually renounced the world, may very conceivably be all in all." [7]

The influence of the literary humanist movement as a school no doubt suffered greatly from the confusion created by the simultaneous advent of " non-theistic humanism " in the theological field of interest. The discussion which this movement stirred up, in a sense, " stole the show " from the other type of humanism.

One of the most serious criticisms of the humanist position, and of the whole school led by Babbitt and More, has been its lack of any sense of economic realities. It has been remote from an interest in and understanding of the economic and social forces which condition existence for millions of people. The whole school has definite resemblances to a cultured company of scholars debating philosophy and classic literature in a cloister, well walled-in from the tragedy of modern civilization. It is like a beautiful ivory tower, around the base of which wind breadlines of the victims of a modern industrial civilization who rarely get into the range of vision of the serene scholars at the top of the tower.

IV

Among the forces which have affected the thinking of the period are what may be called the " new history " and the vogue of biography, following, in most cases afar off, the model set by Lytton Strachey. History dealing with the social conditions and economic influences as being far more vital in the record of humanity than superficial political and military narrative, has made large contribution to the attitude of critical realism, including the work of such historians as Frederick J. Turner, Charles A. Beard, Carl Becker, James Harvey Robinson, Sidney B. Fay. The influence of Spengler, even when his dogmatic theory of cycles of doom is not accepted, has undoubtedly made for a pessimistic view of history and civilization. His conception of history as a living organism and the attempt to show by analogy that our Western culture must pass through the same stages that all growth goes through, those of youth, maturity, old age and death, presents a strong counteractive to romantic optimism. One lasting value of Spengler's influence has been his demonstration that the World War was not a case of mass murder but collective suicide.

Another influence has been the development of a type of literary criticism and history which traces the relation between the environment and background and the literature of a period. This has taken literature out of a social vacuum, where it had frequently been put, and placed it in the soil from which it grew. Van Wyck Brooks was a pioneer in this fruitful type of criticism. Vernon L. Parrington made notable use of it in his three volumes of *Main Currents in American Thought*. This method of criticism has recently been exemplified in significant volumes such as Lewisohn's *Expression in America* and Blankenship's *American Literature*. A significant recent volume is the economic interpretation of American literature supplied by V. F. Calverton in his *Liberation of American Literature*. It is a book notable not only as the first Marxian interpretation of American literature but for much shrewd and original comment. It illustrates, however, much muscular forcing of two centuries of literature into the narrow bed of an economic formula and interpretation. " The bed is shorter than a man can stretch himself in." A more recent and very suggestive treatment of American literature from the Marxian viewpoint is Granville Hicks' *The Great Tradition,* 1933.

On any list of the most important books of the generation, no matter who made it up, would be Lincoln Steffens' *Autobiography*. In a very real sense it is a pilgrimage of America, not, alas, into a Promised Land, but at any rate through many defeated hopes and trusts and through many comforting illusions. Beginning newspaper life from the background of specialized study in ethics, Steffens went through the chief movements of his time. Like many others he " fought for reform in a faith that the machine had not upset the processes of democracy." That faith he was forced to give up. From the romantic idealism of the West into which he was born, he went through progressive disillusion.

He was inspired with hope of change during his muck-raking era, still feeling that to put good men in office would bring an end to corruption. With extended experience he found evil intrenched at a deeper level than that of office-holding, and came to complete despair of any real transformation without a change in the basic economic order, obliterating the corrupting power of wealth and profit.

V

Allied to this literature of criticism, in effect and to some extent in spirit, has been the production during the last few years of satire in the form of drama. Satire, as opposed to comedy or farce, had been almost wholly absent from the American theater before the war. Since that time there has been a group of satirical dramas, serious in intent and effective in execution, indicative of a new spirit of skepticism toward many sacred cows of popular veneration. Some of the best work of Elmer Rice, Maxwell Anderson, Marc Connelly and George S. Kaufman, and John Howard Lawson has been done in this type of drama.

To the Ladies, 1922, by George S. Kaufman and Marc Connelly, contained rollicking ridicule of the solemn hokum of big business, including its pretensions of reward of service in decorating with a bronze button an employe for twenty years of faithful service! *The Beggar on Horseback,* 1924, by the same authors, is a spirited and humorous attack on the superstitions of business. Rice's *Adding Machine,* 1923, was an impressionistic drama of what has come to be known as "technological employment," with its resulting human tragedies. The mass of hypocritical pretense and inanity in the motion picture business is caricatured in Harry Leon Wilson's *Merton of the Movies,* 1922, and Kaufman's *Once in a Life Time,* 1931. *Of Thee I Sing,* 1931, Kaufman and Ryskind's satirical play dealing with politics, is more of a farce than a satire. Underneath its horseplay however there is a withering criticism of politics. Maxwell Anderson's *Both Your Houses,* 1933, is a real drama, not a farce; restrained in tone, biting in its satire. It pictures the ruthless brigandage of legislatures, in following the fortunes of an appropriations bill through both houses of Congress. It is significant of the spirit of the times that these two latter plays received the Pulitzer Prize for drama.

This whole critical movement since the war has been performing a function which historically often has been and always ought to be a function of a vital religious group — that of a critical minority. It is a rôle played by first-century Christianity before it degenerated into the official religion of the majority. It is a rôle which organized religion must play if it is to be a real factor in the ethical and spiritual life of the future.

[1] Small, Maynard & Company.

[2] "Columbian Ode," by Harriet Monroe. The Macmillan Company.

[3] *America Comes of Age,* by Van Wyck Brooks. E. P. Dutton & Company, 1917.

[4] *Sketches in Criticism,* by Van Wyck Brooks. E. P. Dutton & Company.

[5] *Humanism and America,* edited by Norman Foerster, p. 30. Farrar & Rinehart.

[6] *The Challenge of Modern Criticism,* by Percy H. Boynton, p. 12. Thomas S. Rockwell & Company.

[7] *Humanism and America,* edited by Norman Foerster. Farrar & Rinehart.

Chapter Eleven

THE SEARCH FOR GOD

THERE is an aphorism of Coleridge which deserves remembrance whenever the attempt is made to single out the characteristic features, literary or social, of any era: "Make any truth too definite and you make it too small." There is always danger of so emphasizing those novel developments of a literary period which make a contrast with the preceding decades that the result is a false sense of simplicity. The truth is thus made too definite and too small. This caution is particularly needed in any effort to estimate the relative interest in religion in the post-war era in the United States. Manifestly, it could not be called an age of faith. Yet too selective an attention devoted to the many evidences of the breakdown of authority and skepticism concerning traditional values may easily give a distorted and false impression. The misleading conclusion may be that these mental attitudes are much more widespread than they have actually been and that interest in questions of ultimate reality has been put under a moratorium.

Any fairly extensive and impartial examination of the literature of the last fifteen years will readily correct such a judgment, particularly if the attention is given less to names and traditional labels, and more to actual experiences, to the states of mind which lie beneath all labels and which

do not fit into standardized theological pigeon-holes, to aspirations which come from unsatisfied spiritual needs.
When these are weighed it becomes evident that men have
not forsworn interest in those questions which have occupied their minds through all recorded history. There will
be found emphatic evidence that, amid all other trends and
moods manifested, the interest in God, the wistful outreach
for God, the quest for God, the " experiment which becomes
an experience," has gone steadily on. It marks some of the
notable literature of these years.

I

This is indicated in the words of one who certainly cannot be called a partisan witness, Irwin Edman: " There is
probably no epithet more unfashionable in contemporary
discourse than the word soul, no theme less congenial to the
current imagination than salvation. . . . Yet the concerns
of the contemporary are precisely what those of his ancestors
were, the soul and its salvation." [1] Even more emphatic is
the comment made in an address at Columbia University, in
the summer of 1932, by Professor Dennis Saurat, of the University of London, discussing the waning of the mode of
cynical literature: " Among the various faculties of the human soul, such as reason, passion, imagination, this modern
school lays the emphasis on sensation; but among all the
sensations it happens sometimes that there is one in particular which seems to have an eternal value; that is, the sensation of God."

What Professor Saurat calls " the sensation of God " has
not been absent from contemporary experience. Bearing on

this is the significant fact that within the field of religious thought there has been a marked swing of interest away from the periphery of incidental and minor questions to the central theological question — God. God has become the dominant issue of religion. The questions of Biblical criticism, the niceties of exact doctrinal formulation, have paled before the looming of one supreme issue — " What kind of God, if any, can we believe in ? " This freshened interest has been intensely stimulated by the vigorous questioning of the validity and rationality of theistic belief. The new emphasis has come about as a result of a situation similar to that which Macaulay observed nearly a century ago concerning Christian missions in India. " What is the use," he exclaimed, " of discussing close communion with a man who has been in the habit of worshiping a cow? " The present parallel to that exclamation is, " What is the use of refinements on theological sidelines in a generation wondering whether it can continue to believe in any God at all? " Allied to this has been a growing discernment, in liberal theological circles, of the weakness of what has been called an " arid liberalism " deficient in passion and theistic conviction. If the present moment is marked, as it seems strongly to be in the political field, by a recognition of the weakness of a tepid liberalism, there has been also a rather widespread feeling of the religious inadequacy of a rather complacent theological liberalism, which has stemmed more from the romantic evolutionary optimism of the nineteenth century than from the religious realism of the New Testament. Generalization on such a long parade as that included in the term " the church " is notoriously dangerous. But there have been many in the church who have asked the question, " What shall it profit a church to gain a whole world of broad-mindedness and urbane liberal opinion and lose its own life, its sense of the momentousness of its message of God? " In the words of Miles H. Krumbine, " We have disinfected religion from superstition, only to discover that man cannot live on disinfectants." Many have discovered also that a thin trickle of sociology is a poor substitute for God.

Preliminary to a glimpse of both the negative and positive forms of this interest in the central theme of religion, there is a certain change in intellectual and emotional climate, within the last five or six years, which ought to be noted as important background. It is intangible, not subject to exact measurement or definition, yet genuine and pervasive and highly important for the immediate future of religious thought, belief and life.

II

This climatic change has been referred to in the opening chapter of this book as the relative exhaustion of the predominant fashion of cynicism, disillusion, the exaltation of freedom, frequently conceived as license, satisfaction with mere negations. One reason is the advent of another generation following that which experienced the war, a generation which has had a chance to observe the meager results in happiness and fulfilment which the mental fashions of the preceding generation brought. This fresh interest in positive convictions and endeavors has made itself strongly felt in both life and literature. It is strongly marked on the college campus, for instance. If prosperity has not been discovered around the corner in the early 'thirties, at least a new seriousness has. This is gauged in the comment of one who has taught undergraduates at Columbia University for the fifteen years since 1918, Irwin Edman:

"The most striking fact to the observer is the resemblance — with a difference soon to be noted — between the generation that was at college just before and during the war and the generation that is now at college during the Great Depression. For the first time in twenty years, almost every undergraduate who thinks at all is thinking once more in terms of the future of the society in which he is going to live and, if possible, to earn his living. It makes almost no difference what is the center of his intellectual interests — poetry or philosophy, languages or medicine. If he is in any direction intellectually alive, he is deeply concerned, and often articulately so, with what is going to happen in a civilization whose traditional values — indeed, whose economic bases — are going to pieces, or at least are passing into fundamental transformation under his very eyes.

"This is by way of saying that the present generation of undergraduates, like their predecessors of twenty years ago, are becoming amateur social scientists or social propagandists or social prophets. In the intervening years, for reasons familiar in the outside world (reasons generally summed up as the post-war reaction), undergraduates were sidetracked into various forms of diversion or despair. The esthetes, the retreating high intellectuals, the counselors of escape, the luxurious wallowers in nihilism and grief, for a while had it all their own way. The voices of all these are heard very faintly, if at all, on the campus today." [2]

Professor Edman's interpretation has been paralleled by that of a score of other observers. Dr. H. S. Canby, for instance, on the basis of observation of the same tendencies predicts a definite swing back to morality, not of narrow Puritanism but of sane purpose. Predicting a new emphasis in literature, he says: "Man will begin to mean more; his adventures, less. Morality will begin to mean more than morale, and may get a new definition. The ego, having passed through the laboratory and been dressed and undressed in every street, will once more become an instrument by which we strive to attain an ideal, although that ideal may differ widely from the ideals popular in books on the will to power, in boy-scout meetings, and the college Y.M.C.A." [3]

It is no matter for wonder that the pendulum is decidedly swinging toward positives. Lest it seem that this assertion is mere wishful thinking, admit into the evidence the testimony of Harry Hansen, a competent observer of the literary world: " The central fact in American literature at the beginning of the 1930's is the complete bankruptcy of the naturalistic movement. Its proud assurance is gone. It has finally made revolt conventional and uninteresting. It is breaking up in disillusionment and futilitarianism. It is on the defensive, betraying its disorder in a continuous series of petty counter-attacks against the advancing force of a movement toward human standards." This truth that life cannot sustain itself on negatives, on poses, or on mere rebellion, has been put amusingly, but with a grim sincerity, by a popular novelist in a letter to a friend: " One can't go on forever being a bright, or smart, naughty young thing. One has to find a direction or fake one."

This change in mode and mood is not to be taken as indication of any religious revival, in the conventional sense. It is not evidence of definite religious belief. But it does make for a temper of mind and an attitude in which positive spiritual values have a far greater chance of fair consideration.

III

This new mood has found many reflections in literature. For one thing there has been a real return to romance as a reaction of a decade of literary sadism.

For several years the contention that fiction must deal with the hard ugly facts of life in a spirit hard and joyless, ruled as tyrannically as the dressmakers' ukase on the length of skirts. As Dorothy Canfield describes it humorously:

" In this, our little period of history, filled with hate and scorn and fear and restlessness as it is, most of the well-written books are naturally those which express hate and scorn and fear and restlessness. To be bitterly, sickly, helplessly dissatisfied with the background of your life, wherever it is laid, is the fashion now, just as in the romantic period of a century ago, tragic and frustrated young love was the fashion. And fashions are infinitely more tyrannical than laws. To conceive of human life as (what it is in many cases) a sordid trap into which inexorable instincts betray hapless men and women to their doom, is a convention of our time that belongs with the unquestioned tabus of table manners." [4]

A break in that standardization was manifested in the great success of such novels as Thornton Wilder's *The Bridge of San Luis Rey*, Elizabeth Maddox Roberts' *The Time of Man*, and Stephen Vincent Benet's poem, *John Brown's Body;* in Leonard Erlich's novel dealing with John Brown, *God's Angry Man;* in such popular fiction as the novels of Walter D. Edwards' *Rome Haul* and *Erie Water*. There has been a growing feeling that what often passed as realism was only a segment, when even that, of reality. It is felt in the passing of the vogue of the debunking biography. There is a renewed interest in the serious effort to understand a man rather than to enjoy a sensational presentation made up of equal parts of fiction, fact and Freud.

A recent cartoon in Punch reflects and, to a degree, explains the change in literary taste. A little girl is shown begging her short-skirted, cigarette-smoking mother to tell her a story "about the time when there weren't any Old Beans, but just ladies and gentlemen."

IV

The problems of ultimate reality, of the existence and nature of God, have been discussed largely in philosophical and religious works which are not included under creative literature. There are two outstanding books however which, in both style and theme, are much more definitely " literature " in the more technical sense than most discussions of ethics and philosophy. These are Walter Lippmann's *Preface to Morals,* 1929, and Joseph Wood Krutch's *The Modern Temper,* 1929. These may be taken as outstanding examples of the serious discussion of religious themes, and strong challenges to theistic faith.

For several years following the publication of these two books, Lippmann and Krutch were given the spotlight of continuous discussion in sermons, lectures, books and magazine articles. In 1931 the president of an Eastern university said to the preacher at a Sunday morning chapel service that there was something strange about the morning sermon, which marked it off from nearly every sermon delivered in the chapel for a year — there had been no mention of either Lippmann or Krutch! Both books are marked by high seriousness, a strong sense of the importance of religious faith,

however impossible faith may appear to the authors to be
for the modern man, and penetrating criticism of many contemporary trends in thinking.

A Preface to Morals has become almost a modern classic
in its delineation of the dissolving of traditional religious and
moral codes and authorities by science and the modes of life
which have come from the progress of science. Lippmann's
very phrase for this dissolving, " the acids of modernity," has
eaten its way deeply into the contemporary mind. Lippmann is primarily concerned with the possibility of finding
a sanction and support for the good way of life without the
authority of religion, which for his thinking has hopelessly
crumbled away never to be erected again as a bulwark of
moral life. The strong feeling of a certain constant nobility
of spirit and elevation of point of view is enhanced by the
author's emphatic contention for the indispensable values of
morality, of the good life. He feels that a religious authority
for morality can no longer be found, that faith in a personal
God is impossible for the modern intellectual. But he differs
from a host of antagonists of religion in that to his mind such
a conclusion is nothing to give a party over. Unlike many,
he does not wind the Maypole in the village green over the
loss of religion. Its disappearance leaves a lonesome place
against the sky, an emptiness which has not yet been filled.
He sees that mere freedom in itself is an empty boon, an illusion more trivial than the " majestic faith " which it has
displaced with many people. He thus pictures the anti-
climax which freedom, as an end of existence, makes:

" The evidence of these greater difficulties lies all about us: in the
brave and brilliant atheists who have defied the Methodist God and
have become very nervous; in the women who have emancipated

themselves from the tyranny of fathers, husbands and homes and, with the intermittent but expensive help of psycho-analysts, are now able to endure liberty as interior decorators; in the multitudes who drug themselves with pleasure; in the young men and young women who are world-weary at twenty-two; in the crowds enfranchised by the blood of heroes who cannot be persuaded to take an interest in their destiny; in the millions now free to think without fear of priest or policeman who have made the moving pictures and the popular newspapers what they are." [5]

As a more adequate substitute for discredited religious faith in laying a foundation for the good life, Mr. Lippmann presents an ethic of disciplined freedom which is not very different from a severe type of stoicism, consisting in " a noble spirit of disinterestedness," " modern humanism," and what he calls " high religion," — the latter being the insight of the " sages both past and present."

Lippmann criticizes acutely both the pleasure-philosophy and the mood of despair which have marked his time. The ideal of conduct which he presents is a noble one and in its ideal of the mature and disciplined personality it has elements which have been stressed by Stoic and Christian teaching.

It is no part of the purpose of the present volume to deal with the philosophy of religion or to attempt any evaluation of Lippmann's long argument. *A Preface to Morals* finds place here as probably the outstanding literary expression, since the war, of the critical rejection of theistic faith. Some pertinent criticisms that have been made, however, may be noted in passing. The Christian faith which Lippmann discusses is that of literalist tradition. The liberal faith of Dr. Fosdick evidently bothers him, for it does not fit with so much neatness into his theory that religious faith is impossible for the educated modern. So long as Mr. Lippmann conceives of Christian faith as a belief in a God continually interfering with nature, it is a comparatively easy task to show that the day of such a faith is over. Mr. Lippmann can and does show that when the belief in a personal God is tied up to such a traditional belief it must be given up. What he evades is dealing with a religious faith in which a non-scientific world-view has no part whatever. Lippmann's moral ideal is a high one, but aristocratic and cold. It gives little promise as an appeal to any large number of people or as an adequate motive power for moral living. As the criticism of the English essayist, Robert Lynd, points out: " There are men who can live noble lives in such a faith as this, and who are content to peer no further into the ulti- mate mysteries. But to most men it will be as unsatisfying a creed as Fundamentalism itself, for amid all his real and superficial changes, man is still, both in his religious and in his irreligious instincts, very much what he was in other centuries." [6]

The ideal man which Lippmann constructs is a hollow figure, lacking in intense feelings of any sort. The com- placency of his ideal figure strikingly appears in the follow- ing picture of the serene moral aristocrat: " Since nothing gnawed at his vitals, neither doubt, nor ambition, nor frus- tration, nor fear, he would move easily through life. And so whether he saw the thing as comedy, or high tragedy, or plain farce, he would affirm that it is what it is, and that the wise man can enjoy it." Can anyone fail to see that the picture of the wise man calmly enjoying " the high tragedy " of life seems a bit unreal?

Lippmann seems most unreal when he is giving voice to

his naïve faith that capitalism will socialize itself automatically. Consider these words in the light of the tragic history of the five years which have passed since they were written: " Modern business is so complex that it has to generate its own inner control; it is too massive for either the dictator or our democratic law-makers." " It is my impression that when machine industry reaches a certain scale of complexity it exerts such pressure upon the men who run it that they cannot help socializing it. . . . It puts a premium on men whose characters are sufficiently matured to make them respect reality and discount their own prejudices." [7]

The answer which the recent history of modern business makes to that beautiful optimism is a vulgar but emphatic " Oh yeah? " It reads more like Grimm's fairy tales than any reality of the actual world.

Krutch's *The Modern Temper* carries through with rigorous honesty the implications of a view of the world stripped of all absolute values, to their logical extreme of despair. He has drawn perhaps the most complete and impressive picture of the ultimate conclusion of an entirely negative philosophy which has been given to this generation. He sees himself as a representative modern intellectual who has " weighed and rejected the moral, esthetic and other values of his predecessors," and who finds only in " the pursuit of knowledge that which makes life worth living." He allows no ray of light to stray into his sun-proof world. He writes of " the successive and increasingly desperate expedients by means of which man, the ambitious animal, endeavors to postpone the inevitable realization that living is merely a physiological process with only a physiological meaning, that it is most satisfactorily conducted by creatures who never feel the need to attempt to give it any other." (The fallacious quality of this type of thinking has been pointed out by H. A. Overstreet who observes that Krutch's statement that " living is a physiological phenomenon," being an evaluation, is in itself much more than physiological). Krutch examines the great human trinity of love, honor and nobility and considers them all illusions. Love is merely a " biological function." Honor and nobility correspond to nothing in the real world. Yet all through the book is recorded the author's sure sense of the tragedy of his own conclusions. It is that, more than anything else, which gives to the book its importance and its pathos. Here is no exultant atheism; no superficial acceptance of science as a more than adequate substitute for religion. Krutch is as dissatisfied with science and liberal philosophy as supports for life as with religious orthodoxy. Courageous but aghast he faces the ultimate dark which falls upon the world when the denial of all spiritual values has been carried to its logical conclusion.

V

When we turn from the consideration of these negations of religious faith to tentative aspirations or more positive expressions, especially in poetry, we are confronted by the fact that much of it could not be included in any church hymnal. Those who identify religion with its historical theological formulations, those who allow no room for growth and change beneath which the essential religious spirit remains unchanged, will find difficulty in discovering much religion in contemporary poetry (as distinguished from that large body of verse loosely called " religious poetry " which is not here considered at all). Yet one who looks for the experience itself will find the very stuff of religion. Canon Charles E. Raven writes: " The basic element in religion is the sense of reality that is outside ourselves and is not relative but absolute, of values which carry compelling assent, of something fixed and eternal, abiding while all else may change and giving to the transient its worth." If that, rather than the acceptance of a creed, be religion, modern poetry has found in religion one of its frequent themes.

The religious element in contemporary poetry is, of course, varied in tone. It ranges all the way from questioning and skepticism to exultant faith.

Painful doubt, a sense of loss in the passing of faith and a stoic resignation in carrying on life without it, have found frequent expression. The problem which suffering brings to faith is thus put with a whimsical turn by Kathleen Millay. It bears the ironical title " Now I Lay Me ":

> Tell me, God, if you were I,
> Lying sick upon your bed,
> Crying while the night ticks round,
> Quivering cold at every sound,
> Burning hot and fever bound —
> Longing to be dead
> Upon your tortured bed!
> Wondering why you cannot die,
> Beat the night and wonder why! —
> God in Heaven, let me die!
> Weeping to be dead —
>
> Would you think that God will care
> For every ill and every woe,

> And bend your stricken knees in prayer?
> Or would you scream your bitter " No " !
> Beat the night and answer — " No!
> He is not anywhere —
> He is not so! " [8]

Again and again in the treatment of the Arthurian legends by Edwin Arlington Robinson, in his *Lancelot and Merlin,* there is a desperate sort of resignation to a fatalism which drives mortals through the course of a life which they do not understand and from the decrees of which they cannot escape. The utmost good which they seem to be able to expect is the possible escape from the delusion of false hopes. In Robinson there is a note of skepticism which is reverential and even deeply religious in quality. It is not the complacent dogmatism of denial; it is rather groping, wonder; at times, hope. There is a stoic and resigned agnosticism in his " Children of the Night ":

> And if there be no other life,
>   And if there be no other chance
> To weigh their sorrow and their strife
>   Than in the scales of circumstance,
>
> 'Twere better, ere the sun go down
>   Upon the first day we embark,
> In life's embittered sea to drown,
>   Than sail forever in the dark.
>
> But if there be a soul on earth
>   So blinded with its own misuse
> Of man's revealed, incessant worth,
>   Or worn with anguish, that it views
>
> No light but for a mortal eye,
>   No rest but of a mortal sleep,

No god but in a prophet's lie,
  No faith for " honest doubt " to keep;

If there be nothing, good or bad,
  But chaos for a soul to trust —
God counts it for a soul gone mad,
  And if God be God, He is just.

And if God be God, He is Love;
  And though the Dawn be still so dim,
It shows us we have played enough
  With creeds that make a fiend of Him. . . .

It is the faith within the fear
  That holds us to the life we curse;
So let us in ourselves revere
  The Self which is the Universe!

Let us, the Children of the Night,
  Put off the cloak that hides the scar!
Let us be Children of the Light,
  And tell the ages what we are! [9]

A note of courageous honesty, of high spirited resignation,
a sense of values remaining even after cherished faiths have
gone, is heard in Sara Teasdale's " Leaves." This undefiant,
undogmatic skepticism, leaving a window open for possible
light, in which the heart at least is on the side of faith, as of
one with the heart in the church and the head outside, is
found in many poets. A typical example is Don Marquis'
" The God-maker, Man."

As the mind of man grows broader, so do his creeds;
And his gods they are shaped in his image and mirror his needs;
And he clothes them with thunders and beauty, he clothes them with
    music and fire;
Seeing not as he bows by their altars that he worships his own desire.

And mixed with his trust there is terror, and mixed with his madness
    is ruth,
And every man grovels in error, and every man glimpses a truth.
For all of the creeds are false, and all of the creeds are true;
And low at the shrines where my brothers bow, there will I bow, too;
For no form of a god, and no fashion
Man has made in his desperate passion,
But is worthy some worship of mine;
Neither hot with a gross belief,
Nor yet too cold with pride,
I will bow me down where my brothers bow,
Humble — but open-eyed! [10]

A different type of poetry dealing with faith is that which
expresses more positively a vague aspiration, a tentative hope,
a genuine seeking after God if haply it may find him. This
poetry is mystical, often finding intimations of God in nature, in beauty, in spiritual uplift. This vague, unformu-
lated, aspiring faith is the theme of one of the noblest poems
of the twentieth century in America, "The Falconer of
God," by William Rose Benet, closing with the lines:

Yet I fling my soul on high with new endeavor,
And I ride the world below with a joyful mind.
  I shall start a heron soon
  In the marsh beneath the moon —
A wondrous silver heron its inner darkness pledges!
    I beat forever
    The fens and the sedges.
    The pledge is still the same — for all disastrous pledges,
      All hopes resigned!
My soul still flies above me for the quarry it shall find! [11]

There are many authentic contemporary echoes of the
Psalmist's cry, "O that I knew where I might find him,"

such as are found in a typical poem of this mood, " God,"
by Gamaliel Bradford:

Day and night, I wander widely through the wilderness of thought,
Catching dainty things of fancy most reluctant to be caught,
Shining tangles leading nowhere presently unravel,
Tread strange paths of meditation very intricate to travel.
Gleaming bits of quaint desire tempt my steps beyond the decent,
I confound old solid glory with publicity too recent.
But my one unchanged obsession, wheresoe'er my feet have trod,
Is a keen, enormous, haunting, never-sated thirst for God.[12]

Indicative of the finding of God in nature is John Hall
Wheelock's " Midnight ":

> Now in the still
> Shadow and glamour of the departed sun
> Beauty's immortal ritual is done,
>   The divine word and will.
>
> Now, lost in lone
> Worship and breathless adoration, lies
> The loving at the beloved breast and cries
>   His prayer up to her throne.
>
> Now thrills the dim
> Heart of compassionate and conquering love
> With solemn pride, and from her throne above
>   Listens, and leans to him.
>
> No sound is here.
> Mysteriously the many are made one. —
> O peace, now the eternal will is done,
>   And God's own heart how near![13]

A similar perception of nature as " the vicar of Almighty
God," to use Chaucer's phrase, is Margaret Deland's mystical poem, " Deaf ":

Oh, Lord, I cannot hear; didst speak, oh Lord?
My soul is deaf; oh, speak so I may hear!

Dawn trumpets on the hills, and draws her sword,
All glittering from its scabbard of the dews,
And, hearing, with a shout Day's hosts arise!
Quick, at Spring's footstep on the April snows
The daffodils pour fragrance to the skies.
The eager seas arise to clasp the land,
Then turn, with joyous patience, to retreat
Back to the deep, at some low-voiced command.
Men answer to the whirlwind and the fire,
And to melodious silences of peace;
To summonings of beauty, fear, desire —
The changing Word of the unchanging Voice
Which gives to Time, Eternity's demand.
All these, Thy children — seas, and stars, and men —
Listen: and answer as they understand;
I do not answer, for no word is clear;
And yet I listen, Lord, I listen, too —
But nothing reaches me!   I cannot hear.
My soul is deaf; Lord, speak that I may hear.[14]

These are only two of many examples of a body of poetry which is the typical expression of the conviction expressed in philosophical language by Professor H. A. Overstreet: " There is in nature an *élan,* a quickening vitality, an urge toward more widely functioning wholes, a trend toward truth, beauty, and goodness, which have within them the lasting power that lies in coherence; and in this everlasting, creative life that moves toward wholeness we find the reality of God." [15]

This approach to faith through the scientific conception of nature, and its law and order, a frequent theme of poetry in a scientific age, is thus expressed by Ellen Glasgow:

> In truth that falsehood cannot span,
>   In the majestic march of Laws
> That weed and flower and worm and man
>   Result from one supernal cause
> In doubts that dare and faiths that cleave,
>   Lord, I believe.[16]

Such poetry is the expression of what may be called unbaptized and unenrolled religion. It is comparable to the faith outside the ranks of Israel which Jesus greeted with joy and to which he paid such high tribute.

VI

Another section of this poetry dealing with religion is that which expresses much more definitely and positively a firmly held faith. Sometimes this faith is in the form of a conviction of the immanence of God, as in Madison Cawein's poem, " Penetralia ":

> I am the warmth, the honey-scent
> That throats with spice each lily-bud
> That opens, white with wonderment,
> Beneath the moon; or, downward bent,
> Sleeps with a moth beneath its hood:
> I am the dream that haunts it too,
> That crystalizes into dew.
>
> I am the seed within the pod;
> The worm within its closed cocoon:
> The wings within the circling clod,
> The germ that gropes through soil and sod
> To beauty, radiant in the noon:
> I am all these, behold! and more —
> I am the love at the world-heart's core.[16]

Sometimes it is much more purely mystical, through feeling rather than through an intellectual process, as in Angela Morgan's, " Kinship,"

> I am aware
> As I go commonly sweeping the stair
> Doing my part of the every day care . . .
>
> I am aware of the glory that runs
> From the core of myself to the core of the suns.
> Bound to the stars by invisible chains,
> Blaze of eternity now in my veins,
> Seeing the rush of ethereal rains
> Here in the midst of the everyday air —
> I am aware.
>
> I am aware,
> As I sit quietly here in my chair,
> Sewing or reading or braiding my hair —
> Human and simple my lot and my share . . .
>
> I am aware of the splendor that ties
> All the things of the earth with the things of the skies,
> Here in my body the heavenly heat,
> Here in my flesh the melodious beat
> Of the planets that circle Divinity's feet.
> As I sit silently here in my chair
> I am aware.[17]

Of particular significance is the fact that one of the poets whose name is one of the peaks of literature in America in the twenty years which followed the poetry revival beginning in 1912, Vachel Lindsay, was essentially an evangelist. He spoke in movements and diction that were novel to poetry. But there was an authentic spell in his music and his idealism and the religious content and background of his

work represented the outlook of multitudes. "General
William Booth Enters into Heaven" is, of course, one of his
greatest poems, as it is perhaps the greatest religious poem of
a generation. He has been an unofficial poet laureate of the
Christian faith and outlook of our time. Lindsay's voice
was not that of a discontented rebel bewailing his time, but
that of one who measured his world against a religious standard and vision. His faith was not an apologetic one, with its
back against the wall, but a lyrical faith, a marching conviction, striving to keep religion from sinking into moral and
spiritual mediocrity. Characteristic of his own faith is his
"Heart of God":

> O great heart of God,
>   Once vague and lost to me,
> Why do I throb with your throb tonight,
>   In this land, eternity?
>
> O little heart of God,
>   Sweet intruding stranger,
> You are laughing in my human breast,
>   A Christ-child in a manger.
>
> Heart, dear heart of God,
>   Beside you now I kneel,
> Strong heart of faith. O heart not mine,
>   Where God has set His seal.
>
> Wild thundering heart of God
>   Out of my doubt I come,
> And my foolish feet with prophets' feet,
>   March with the prophets' drum.[18]

His conception of the church, in his poem, "The Illinois
Village," is more than one man's imaginative picture of a

deep seated devotion; it represents the mood and heart of
multitudes of people:

> Who can pass a village church
> By night in these clean prairie lands
> Without a touch of Spirit-power?
> So white and fixed and cool it stands —
> A thing from some strange fairy-town,
> A pious amaranthine flower,
> Unsullied by the winds, as pure
> As jade or marble, wrought this hour: —
> Rural in form, foursquare and plain,
> And yet our sister, the new moon,
> Makes it a praying wizard's dream.
> The trees that watch at dusty noon
> Breaking its sharpest lines, veil not
> The whiteness it reflects from God,
> Flashing like Spring on many an eye,
> Making clean flesh, that once was clod.[19]

To take one final example, there is James Oppenheim's
striking poem, " Night," in which a poet, a scientist and a
priest each gives his interpretation of reality. The voice of
faith finds expression in the reply of the priest to scientist
and poet:

Man of Song and man of Science
Truly you are as people on the outside of a house,
And one of you sees only that it is made of stone, and its windows of
    glass and that fire burns on the hearth,
And the other of you sees that the house is beautiful and very human.
But I have gone inside the house,
And I live with the host in that house.
And I have broken bread with him and drunk his wine
And seen the transfiguration that love and awe make in the brain,
For that house is the world, and the Lord is my host and my Father:
It is my Father's house.

And again the priest speaks to the poet and the scientist:

Enough? I see what is enough!
Machinery is enough for a Scientist,
And Beauty is enough for a Poet;
But in the heart of men and women, and in the thirsty hearts of little
    children
There is a hunger, and there is an unappeasable longing,
For a Father and for the love of a Father . . .
For the root of a soul is mystery,
And the Night is mystery,
And in that mystery men and women open inward into Eternity,
And know love, the Lord.
Blessed by his works, and his angels, and his sons crowned with his
    glory! [20]

Poetry dealing specifically with Jesus is even greater in
bulk and comes from writers of the widest variety in religious conviction or lack of it. Anna Hempstead Branch's
line occurring in a poem addressed to Jesus, " Thou art the
great Blood Brother of my heart," is a confession in which
many have shared. Two poems, far separated in spirit and
tone, from poets as far apart in temperament as possible, may
be cited as examples of recording the sense of the diffused
presence of Jesus and his universal significance. The first
is Harry Kemp's " The Voice of Christmas " (the last four
of the six verses are quoted):

I cannot put His presence by, I meet Him everywhere;
I meet Him in the country town, the busy market-square;
The Mansion and the Tenement attest His presence there.

Upon the funneled ships at sea He sets His shining feet;
The Distant Ends of Empire not in vain His Name repeat —
And, like the presence of a rose, He makes the whole world sweet.

He comes to break the barriers down raised up by barren creeds;
About the globe from zone to zone, like sunlight He proceeds;
He comes to give the World's starved heart the perfect love it needs —

The Christ, whose friends have played him false, whom Dogmas have
    belied,
Still speaking to the hearts of men — tho' shamed and crucified,
The Master of the centuries who will not be denied! [21]

The other is the familiar "White Comrade," the war
poem, by Robert Haven Schauffler, ending with the lines:

> Those bullet-holes in the patient hands
> Seemed to transcend
> All horrors that ever these war-drenched lands
> Had known or would know till the mad world's end.
> Then suddenly I was aware
> That his feet had been wounded too;
> And, dimming the white of his side,
> A dull stain grew.
> "You are hurt, White Comrade!" I cried.
> His words I already foreknew:
> "These are old wounds," said he,
> "But of late they have troubled me." [22]

The poet's interest in Jesus and the use of Jesus as theme
and inspiration of poetry have been steadily increasing since
1900. Evidence of the large volume and wide variety of the
poetry dealing with Jesus is to be found in two valuable
anthologies, *The Master of Men,* edited by Thomas Curtis
Clark, and *Christ in the Poetry of Today,* compiled by
Martha Foote Crowe and Elvira Slack. Very valuable also
is *Lyra Mystica,* edited by Charles Carroll Albertson, the last
one hundred pages of which are devoted to contemporary
American poetry.

Longer narrative poems have also evidenced this interest.

Among these are Lola Ridge's *Firehead,* dealing with the trial and execution of Jesus, Sara Bard Field's *Barabbas,* and Robinson's *Nicodemus.*

One particular type of poem, not explicitly dealing with religion but nevertheless having important religious implications, may be mentioned in this connection. There are many poems of love in which the experience of human love has such an absolute value that it furnishes evidence to the poet of both its permanence and its origin in the divine. "The excellent becomes the permanent." Edgar Lee Masters' poem, "My Light and Yours," is one of this type, as indicated in its last lines:

> When folly and wisdom are no more
> And fire is no more
> Because man is no more
> When the dead world slowly spinning
> Drifts and falls through the void
> My light with yours
> In the Light of Lights forever.[23]

Another is Odell Shepard's poem, "Vistas":

> Street after street, as I passed
> Lured me and beckoned me onward
> With memories frail as the odor
>   Of lilacs adrift on the air.
> At the end of each breeze-blurred vista
> She seemed to be watching and waiting
> With leaf shadows over her gown
>   And sunshine gilding her hair.
>
> For there was a dream that the kind God
> Withheld, while granting us many —
> But surely, I think, we shall come
>   Sometime, at the end, she and I,

To the Heaven He keeps for all tired souls
The quiet suburban gardens
While He Himself walks in the evening
Beneath the rose-dropping sky.[24]

Arthur Davison Ficke's beautiful and moving poem,
"Prayer for a Lady," suggests some relations of love poetry
to religion.

Here in the high midsummer hour
I call upon Thy Grace and Power.

O Lord, Thy benefice confer
On me — but most of all on her

Whose delicate untroubled face
Is as the mirror of Thy Grace —

A gift not to be known or spoken,
A light, a miracle, a token

Of love we shall not wholly say
Through the long eloquence of the day.

This prayer I offer unto Thee
Aware of its futility.

Full well I know Thou canst do naught,
Being but a figment of my thought.

It is a folly, that I seek
Thy Voice where there is none to speak.

And yet, dear Lord, so much her worth
In the confusions of the earth

That prayers for her sake must be said
Even though God himself be dead.

Wherefore, dear Lord, Thy blessing give
On her, Thy angel-fugitive.[25]

Human love as a pathway to faith in God and experience of God is thus described by Harold Trowbridge Pulsifer, in " The Mantle of God ":

> I pray to a God with a woman's face.
>   (My mother's face is wondrous fair!)
> The wide world is an altar-place,
>   And love-in-life the only prayer.
>
> I work for a God with a woman's hands.
>   (My mother's hands are cool and strong!)
> I sing for a God who understands
>   The worker's work and the singer's song.
>
> I live for a God with a woman's eyes.
>   (My mother's eyes have made me whole!)
> The very walls of paradise
>   Are compassed in a single soul! [26]

In the drama two interesting " Passion plays " are those of Don Marquis, *The Dark Hours,* and the one-act play of Charles Rann Kennedy, *The Terrible Meek*. Though written several years earlier, *The Dark Hours* was first produced on the stage in 1933. It is more successful as poetry than as drama. It is reverential in spirit, and marked by beauty and skilful characterization. In the face of the convention of the theater opposed to the attempt, the play introduces the figure of Jesus on the stage, a hopeless piece of daring which is not dramatically effective. A chief theme of the play is Judas and the motives which led to his betrayal of Jesus. The defense which Judas makes of his action is largely that of helplessness, that he was a compelled figure in a scheme of salvation. As Judas complains to Caiaphas in the first act, Jesus has " cast a spell " on him till he is " a city full of spirits and they riot in the streets." " I am bewitched," he cries, "I am a cavern full of ghosts which war with one another, and they cry out and make a windy tumult in my head." Yet that is not the whole story. Mr. Marquis, in his interpretation of Judas, allows play of the motive of the lust for money and the thwarting of ambition. Thus Judas explains himself to Caiaphas, "I thought that He was to be king of the Jews, and had this been so, I should have been His chamberlain. It was I who carried the money and kept the accounts of His company. I planned to be His bursar when He came unto His throne. There was a night when I stood upon a hill and saw the world swirl past me. Cities and armies, tribes and senates and navies all melted to a mist and went swirling by beneath the stars. The wind and sound beat upon mine ears and I guessed something of the iron delight of power." The final scene at the foot of the cross is eloquently powerful.

The Terrible Meek by Charles Rann Kennedy, produced first in 1912, takes place entirely at the foot of the cross. It may be called a propaganda play in a sense that *The Dark Hours* is not, for it interprets the crucifixion in terms of present-day pacifism. The stage is dark, the figure on the cross is not seen. The voices of three characters are heard speaking in the language of modern conversation, a captain and a soldier who have executed a man under a criminal sentence, and the mother of the man. Only at the end of the play, when the light comes on revealing the characters dressed in the costumes of the time of Christ and making visible three crosses, is it explicitly shown that the execution has been that of Jesus. The concluding speech of the soldier to the mother of Jesus states impressively the theme of the play:

" Captain: I tell you, woman, this dead son of yours, disfigured, shamed, spat upon, has built a kingdom this day that can never die. The living glory of him rules it. The earth is *his* and he made it. He and his brothers have been moulding and making it through the long ages: they are the only ones who ever did really possess it: not the proud, not the idle, not the wealthy, not the vanishing empires of the world. Something has happened up here on this hill today to shake all our kingdoms of blood and fear to dust. The earth is his, the earth is theirs and they made it. The meek, the terrible meek, the fierce agonizing meek, are about to enter into their inheritance." [27]

Eugene O'Neill's *Lazarus Laughed,* published in 1928 but not yet produced on the commercial stage, is a treatment of the triumph of love and joy over death and the fear of death. It is daring in its attempt to put into dramatic form the life of Lazarus after his return from his three-days sojourn in the grave. At climactic points in the drama he delivers his message, " There is no death." The symbol of his deliverance from fear is a low musical laughter in which he continually indulges. He has looked into the eyes of Christ and has learned Christ's secret of the powerlessness of death and the power of love. Through many scenes he passes, overcoming the paganism of Greece and Rome, even the Empire as represented by Tiberius.

Like so much of O'Neill's dramatic work, the meaning cannot be squeezed into any exact statement. Very evidently it is not the Christian doctrine of personal immortality which O'Neill is representing in this drama of Lazarus. Yet it is marked by spiritual sensitivity and deep insight, such as his portrayal of the fate of one who carries the spirit of Christ to a world not yet prepared for it, and the human anti-climax of fear and selfishness causing forgetfulness of the high hours of spiritual understanding. It is an effective presentation of the difference which a faith in the final triumph of life over death ought to make in the attitudes and actions of daily living.

Channing Pollock's *The Fool* and Benn W. Levy's *The Devil Passes,* 1932, are examples of popular plays dealing with religious themes. Pollock's play deals with the industrial conflict. In spite of sentimentalism and melodrama, it has strong scenes of dramatization of the struggle between justice and greed. The theme of *The Devil Passes* is the resistance of a group of people to particularly attractive limitations laid before them by the Devil in the form of a curate. They resist by virtue of some intangible power which holds them back, perhaps God.

Both in great popular success and in artistic power and spiritual understanding, *The Green Pastures,* written by Marc Connelly, adapted from Roark Bradford's stories, *Old Man Adam and His Children,* ranks high in treatments of religious subjects in drama. It presents the familiar scenes of Old Testament history as they are supposed to be conceived in the tradition of Bible story telling and preaching among the Negroes of the Southern states. It was a theme with a hundred pitfalls. Mr. Connelly has dexterously skirted every one. His episodic drama has rich humor but no buffoonery; it is daring and yet reverential. A measure of the dramatist's remarkable achievement is to be found in a comparison of the play with the stories of Mr. Bradford, which formed its basis. There is plenty of humor and appreciative understanding of the Negro in Bradford's work. But the art by which the play is lifted up above the level of humor, the poetic sense which gives the drama beauty and power, above all, the deep spiritual understanding, its really profound pic-

tures of the growth of the idea of God as the experience of
the Hebrews goes on, a growth from a magic-worker to the
high spiritual conception expressed in Hosea and Jesus —
all these elements are due to Mr. Connelly. It is just these
features which have given the play its spiritual quality.
Much credit is also due to the unique talent and personality
of the actor who played the rôle of God, Richard B. Harrison.
There is deserved tribute both to dramatist and actor in the
statement of Clayton Hamilton that never in the history of
drama had an actor been able to come upon the stage and
say to the audience, through his acting, " I am God — God
is like this," and be accepted sincerely and unanimously.
The scene in which the idea of a suffering God first appears
is marked by great beauty and insight. The climax swiftly
and powerfully suggests the rôle of Christ in the revelation
of a God of love:

" Seated in an armchair near the center of the grounds God is star-
ing thoughtfully into space. His pensiveness worries Gabriel. He has
been sittin' that way an awful long time. Is it somethin' serious that
is worryin' God? It is, God admits, very serious.

" GABRIEL (awed by his tone) — Lawd, is de time come fo' me to
blow?

" GOD — Not yet, Gabriel. I'm just thinkin'.

" GABRIEL — What about, Lawd? (Puts up hand. Singing stops.)

" GOD — 'Bout somethin' de boy tol' me. Somethin' 'bout Hosea
an' himself. How dey foun' somethin'.

" GABRIEL — What, Lawd?

" GOD — Mercy. (A pause.) Through *sufferin'*, he said.

" GABRIEL — Yes, Lawd.

" GOD — I'm tryin' to find it, too. It's awful impo'tant. It's awful
impo'tant to all de people on my earth. Did he mean dat even God
must suffer? (God continues to look out over the audience for a moment and then a look of surprise comes into his face. He sighs. In
the distance a voice cries.)

" THE VOICE — Oh, look at him! Oh, look, dey goin' to make him carry it up dat high hill! Dey goin' to nail him to it! Oh, dat's a terrible load for one man to carry! (God rises and murmurs ' Yes! ' as if in recognition. The heavenly beings have been watching Him closely, and now, seeing Him smile gently, draw back, relieved. All of the angels burst into ' Hallelujah, King Jesus.' God continues to smile as the lights fade away. The singing becomes fortissimo.)

" THE CURTAIN FALLS " 28

1 *The Contemporary and His Soul,* by Irwin Edman. Cape & Smith.
2 New York Herald Tribune, Sept. 11, 1932.
3 Century Magazine, Vol. 107, p. 577.
4 Book of the Month Club Bulletin, May 1933.
5 *A Preface to Morals,* by Walter Lippmann. The Macmillan Company.
6 London Daily News, Aug. 1927.
7 *A Preface to Morals,* by Walter Lippmann. The Macmillan Company.
8 *The Beggar at the Gate,* by Kathleen Millay. The Liveright Publishing Corporation.
9 *Children of the Night,* by Edwin Arlington Robinson. Charles Scribner's Sons.
10 *The Awakening and Other Poems,* by Don Marquis. Doubleday, Doran & Company.
11 *The Falconer of God,* by W. R. Benet. Yale University Press.
12 Gamaliel Bradford.
13 *Dust and Light,* by John Hall Wheelock. Charles Scribner's Sons.
14 Used by permission of the author.
15 *The Enduring Quest,* by H. A. Overstreet. W. W. Norton & Company.
16 Madison Cawein. The Macmillan Company.
17 Dodd, Mead & Company.
18 *Collected Poems,* by Vachel Lindsay. The Macmillan Company.
19 Ibid.
20 A. C. McClurg & Company.
21 Brentano's.
22 Reprinted from The Outlook, now The New Outlook, New York.
23 *Toward the Gulf,* by Edgar Lee Masters. The Macmillan Company.
24 *A Lonely Flute,* by Odell Shepard. Houghton Mifflin Company.
25 *Escape to the Hills.* Used by permission of the author.
26 Used by permission of Houghton Mifflin Company.
27 *The Terrible Meek,* by Charles Rann Kennedy. Harper & Brothers, 1912.
28 *The Green Pastures,* by Marc Connelly. Farrar & Rinehart.

INDEX

293